## KINSHIP, LAW AND THE UNEXPECTED

How can we hold in the same view both cultural or historical constructs and generalities about social existence? In response to this anthropological conundrum, *Kinship, Law and the Unexpected* takes up an issue at the heart of studies of society – the way we use relationships to uncover relationships. Relationality is a phenomenon at once contingent (on certain ways of knowing) and ubiquitous (to social life).

The role of relations in western (Euro-American) knowledge practices, from the scientific revolution onward, raises a question about the extent to which Euro-American kinship is the kinship of a knowledge-based society. The argument takes the reader through current issues in biotechnology, new family formations and legal interventions, and intellectual property debates, to matters of personhood and ownership afforded by material from Melanesia and elsewhere. If we are often surprised by what our relatives do, we may also be surprised by what relations tell us about the world we live in.

Marilyn Strathern is William Wyse Professor of Social Anthropology at the University of Cambridge and Mistress of Girton College, Cambridge. She has carried out fieldwork over several years in the Highlands of Papua New Guinea (Melanesia). She is the author of *The Gender of the Gift*, *After Nature* and *Property, Substance and Effect*.

# Kinship, Law and the Unexpected

*Relatives Are Always a Surprise*

MARILYN STRATHERN

University of Cambridge

CAMBRIDGE UNIVERSITY PRESS
Cambridge, New York, Melbourne, Madrid, Cape Town, Singapore,
São Paulo, Delhi, Dubai, Tokyo

Cambridge University Press
32 Avenue of the Americas, New York, NY 10013-2473, USA

www.cambridge.org
Information on this title: www.cambridge.org/9780521615099

First published 2005

*A catalog record for this publication is available from the British Library*

*Library of Congress Cataloging in Publication data*
Strathern, Marilyn.
Kinship, law and the unexpected : relatives are always a surprise / Marilyn Strathern.
p.   cm.
Includes bibliographical references and index.
ISBN 0-521-84992-6 (hardcover) – ISBN 0-521-61509-7 (pbk.)
1. Kinship.   2. Kinship (Law)   3. Domestic relations.   I. Title.
GN487.S767   2005
306.83 – dc22            2005000153

ISBN 978-0-521-84992-0 Hardback
ISBN 978-0-521-61509-9 Paperback

Transferred to digital printing 2010

# Contents

# Preface

Anthropologists use relationships to uncover relationships. The device is at the heart of social anthropology, and anthropologists also find it at the heart of kinship. This book would not have been possible but for the wave of anthropological writing that has gone under the name of 'the new kinship' (studies), although it does not fall into the genre. I wish to add a footnote about the role that appeals to relationality play in anthropological studies of social life and suggest why we should be interested in it. Appeals are made to a phenomenon at once contingent (on certain ways of knowing) and ubiquitous (to human society).

One of the enduring methodological conundrums of anthropology is how to hold in the same view what are clearly cultural and historical constructs and what are equally clearly generalities about social existence. The trick is to specify each without diminishing the other. If this is an attempt, by its very nature the present work must be incomplete precisely because of the specific circumstances that have suggested kinship as an intriguing field for investigation here. The field already limits ('constructs') the exercise.

The specific circumstances are epitomised in the new kinship. Studies under this rubric focus on the reflexive nature of analytical constructs, and very often on people's dealings with one another under new technological regimes, with the stimulus to indigenous reflexivity that brings; people come to make new kinds of connections between their lives and the world they live in. Much of the substance of what follows would be familiar to such concerns, especially in the first part. Part I touches on contexts in which the new medical technologies have posed questions for families and relatives. These contexts become, in Part II, a foil for comparative analysis. The essays thus move from materials lodged largely in the United States and the United Kingdom, and in the first chapter white Australia, to creating the grounds for talking about Melanesia, Amazonia and (briefly) Aboriginal Australia. They describe the consequences of relationality, both in the data and in the organisation of it; several of the essays are illustrative in this sense, deploying the term no differently from its use in much anthropological writing.

Indeed, relationality – as an abstract value placed on relationships – is highlighted in a recognisable and conventional manner through attention to the law. Running through these essays is a commentary on the way modernist legal thinking at once opens up and closes down predispositions to think in terms of relations. Part I introduces Euro-American law on its own home territory, so to speak, in both creative and regulative mode, whereas Part II shows legal categories being introduced in situations otherwise foreign to them, in some cases in the name of governance, in others as an analytical device on the part of the observer. Either way, one should not overlook the imagination and ingenuity of lawyers in dealing with new issues. Concepts developed in the name of intellectual property offer a rich seam for mining here and are in the foreground or background of several chapters. 'The law' is thus depicted in different guises, whether contributing to the conceptual resources through which people approach problems entailing ownership or rights, or intervening in disputes, crystallising certain cultural moments for the sake of advocacy, and so forth.

There is a particular purchase to bringing in legal thinking. It is a discipline and a practice that has to deal with different kinds of relationships. After all, in European mythology, the law is the classic locus for situations where categorical and interpersonal relations confront each other, as – in her lectures of the name – Judith Butler (2000) reminds us was true of Antigone's claim. Ajudications in the courts, pleas on the grounds of human rights: the law deals with persons in relation to categories. We shall see the significance of this.

The essays are intended to convey the embeddedness of relational thinking in the way Euro-Americans come to know world, and the descriptions of social life this embeddedness has made – and continues to make – possible. It offers us truths of a very special kind. In turn, such relational thinking is successful to the extent that it capitalises on a common capacity or facility in the making of relations that exist in other registers altogether. From here comes the attempt to hold in the same view what are clearly cultural and historical constructs and what are equally clearly generalities about social existence. The Introductions to the two parts, Divided Origins and The Arithmetic of Ownership, spell this out.

## DEBTS

Separate acknowledgements are recorded at the end of each chapter, as each originated at a particular event or for an occasion. (To this extent, they may be read as independent pieces.) This is to record more generally my intellectual debts to colleagues whose work makes superfluous any further rehearsal of the turn to kinship; that micro-history within anthropology has been well written. I include Janet Carsten's *After Kinship*, which rewrites the debates that shifted the study of kinship from a mid-twentieth-century preoccupation to an arena of much future promise; Sarah Franklin's and Susan McKinnon's collection of essays on new locations for new interests, *Relative Values: Reconfiguring Kinship Studies*, and the reader edited by Robert Parkin and Linda Stone, *Kinship and Family*, that brings a span of diverse materials into provocative relationship. Of ethnographically based monographs, Jeanette Edwards' *Born and Bred: Idioms of Kinship and New Reproductive Technologies in England* is foremost. All these include reflections on the substantial materials, theories and analyses that are constantly re-drawing kinship studies today.

This book is not only about kinship, and there are other debts; for the stimulus of many conversations, Françoise Barbira-Freedman, Debbora Battaglia, Joan Bestard-Camps, Barbara Bodenhorn, Corinne Hayden, Caroline Humphrey, Alain Pottage, Paul Rabinow, Christina Toren, Eduardo Viveiros de Castro. Benedicta Rousseau is owed special thanks. Much of the thinking occurred in the environs of Ravenscar in North Yorkshire, under Jenny Bartlet's stimulating hospitality, and it is not inconsequential that Ru Kundil and Puklum El from Mt. Hagen have stayed there too.

Chapter Three and the three chapters of Part II were first written under the auspices of Property, Transactions and Creations: New Economic Relations in the Pacific. This was a three-year investigation (1999–2002) funded by the U.K. Economic and Social Research Council (award R000 23 7838), and acknowledgement is gratefully made. The arguments here owe much to Eric Hirsch, co-convenor, and to Tony Crook, Melissa Demian, Andrew Holding, Lawrence Kalinoe, Stuart Kirsch, James Leach and Karen Sykes, as well as to Lissant Bolton and Adam Reed, and to the ephemeral association that called itself the Trumpington Street Reading Group.

Permission to reprint or draw upon papers published elsewhere is gratefully acknowledged.

Chapter Three *Abridged* as Emergent relations, in Mario Biagioli and Peter Galison, eds. 2003. *Scientific authorship: Credit and intellectual property in science*. New York: Routledge, pp. 165–94.

Chapter Four *From* the journal *Theory, Culture and Society* 18: 1–26, 2001; also pub. in Christopher Pinney and Nicholas Thomas, eds. 2000. *Beyond aesthetics: Art and the technologies of enchantment: Essays for Alfred Gell*. Oxford: Berg, pp. 259–86.

Chapter Five *From* Martha Mundy and Alain Pottage, eds. 2004. *Law, anthropology and the constitution of the social: Making persons and things.* Cambridge: Cambridge University Press, pp. 201–33.

Chapter Six to appear in Bill Maurer and Gabriele Schwab, eds. In press. *Accelerating possession: Global futures of property and personhood.* New York: Columbia University Press.

## MANDA

Among several interesting developments in social anthropology at the moment, a particular trajectory directly affects the substance of this book and leads to a different kind of acknowledgement. It is invariably to one's benefit that one consumes the work of colleagues, critical or otherwise, and there is a temptation to be like the marketing executive or policy maker in this era of ready responsiveness and absorb criticism the moment it is articulated. Indeed, ethnographers these days will tell you that hardly have they jotted down observation or comment and their subjects will have come up with their own analysis. I am sorely tempted, for example, to take on board a piece that Alberto Corsín Jiménez (2004) generously sent me; informed by James Weiner's prescience, it is a critique of relationality with which I find myself at almost every step agreeing. I might not have fallen in with the criticism so readily had I not been warmed up to the task first by Iris Jean-Klein, and Annelise Riles, and then by Tony Crook's (2003) work on unmediated relations in Angkaiyakmin, Bolivip, by Monica Konrad's (2005) account of nameless relations in Britain, and by Andrew Moutu's (2003) study of kinship and ownership in Iatmul. I think, though, that I can best serve the new radicalism by my own conservatism, and thus conserve what will then become an original position rather than consume new ones! So I endeavour to remain true to a point of view not because I defend it but because there is some mileage to be gained from specifying – precisely at this juncture – what is so interesting about it that it could become important to leave behind.

The Melpa (Hagen) term *manda* means something along the lines of 'enough said', 'sufficient for the present', 'let's stop for now' – an exhortation to shut up, recognise an end, acknowledge a finish, even though everyone could go on talking forever.

Marilyn Strathern, August 2004
Girton College, Cambridge

PART ONE

# DIVIDED ORIGINS

# Introduction: Divided Origins

*T*HE U.K. HUMAN GENETICS COMMISSION'S PRELIMINARY DISCUSSION document (HGC 2000) on the use of personal genetic information singles out children as a category with special interests. Given that ethical procedures in medicine rest crucially on the principles of informed consent and confidentiality, genetic testing poses a particular nexus of problems where children are concerned. Of course, both the question of young persons being incapable of giving consent in their own right and the need for parents to be informed of medical facts about their offspring long pre-date the new genetics. But genetic medicine introduces a particularly challenging set of issues, such as the testing of children for conditions for which they show no symptoms or for conditions that may only be relevant in adult life; the kind of understanding families might have about Mendelian inheritance; the implications of parentage testing and of who owns knowledge about a child's genes. Generally lumped together as posing ethical dilemmas, these add a significant dimension to the status of being a child. Yet, although they are important, it is arguable that they impinge on relatively few people and are in that sense exotic. I take the contrary view and suggest that such dilemmas arise out of and contribute to some very general currents of thinking in contemporary Euro-American societies.[1] We might then say that these general currents simply point to a recent phenomenon, a self-consciousness about living in a society in which communications and the so-called knowledge economy mobilise whole constellations of values that clamour for attention. But I would take the same step again and argue that this, in turn, is a recent version of a long standing preoccupation with knowledge.

Similar steps recur throughout this volume, old positions recaptured on new terrain, and I make no apology for the not-quite replication of issues. It is one way of working through a culture and its preoccupations, now explicitly linked, now implicitly so. Some of the many relationships between knowledge and kinship are the subject of the first part of this book. To make the concerns concrete, I introduce a (seriously) playful vignette, although the precise cause for parental anxiety depicted here may be a little behind the times.

### THE CHILD'S TWO BODIES

To be self-conscious about knowledge is in Britain a largely middle class predilection. Miller (1997) describes how, in bringing up their children, middle class mothers in 1990s North London used their knowledge of the world to shape the way they would like their children to grow. They cannot do anything about the genes; they can do everything about health, hygiene and many common afflictions; they chat about what food children should eat and what toys they want to play with. The outcome is that mothers come to regard the child's growing up as a series of defeats. The first enemy was sugar, then sweets and biscuits, then brands such as Coca Cola, and bigger temptations such as Barbie dolls and the ubiquitous gun: 'an unceasing struggle between what is regarded as the world of nature and the artificial world of commodity materialism' (1997: 75). The battles over diet and gender are regarded as efforts to resist commercialism and consumerism, efforts that invariably end first in capitulation and then in the withdrawal that characterises the grandparental generation, who find it easier to allow the child freedom to choose its own style.

Why struggle in the first place? As I see it, the young mother is placed in a position of responsibility *by her knowledge of* the effects of these substances and toys on the growing body, and on the growing mind and sets of behaviours. In other words, the child's condition depends on how the mother acts on her knowledge of the world. If the child is fed on sugar-free food he or she will be more healthy; love the child now and he or she will be able to love in the future, and so forth. At the same time, what the mother sees in the way the child grows up is her own half-hearted capacity to hold (say) the world of commerce at bay – or embrace it for that matter.

Parents do not give up without a struggle, within which their concept of biology plays a major role. It is very common for such parents to insist that their infants have an allergy to anything artificial. It is as though the infants' bodies have antennae attuned to the mothers' ideology of nature. Infants are said to come out in spots as soon as they ingest any kind of additive or the wrong E-number. If the children do not oblige (with spots) then the parents may claim these additives cause behavioural problems, which is a harder claim to contest.

Miller 1997: 76

Although Miller does not put it in these words, the child seems to embody the conscientiousness with which the mother has acted on her knowledge and stuck to her principles. She must carry on until the child itself is properly informed about things. In the interim, its development reflects the application of her own knowledge.

Such a parent, in this view, shares body with the child twice over. First is the body of genetic inheritance, a given, a matter regarded colloquially as being of common blood or common substance. Second is the body that is a sign of the parent's devotion – or neglect – and in this middle class milieu it is above all through the application of knowledge that the parent's efforts make this body. Miller reports that in the neighbourhood circles he observed what the child ate or played with reflected back on to the mother's local reputation. He jokes that the child grows the mother.[2]

These mothers have to go through the same process with the next infant too; their socialisation is not in that sense ever complete. However, there is a gradual attrition of the effect that parents feel they have on the child. Whereas they can mould the first child, the second already grows up under the shadow of the first child's victories. The parent learns how to take defeat. In accepting defeat the parent is of course acknowledging the growing autonomy of the child. And what will cap it will be the fact that for all the struggle to impart a world view, to teach the child to know the world that the parent knows, knowledge will in the end divide them. In many senses, they may come to share similar suppositions about the fundamental nature of the universe, about biology for instance, but ultimately it will be the child's knowledge that separates him or her from the parent. This will be partly because information is changing all the time and people keep up to different degrees, partly because the child must come to be keeper of knowledge about him or herself. Here is the significance of confidentiality and the age of consent. But until there is understanding, the parent must take on the monitoring task on the child's behalf. Parents are a special case because of all a child's caretakers and teachers only parents share both bodies with the child.

The two bodies are regarded as belonging to the same world (after Viveiros de Castro 1998a; 1998b), traditionally rendered as at once given and constructed. The simultaneity is captured by Latour's (1993: 6) famous aphorism that one will never find any network of events that is not at once 'real, like nature, narrated, like discourse, and collective, like society'. Whether in affirmation or denial of its importance, people thus imagine themselves confronting reality; nature (as in Miller's account) might be the epitome, but that order of reality can be extended to any givens of existence. Yet this really-existing universe is inextricably bound with ways of knowing it; the world is *also* the world they know that they create by their knowledge. It is the same world in which children are explicitly tutored (tautologously, acquire knowledge about). Kinship gives an added twist: even when people know that the routes to knowledge are divergent, the knowledge itself imposes an obligation on the knower in relation to those around him or her. It is a cause of moral action and creates a compulsion to act. Such at least would appear to be the implication of this mode of thinking. This doubled world is of course inhabited not only by these English-speakers but also by Euro-Americans at large.

In this vignette lies just the kind of material that would fuel continuing debate, within anthropology and beyond it, over the respective roles of the social and the biological in kin relations. However, I wish to locate its message rather differently – in what it tells us about knowledge practices – and in doing so to introduce a difference between two modes of relating. For the mother has to see the child as not only an extension of herself but also an extension of the world, and that she visualises through specific concepts that link the child to this world. In other words, the child, or aspects of his or her condition or behaviour, becomes a category, an exemplar of a type, as when it is conceptualised as prone to this or that. An example of such categorisation would be seeing one's offspring as a typical urban child, prone to allergies linked to eating habits, supermarket advertising, peer pressure from the playgroup, and such like. These all need to be brought in relation to one another, and the mother is the one to do it. In this (Euro-American) world view, persons can thus act on other persons in the same way as they act on the world, a folk model of the way in which 'we engage others in the processes of our own becoming' (Toren 2002: 189).

## A TOOL

So there is indeed a footnote to be written to kinship studies. It has little to do with the substance of kinship thinking or its relevance to contemporary concerns; it does not enlarge our sensibilities about diversity or the ingenuity with which people work things out for themselves. It points to what people have in common rather than what makes them distinctive. Moreover it is not on the face of it very interesting: more a truism than a reflection, more surface observation than deep analysis, and of little theoretical (model-building) purchase. It has all the triviality of a universalism. Nonetheless, it gives present concerns another dimension. By way of shorthand, I shall refer to it as a tool. It works by virtue of its duplex character.

The idea of the tool[3] I have in mind is not unlike the enzymes that tailor and splice genes, the central tools of recombinant DNA in the words Pottage

(2004: 272) takes from Rheinberger. He adds: 'biotechnological inventiveness splices life into life', thereby 'dividing life into the two asymmetric regions of technique and object'. Life is put to work on life, much as anthropology uses relations to explore relations. The anthropologist's tool is a duplex that divides as it combines.

One of those present concerns we regard as contemporary comes from scholarly practice. Although anthropologists want to go on deploying the notion of kinship and although common sense tells them that they must find it everywhere, their analytical constructs keep pushing kinship back into the contingencies of the constructs themselves. In particular they (the con-structs) regularly founder on the ubiquity or otherwise of 'biology', 'substance', 'conception', and so forth, notions evidently part of cultural thinking. For without that substratum, what then distinguishes kinship from any other phenomenon? This was the old question. Yet anthropologists are not easily going to say that there are peoples without kinship. So what is it that they go on finding everywhere? It cannot be these locally laden notions, obviously, but must be something else. It is not necessarily going to be useful to call it *kinship* either. However, and arguably, such being the compulsion of anthropology's own kind of relational knowledge, the *search for* kinship invariably throws certain forms of sociality into relief.

Perhaps what anthropologists find everywhere are two kinds of relations. Or rather, the realisation that relationality summons divergent thinking. A homely example in Chapter One is phrased in terms of connections and dis-connections between persons who may or may not be counted as relatives; the one process implies the other. Now the relation is divided (into two kinds) in a particularly powerful way that I want to call 'anthropology's relation'. The two kinds that principally interest me here comprise the conceptual (or categorical) and the interpersonal. On the one hand are those relations seen to make connections through a logic or power of articulation that acquires its own conceptual momentum; on the other hand are those relations that are conducted in interpersonal terms, connections between persons inflected with a precise and particular history. We may focus on the division that is presupposed in the two kinds or on the routine social fact that they are man-aged in tandem. Either way, *it is the facility to deal with both together,* to operate two kinds of relations at the same time, that is the tool. This in-volves more than the cognitive ability to combine and discriminate, more than the content or ontological field (relations/relationships) being sum-moned, and more than the particular outcomes in terms of conceptual and interpersonal orientations. Rather, all these together define the implement by its usefulness. It is a tool, *tout court,* for social living. It simultaneously compels social imagination and social action, theoretically trivial, immensely useful.

Both the mutual formula of connection/disconnection and the conceptual/interpersonal tandem may be exemplified in kinship systems. As far as Euro-American kinship is concerned they are joined by a third duplex, to which I return, namely a highly developed contrast between relations already in existence and those that must be deliberately created. Now the particular tool I am calling anthropology's relation, the divergence between the conceptual and the interpersonal, is composed neither of mutually referential opposites (as in connection/disconnection) nor of explicit features of any one cultural repertoire (as in the third case, which yields a contrast between the given and the constructed). Rather, only the work of anthropological exegesis will show how the one relation is folded into the other. We come to see that it is through interacting with persons that diverse interactions and further connections become intellectually conceivable, while it is through creating concepts and categories that connections come to have a social life of their own. The latter observation was presaged by Godelier (1986) in his search for the origins of kinship. Kinship appears where one can imagine – make an abstract image of – the relative of a relative, relationships between relationships. Kinship appears again where people make an imperative out of so doing. The imperative is logical and moral at the same time.

In sum, as anthropologists use it, their sort of relation is a tool for investigation that the discipline has borrowed from widely shared features of social life. What gives it purchase is the facility it offers for switching, as the North London mothers did, between relations of two kinds. The child who is the extension of the mother is also an extension of the world she inhabits. These mothers were involved in other switching too, as I comment in a moment.

For myself, there is a further source of interest in this duplex. It comes from submitting to the temptation to explore the (cultural) contingency of the very notion of relation. After what I have just said, it would be patently absurd to see the duplex as the creation of any one locale, let alone a creation of the scientific revolution (as Chapter Two might imply); however, it seems to have been pressed then into service in new ways, and specifically in the pursuit of knowledge for its own sake. This kind of knowledge I take as information attached to its source in some demonstrable manner. The point is, its formulation, use and circulation *in specific knowledge practices* is definitively contingent. Contingency does not make it un-useful; rather, it gives the duplex a specification of its usefulness. Thus a focus on the relational remains one of social anthropology's key strengths, and it does so among other things because of anthropology's willingness to move between conceptual and interpersonal relations in its descriptions of social life. I believe anthropology thus arrives at a certain truth about sociality that could not be captured in any other way.

There is clearly an account to be written about all of this, and the present one is not quite it. (The artefactualisation of 'the relation' is particularly clumsy, but it perhaps has some use as shorthand.)[4] At the same time some of the account might already have been written, which is what this collection, drawing on the works of many others, is meant to indicate.

## DIVIDED ORIGINS

Because they were formulated at different times, it may be helpful to be explicit about the connections between the chapters.

Anthropologists are of course latter day users of the relation (anthropology's relation) as a tool. Others have seized on it before them, and Part I hazards giving a special place to its development in the scientific revolution and its facilitation of that revolution. It helped produce among other things what I venture to generalise as 'science's relation', the third duplex. In fact, the duplex that I call anthropology's relation is not the only source of divergent ways of relating in anthropology itself. The discipline has drawn substantially on science's relation as it developed in tandem with new knowledge practices that came to describe the world in divergent ways, echoed in the North London mothers' anxieties over the effort to make the child as natural as possible.

The first three chapters contain a footnote within a footnote, namely a comment on what Carsten (2004: 165) calls Schneider's 'key perception about the relation between scientific knowledge and kinship'. This was that the more (Euro-)Americans learn about the biological facts of procreation, the more they feel informed about the facts of kinship.[5] Chapter One starts with a discussion that could have been composed of many elements, drawn from anywhere in the Euro-American world. The combination put together here is intended to illustrate ways in which people see science as affecting their lives, and specifically biotechnology. It thus moves over terrain familiar to a Euro-American readership and familiarly opens with an assumption about who *we* and *us* are. If it speaks with a Euro-American voice, Euro-American is spoken in many places and the action in this chapter takes place largely in Australia, from early days a country at the forefront of developments in assisted conception techniques. This aspect of biotechnology is prime material for prevalent and media-fanned assumptions about the increase of individualism that biotechnology supposedly brings in its wake.

In taking off from people's preoccupations, as reported in the press and elsewhere, Chapter One shows something of the value given to people's choices and rights in how they manage their lives and how this chimes with knowledge about the given nature and obligations of heredity and family. Knowledge brings responsibilities. However, the anthropologist is as interested in what is not said as in what is said. The bulk of the account is taken up with a (positivist) understanding of individuals as entities prior to relationships, so to an age that thinks of itself as individualistic, the revelation of relationship can come as something of a surprise. The person as an individual turns out to be the person as a relative. This occurs in two distinct locations: one in the turbulence of family arrangements and one in the procreative obligations kin are (newly) imagined owing one another. And right at the end I present academic arguments that presuppose relational thinking. These last are interestingly complicated by the substance of the debate they address, the separateness or otherwise of pregnant mother and fetus. The example presses home the point that the concept of relationship asks us to think about connections and disconnections together. The duplex is left at that and not further elaborated.

Chapter One thus documents an arena that has brought families and their relatives into the spotlight in the way ethicists and medical administrators approach guidelines for the deployment of new technologies. Alongside Australian reports and reportage, U.S. and British materials point to how law and biotechnology work together (a parallelism in their effects and fabrications), and how law and kinship often do not (notions of the embodied and distributed person sit uncomfortably with the legal subject). At the same time, Chapter One introduces science (biotechnology) largely where folk parlance would conventionally locate it, something to be drawn 'into' society. Chapter Two opens up current discussions (among scientists, policymakers and others) about science and society that challenges this location. However, Chapter Two takes the challenge in an unexpected direction, asking us to imagine science as already embedded in society. But there is also a second challenge here. It was the anthropologist's pre-existing interest in relationships and indeed in a relational account that led me to spring two 'surprises' in Chapter One. We might ask how relationism comes to be embedded in anthropological analysis in the first place.

Social anthropology is an Enlightenment-inspired, information-gathering discipline; the first task is to grasp the role of relations in (Euro-American) knowledge-making. Chapter Two embarks on a case for the special status of relations in scientific epistemology. To repeat the point, it is obviously absurd to claim that what the scientific revolution created was a relational view of the world, which is the condition of social being in the first place. So, what *was* being created? Perhaps one could say that 'the relation' (and

I am talking of anthropology's relation) was being appropriated for particular, in this case *epistemological*, ends. Of course this points to little more than tautology – new practices of knowledge whose suppositions about relationships evidently developed in new ways. But if one can talk in these terms at all, then just such an appropriation, leading to a particular kind of (scientific) knowledge-making, would be the kind of cultural contingency for which I was looking.

At any rate, what emerged was knowledge with divided or divergent origins, that is, knowledge capable of looking to more than one source.[6] Truth might rest in the persuasiveness of concepts, as logically connected to other concepts, or truth might rest in the persuasiveness of persons, bringing with them the guarantee of professional expertise, and in either case relations had to hold. We shall come on to that in Chapter Three. In the meantime, Chapter Two explores the specific duplex I call *science's relation*.

Science's relation is exemplified in a trope that Schneider also used, though I deploy it for different ends. I refer to the distinction between discovery and invention, between unfolding relations already there (co-implications) and making new relations (meaningful connections).

The distinction allows Euro-Americans two ways of getting at relational knowledge: uncovering what is in nature and making new knowledge through culture. A couple of contexts render this divergence apparent. (There is no significance in there being a couple.) Thus Chapter Two considers the way science's relation informed a relational view within the discipline of social anthropology itself. It also considers the echoes of scientific relationism in indigenous, here English, kinship relationships. In both cases, what is of interest is a division between modes of knowledge about the world (or about oneself as part or not part of that world). In both cases, scientific knowledge practices appear an explicit model for the interpretation of certain elements. On much less certain ground, the argument about an implicit or embedded science is made in a thoroughly speculative manner. However, if I am driven to take the risk (of error, logical and otherwise), an indigenous ethic in modern epistemology is at my heels. Uncovering connections and making connections can both have the force of a moral imperative, in the first case to exploit or conserve but otherwise acknowledge the world as it is and, in the second, as Wagner (1975) pointed out long ago, to make human life work as social life, the grand project of creating society. Nature and culture! The contrast appears at once foundational and as requiring attention. And whether in terms of the verification of abstract knowledge or for the personal responsibilities that knowledge brings, the theme of accountability runs through Part I.

Chapter Two is broad brushed. It is science's emphasis on particular modes of knowing that suggests we might talk of a scientific kinship system, of Euro-American kinship as the kinship of a knowledge-based society. Chapter Three attempts some detail (and becomes localised to the English-speaking world). In particular, it attempts to justify the directionality I gave to scientific thinking as a possible model for aspects of kinship thinking. Although the intention in Chapter Two had been somewhat mischievous, taking off from contemporary yearnings to see science in society, this chapter is altogether more sober. (The reader is asked to forgive the attempt at streamlining the main argument that leads to an overburden of endnotes.) With natural science as one source of divergent ways of conceptualising relations in the background, it argues a general case for *anthropology's relation*, a duplex that does not rest on nature and culture. At the least it presents materials whose questions will hopefully linger even if the effort at answering them proves transient.

Its impetus goes back to a 'discovery': the verbal crossovers that the English language allows between conceptual and interpersonal relations. It was the inter-twining that started me off in the 1990s (Strathern 1995). Although I was not aware at the time, Sahlins (1993: 24–5) had drawn attention to Locke's dictum that we necessarily know things 'relationally' by their dependence on other things; a brief foray into how Locke made the concept concrete is at the centre of this chapter. The divided modes of relationality that figure in Chapter Two make an appearance in Chapter Three in the discussion of conceptual relations. Whether entities pre-exist relations or are brought into existence by them is another way of referring to the contrast between applying the creative work of the relation (invention) or uncovering its prior status (discovery). But this does not exhaust the interest of conceptual relations; above all they can be invested with creative or generative power.

If Locke is at the centre of Chapter Three, impetus also comes from the sidelines: a dreadful pun heard not so many years ago in an American court that referred to parents as the mental conceivers of a child. The part that knowledge plays in the perception of contemporary kinship (again the directionality is deliberate) is rendered dramatic by present-day discussions in the context of new procreative technologies. Here it follows through issues introduced in Chapter Two about the sensitivity of personal information, of great interest to the law, and expands on the work of Dolgin and her formulation of the genetic family mentioned in Chapter One. The creativity of lawyers and a commentary on forms of reproduction – both logical and procreative – offers some contrast with the end of that chapter, which had concluded with a lawyer complaining of the law's limitations.

The cultural contingency of interest here is anthropology's ability to forge a discipline out of relationality. It seems I have woven back and forth between conceptual clarifications and concrete instances, neither of which seems quite up to the measure of the other. Yet that incommensurability has to be right. All I stress in conclusion is that the duplexes mentioned here (connection/disconnection, categorical/interpersonal, given/constructed) that belong to no single logical order, and appear to summon such diverse materials, are all tools for grasping aspects of one world. That world is known not only from different viewpoints but also from specifically divergent, that is, related, ones. Any of the divergences (and there will be others) produces 'the relation'.

The contingency is the pivot or turning point that directs us to Part II. The kinds of objects Euro-Americans make of relationality is there elucidated with Melanesian materials in mind, where relationality is objectified, reified, in other ways. For all the relational inventiveness that Euro-Americans pour into their systems of knowledge, or the work that goes into making society, or the passion of a judge's plea that one-time parents give heed to their relation with a child, the law does not recognise a relationship as a legal subject. Only individuals (individual persons) can be legal subjects. It would not be too far off beam to say that in Melanesian ways of thinking, relationships *are* the equivalent of legal subjects, insofar as they are embodied in persons subject to politico-ritual protocols and public attention.

Together the chapters in Part I comment on a particular Euro-American appropriation of the capacity to manage two kinds of relations, two modes of relating, at once. I have ventured in turn to discriminate between the divergences offered by science's relation and by anthropology's relation. Of course we can only see this process refracted through the very knowledge practices that are built on it. Here we become particularly conscious of the creative and productive, that is, generative operations summoned by science's relation. So, for example, the difference between discovery and invention is not just a scientific (or as we shall see a legal) distinction but is axiomatic to a view interested in knowledge about the world that sets up relations between the given and the made. This key relational nexus is replicated in similar if not identical fashion across diverse arenas, which is why it is so hard to get away (despite best efforts) from its specific location in nature and culture, biology and society, that seems to speak for everything else, including kinship. Highly productive in advancing knowledge of the world, enabling of anthropology among many other disciplines, it remains the case that every insight about (knowledge about) such relationality also obscures. The theoretically more generative, and in this case more creative of systemic thinking, the more knowledge must insist there are things beyond its ken.

Social anthropology has pointed out some of the force of such conceptual or categorical thinking, while its interest in situations where people are simultaneously dealing with interpersonal relations draws it in other directions. Can its own management of relations (conceptual and interpersonal) in fact hold up outside the Euro-American world that anthropology indigenously inhabits? Sometimes it likes to think its practices have origins elsewhere, too.

### ACKNOWLEDGEMENTS

I am grateful to Christina Toren for her encouragement at the 2001 conference on *Children in their Places*, convened at Brunel University by Suzette Heald, Ian Robinson and Christina Toren; parts of both Introductions were, to my considerable benefit, aired there under the panel rubric 'Children in an information age'.

# Relatives Are Always a Surprise: Biotechnology in an Age of Individualism

> We are living in an era of intense individualism.
>
> Margaret Somerville, on stem cell research, in conversation
> with Peter Singer. ABC TV *Dateline*, 16 August 2001

W HAT KIND OF PEOPLE IS BIOTECHNOLOGY TURNING US INTO? 'WE' are no more or less than the users of it, who might be anywhere, although the attendant issues discussed here reflect specifically Euro-American aspirations and concerns. Over the past twenty-five years, biotechnology has provided some powerful food for thought, challenges to how we users of it imagine society and how we imagine our relations to one another. Public opinion has, for example, seized on the idea that the new genetics is making new kinds of persons out of us.[1] Some see these new persons as ultra-individuals. But the new genetics also makes new connections, and here there are some surprises – people find themselves related in unexpected ways. Then again, the kind of people we might be becoming will depend a bit on what we already are, and we are not always quite what we seem.[2] If ours is an age of individualism, as we constantly tell ourselves, and biotechnology feeds into that, then what exactly is biotechnology feeding? Let me start with a case.

## AN AGE OF INDIVIDUALISM

Here is a slice of 'ordinary life' (after Edwards 2000), even if the circumstances that bring it into public view are not ordinary. It concerns grandparents and grandchildren – two girls – and how much they see of one another. The parents separated just before the birth of the second girl, and the father lived at home with his parents, so these grandparents used to see a lot of the two girls.

Grandparents are not the kind of relatives expected to frequent the law courts.[3] But it was as grandparents that the couple petitioned for visiting rights to their grandchildren (Dolgin 2002). Some 18 months after the girls' parents separated, their father died. The girls continued to spend time with their father's parents, but the mother thought it was excessive and wanted to limit it and not allow overnight visits. This is what brought the grandparents to court. The trial court ruled that although the children would benefit from spending quality time with the grandparents, it should be balanced with time spent with the children's 'nuclear family'. The case went to several appeals (the mother appealed, and then the grandparents appealed against the reversal of the trial court's decision).

At the final appeal, the conclusion followed the common law assumption that the courts should not interfere in a parent's right to raise children as he or she wishes.[4] The 'nuclear family' was invoked, and the grandparents were outside it. The U.S. Supreme Court (ultimate court of appeal) 'found wanting the trial court decision that favored a family of extended kin because that choice failed to defer adequately to the decision of a fit mother about her children's familial relationships' (Dolgin 2002: 383). Although observations were made about extra-familial support being important in situations in which there was only one parent – statistics were quoted by the appeals court judges (in 1996, 28% children under 18 lived in single parent households [population not noted]) – the final ruling found in favour of the mother and her authority over her daughters. This did not just mean that the mother's wishes took precedence over the grandparents' but that her individual right to be the kind of parent she wished to be was endorsed.

The judges rejected an atomistic view of family life,[5] but they did endorse parental determination. Many see 'biotechnology' doing what the law did.

Primarily in the form of assisted conception techniques, advances in reproductive medicine have enhanced parental freedom of action. In vitro fertilisation (IVF) and associated procedures have been offered in the name of the nuclear family, enabling couples to have the children who will complete it (see especially Haimes 1990; 1992); in the name of single parents, allowing them to have children without entering into partnerships; and in the name of reproductive choice, recognizing the very determination to have children as possible grounds for claiming parentage. The kind of parenting involved in the court case involving the grandparents is all about social arrangements, whereas biotechnology attends to biology and the body's capacities. One is about rearing children, the other is about having them in the first place – nurture and nature, if you like, or rather nurture-helped-by-the-law and nature-helped-by-technology. But either can be seen as encouraging an individualism of a kind.

This individualism may involve other people, but it is the individualism that refers to the self as the source of choice-making and to the virtues of autonomous action.[6] Parental determination is also parental autonomy. From some points of view, this may look selfish. Actually, the daughter-in-law read selfishness into her in-laws' motives. She thought that the grandparents were thinking of themselves first and trying to turn the girls into some kind of substitute for their lost son.

### ADDING DEBATE

What is interesting about adding biotechnology to such ordinary situations, if I can put it like that, is that one adds debate. Debate has become part of the changing social environment in which the new genetics finds itself (Franklin 2001 b: 337). A doctor talking about the world's thirteenth IVF baby, born in Victoria, Australia, now turned 21, said:

> The issues have also changed. Twenty-one years ago doctors were concentrating on women's early morning dash to the hospital for the collection of eggs. Now they are debating the ethical and moral dilemmas of stem-cell research and single women's rights to IVF.
>
> *The Age* (Melbourne), 24 July 2002

Because of the visibility of the 'new' techniques and the problems they pose for decisionmaking, little is left unquestioned. Indeed, the media constantly draw attention to the circumstances under which people choose reproductive interventions, for these appear test cases for the validity not just of this technology but sometimes (it seems) of all technology.

Among other things, biotechnology has turned us into people who are not surprised if intimate medical matters concerning third parties are debated in public and who in an arena heavily dependent on the expertise of the clinician or scientist see the need to weigh different values, bringing together public and private moralities. After all, 'even if one considers a union a private affair, not necessitating [registry] papers, the birth of a child is always a public event' (Segalen 2001: 259). The role of the expert here has turned quite complex.

It is not just a case of science producing dilemmas for society to solve; biotechnology has become an arena in which society speaks back (Nowotny, Scott and Gibbons 2001; cf. Franklin 2001 b) and in which the public takes an interest in experts' agendas, including their research agendas. Of course, scientists are not the only experts in the field; biotechnology is making us into people who listen to ethicists and philosophers and lawyers as well. And that is not just because their interventions affect individual lives at the points at which people have to make difficult decisions but also because of what often *makes* those decisions difficult. This includes the very fact that we imagine these interventions will affect the kinds of persons we are,[7] for example, how we choose to 'be human'. What is remarkable about the arena of biotechnology is that such a question does not, on the face of it, have to do with excessive violence, greed or the violation of rights but with applications that can lead to advances in medicine. In truth, violence, greed and violation have all been read into the development of biotechnology, but as the obverse of what we are assured are bound to be benefits, both in terms of medical treatment and in keeping at the forefront of research. What emerged as a contentious issue from the outset (at least in the United Kingdom with the Warnock Report in 1985 [Warnock 1985]), the question of limits and where to impose them, is still present.

In a lesser register, if Euro-Americans do not ask the question (What kind of people are we turning into?) about humanity then they may ask it about society; what consequences do people's decisions have for the kind of society they would like to live in? Here individual self-interest emerges as the contentious issue. Techniques welcomed to solve the problems of potential nuclear families may be regarded as suspicious if their end result is more single parent families. Although the desire to have a baby may be taken positively as thoroughly natural, the desire to have a child of a particular kind or for a particular purpose can be taken negatively as an example of parental selfishness.[8] Contemplating the implications for Humanity or for Society is unlikely to be where those closely involved find most difficulty but, fanned by the zeal of the press, which constantly puts these cases into the public eye, it does make difficult how everyone else is to *think about* the phenomena.

The year 2002 brought reports of a deaf couple who intentionally had a deaf child to match their own condition, their second, the first being four years old. This was by sperm donation and need not have involved any 'biotechnology' at all, but the story fits into the genre of stories about 'genetic manipulation'. It also was about same-sex parenthood because the partners were women. 'Babies, deaf by design' was one headline, to echo debate over designer babies raised by the new genetics (*The Australian*, 16 April 2002).[9] 'Being [born] deaf is just a way of life. We feel whole as deaf people and we want to share the wonderful aspects of our deaf community'.

Commenting on these words from one of them, *The Australian's* reporter observed that the parents turned deafness from disability into cultural difference. Their decision thus highlighted the enigma of autonomous choice. What for the couple was design for perfection for others was design for disability. Note that the couple's design for perfection was not to have themselves reproduced, which would have been dependent on the vagaries of genetic recombination, but to create children who replicated their shared *elective* characteristic of deafness. It was the one characteristic that they wanted to see in their child. They said they felt they could nurture a deaf child with more understanding than a child with normal hearing.

The couple was portrayed as selfish for not thinking of the child. Where they stressed the sense of belonging and sharing that came from being with members of their 'deaf community', the newspaper stressed the fact that the deaf are cut off from mainstream society. 'Sooner or later their children will have to face up to the hearing world', observed the journalist who described the huge technical backup system that assists them to communicate (for example, over telephone). Interests in common at once unite and divide, and mainstream society has sufficient interest in these children to pass highly evaluative judgements on the parents' decisions.

The case, from Maryland (United States), was reported in the Australian press as it was across the world. The question it raises for the public – how we are to think about the parents' decision? – is seemingly ubiquitous. Although these types of questions are debated with local issues in mind and although the regulatory regimes are different, they strike similar chords. The dilemmas travel with the technology, that is, the debates crop up in surprisingly similar forms in many otherwise different contexts.[10] I already have in mind that, based on her study of couples trying to create families through assisted conception, Bonaccorso (2000) had come to this conclusion about Italian practices. Procedures of litigation may differ, but the way in which values are weighed in favour of certain kinds of family arrangements seems very familiar, amid a general consensus about the causes for both congratulation and disquiet.

Now the plight of the deaf couple might lead one to pit individual choice *against* general public values. However, I would put it rather that we see an interplay between what are in effect two sets of public values, which in turn may either chime together or clash. On the one hand lies autonomy and the individualism it promotes, and on the other hand lies altruism and interests in common.[11] Both values are written into public reactions to biotechnology; either can be taken in a positive or a negative direction.

## INDIVIDUAL AND COMMON INTERESTS

By way of example, I focus briefly on issues concerning genetic make-up. Western (Euro-American) imagery routinely represents individuality through people's unique and singular bodies, echoed in understandings of the unique genetic template. No one else has quite the same combination of genes, bar identical twins. The perception of individuality and the value of individualism go together, and the significance of the unique genetic template is repeated over and again, a twentieth century discovery so easily absorbed into pre-existing notions about individuality that it is – among other things – the possibility of compromising that uniqueness that makes cloning so threatening.[12]

Bodily uniqueness is a sign as much as a Euro-American symbol of auto-nomy and of respect for the person as an individual (for recent discussion, see Davies and Naffine 2001; James and Palmer 2002). Indeed, the integrity of the body is itself the subject of rights. Thus much current questioning over embryo stem cells recalls earlier anguish over embryo research. Paradoxically, the biotechnology that in the eyes of some destroys individual beings also becomes one of the vehicles through which the very 'individuality' of em-bryonic features become apparent. And it is the interventionist character of biotechnology that has us formulate obligations: how to treat others.[13] Here the embryo may be depicted as a fragile and vulnerable member of the species who needs special protection.

The individuality of a person's make-up is also made visible through his or her profile of likely health, with an interesting qualification. That genetic diagnosis offers the possibility of being able to make sense of the person's own genome has at the same time stimulated great interest in the role that heredity – inheritance from others – plays in the transmission of disease. Nonetheless, it is what comes together in the individual genome that will count for the pa-tient, which can be seen as both positive and negative. Chapter Three touches on people's urge to seek out relatives beyond the nuclear family in order to recover information about themselves and their medical prospects. There is also evidence, largely from the United States (Dolgin 2000; Finkler 2000), to suggest that some people trace relatives simply to gain this vital informa-tion and give little regard to the possibilities of starting up relationships with them.[14] This creates (the phrase is Dolgin's) 'genetic families', whose members are first and foremost linked through the information their bodies hold about one another. Individualism flourishes to the extent to which these genetic ties can be disarticulated – severed – from social ones.[15]

On the other side, of course, genes are not unique at all. Again, we find both positive and negative values. The combinations might be unique, but the genes themselves are replicas. People share the same range with everyone else on the planet, and the same basic genetic mechanism with all living things – even as they share the genetic make-up found in millions of human bodies built in similar ways, almost but not quite identical to one another. For however long this has been true, it is biotechnology that moves people to make declarations about genetic solidarity. Heredity become heritage, and the appeal is to the macro community this creates:

The concept of genetic solidarity and altruism might be summarised as follows: We all share the same basic human genome, although there are individual variations which distinguish us from other people. Most of our genetic characteristics will be present in others. This sharing of our genetic constitution not only gives rise to opportunities to help others but it also highlights our common interests in the fruits of medically-based genetic research.

HGC 2002: 38

What comes to mind are objections to 'patenting genes' (DNA), which, some argue, puts common resources into private hands.[16] The argument was heard over the decoding of the human genome and the spectre of patenting, a race fuelled by visions of public against private property, the common interests of humankind against capital accumulation by a few. There are in fact two rather different positions here. Membership of the human species confers belonging, common membership arousing a sense of identity with other human beings. The notion of common interests, however, starts raising questions of ownership of a quasi-property kind.[17] That is, insofar as the features of a common humanity can be made to yield a resource, there is some competition as to who should enjoy its fruits: what disabilities should be treated, who has access to the information it yields, who can benefit from the development of pharmaceuticals. It also makes clearer what is implicit in the model of common humanity, that a sense of inclusiveness at one level (we all have [more or less] the same genome) is exclusiveness at another (other species do not count).

Now the case of heredity concerns people working out the consequences of discovering genetic connection, whereas the case of heritage amounts to abstract justifications for ethical behaviour. Despite these differences, I suggest that both prompt attitudes that are thoroughly familiar from Western (Euro-American) images of the 'nuclear family'. Now on the face of it nothing could seem further apart than the dispersed network of relatives in which ties are treated instrumentally (the so-called genetic families) with only the tiniest units coming together to form (nuclear) families, and the inclusive body of human beings that form a unity[18] at a fundamental level no one should tamper with. Yet shift perspective a bit, and if the exclusive family appears like an individual writ large, then the community of humankind – in this view internally undifferentiated – appears like an exclusive family writ large. Whether, as in the instance of the Washington grandparents, close relatives do not count, or whether protection extends only to the notion of what we share with other human beings, the family looks after its own.

Some of the hold that biotechnology exercises over the imagination is its power to intervene in realities that already play a role in the way people think about themselves. Heredity or heritage, one can think of genes in narrower or broader contexts in human affairs. And the boundary images of 'family' do their job twice over. At the same time this particular imagery is highly selective. There are many other things we know about families. So let us not assume what they are; let us stand back a second time, then, and return to the ordinary family we have already encountered.

### RECOMBINANT FAMILIES

Here lies a surprise. The Washington grandparents who petitioned for visitation rights found that the courts put different weight on the nuclear family. But what was this nuclear family?[19] By the time of the first hearing, the mother had already remarried. The family household in which the girls were now living included their mother, her new husband who subsequently adopted them, a child from the new marriage, three children from an earlier marriage of hers, and two children from the new husband's previous marriage: eight offspring in all, although none of the couples had had more than two or three together. In fact, a British anthropologist, Simpson, punned of similar kinds of arrangements in the United Kingdom that the resulting constellations produce families that are 'unclear' rather than 'nuclear'.

Simpson (1994; 1998) was commenting on a phenomenon that appears in many post-divorce arrangements in Britain. There does not immediately seem anything untoward about such family arrangements – similar ones can be found in many times and places, as for instance in the French example of repeated divorces over three generations given by Segalen (2001 : 262–3) – except that it does not fit into the model of the 'family' we have been considering. It is neither narrow nor wide, it has no clear boundary. Rather, bits originating in other families have come together to make a new one. The surprise is in seeing what is happening: dissolution often leads to recombination (cf. Bell 2001 : 386).

The background is familiar enough. Britain has the highest divorce rate in Europe[20]; with more than half of divorced couples in 1990 having a child under sixteen, it may now have reached a plateau, but it is a plateau with a distinctive configuration. Despite the break-ups, both families and marriage remain popular (one in three marriages is a remarriage) (Simpson 1998: viii). That same figure is true of Australia (roughly a third of all marriages is a remarriage).[21] 'Ten things you didn't know about Australian families' is how the *Sun Herald* (Sydney) (23 January 2000) greeted a swathe of statistics, dating to 1996–1998, intended to provoke surprise both at how traditional Australian family arrangements persist *and* how prone to change they are. The changes are, for instance, in the direction of rising divorce rates (40% of all marriages after 30 years, edging to the United Kingdom's 50%) and a rising age of women having children, yet tradition is evident in the fact that most children are born to parents who are married (70%), and over 70% of children under 18 who currently live with their parents live in a nuclear family (mum, dad and the children they had together).[22] However, a sense of change is introduced by the *projection* that 30% children under four will be in single parent families by 2021 (the present figure is 20%, of which the majority are single mother families). The traditional and non-traditional exist side by side.

It is nothing new to observe that there seems as much value put on marriages and families as ever; *how* they are made up is another matter. In Australia, a high proportion of children live with both 'biological' parents, but there are also many who live with only one. It may be in a single parent family, or it may be in a recomposed one. 'Recomposed' is Segalen's (2001: 259) word for families, as in the Washington instance, that form after the break-up of previous ones.[23] The high degree of divorce in present times throws those recomposed families into relief, and makes them visible. 'Divorce is the point at which marriage is officially dissolved but it is also the point at which the principles, assumptions, [and] values . . . surrounding marriage, family and parenting are made explicit' (Simpson 1998: 27). Indeed, Simpson suggests that what is new is the extent to which such recompositions have become part of the fabric of society. Marriages might dissolve and many would regret the rate it has reached, but families reform. Creeping up on us, as it were, is a new realisation of ways of arranging the relationships.

Embedded in these ordinary circumstances are pointers to what is also interesting about biotechnology. It has become part of the social fabric: 'ART [assisted reproductive technology] is now clearly an integral part of society', to quote an observation from Western Australia (Cummins 2002). What has been creeping up on us is a world in which, for example, the thought of replacing parts of bodies – or even the bodies of lost persons – follows not far behind knowing about techniques of organ transfer or hearing of claims on a deceased spouse's reproductive material. Assisted conception procedures that offer remedy to those unable to have children also encourage people to organise careers with an expectation of late parenthood. Obviously in this area (of assisted conception), but also where family members must make decisions in relation to one another, for example over prolongation of life at birth or death, biotechnology has itself become a factor in the way people manage their lives. It adds its own field of recombinations in what it takes to conceive children. And it is partly the degree to which the applications of biotechnology have in turn intervened in the formation of families that has given us recomposed families. From her French perspective, Segalen writes:

[By adopting] new legal dispositions reflecting the new attitudes towards marriage, and also echoing the development of biotechnologies since the 1970s, jurists have disarticulated marriage and filiation [the recognised relation of succession between parent and child]. More children . . . enjoy the benefits of a paternal presence though the father [is not what he seems]. . . . The father, according to the Napoleonic Code, was the man who gave his genes, gave his name, and daily raised the child in his home. These three components of filiation have been disassociated in recomposed families.

Segalen 2001 : 259[24]

The jurists might have taken apart marriage and filiation but, as people tell themselves, reproductive technology has already taken apart filiation and conception. If you look at the regular nuclear family, you may well find that the parents have been helped by a donor. What is true, then, of families legally recomposed through divorce and adoption is also true of biotechnological parentage, at least insofar as the fertile components that go to make up a child may be drawn from diverse sources, diverse bodies.

We might surmise that families composed of other families, with children already conceived, would be largely distinct from families seeking augmentation through gamete donation or IVF. But the two kinds of recomposition can come together. Again, divorce or separation makes that coming together visible, and following the break-up of partnerships we hear much about, for example, disputed rights of disposal over frozen embryos.[25] This is the moment at which combinations have to be disentangled.[26] To take one example, the judgement in the Washington grandparents' petition was subsequently cited in a Rhode Island case involving a same-sex couple who had separated, in which one of the pair applied for visiting rights to a child born to her partner through artificial insemination that she had helped organise (Dolgin 2002: 402–4). What weighed with the judges was the 'parent-like relationship' she had had with the child for the four years they lived together, even though once the visitation privileges had been won she forfeited her claims to parentage as such. In this case, the authority of the child's 'biological mother' had to be balanced against the interests of the other party asserting co-parental rights.

A complex nexus of possibilities is afforded not just by the law, then, but also by biotechnology. Indeed, and to follow Franklin's (2003:81) use of 're-combinant' as an epithet for certain kinds of conceptual relations, we might borrow the metaphor again: such families are nothing if they not recombinant. It would be to draw on a simple notion from a complex cellular process, namely, that the techniques involving recombinant DNA were, at least when new, described as permitting the 'combination of genetic information from very different organisms' (Berg et al. 2002: 320). Biologists' ability 'to splice and recombine different DNAs' dates from 1973 (Reiser 2002: 7).

'Recombinant' is an apt term for the social forms these new families take[27]; their formation is not just a matter of shuffling parts around or submerging parts in an undifferentiated whole but of cutting and splicing so that elements work in relation to one another in distinct ways. To some extent, the elements can be kept conceptually discrete. (You cannot undo a conception, although a baby's DNA will carry imprints that can separately identify each of its parents.[28] You can block the social connotations of that conception, as routinely happens when donor anonymity cuts off donors from their reproductive act.) I mean recombinant, then, in the sense that in taking apart different components of motherhood and fatherhood one is also putting them together in new ways, in both conception procedures *and* in rearing practices, and then all over again in combinations of the two.

### THINKING ABOUT RELATIVES

There is much more going on than the 'fragmentation' of society. Euro-Americans know that the thought of biotechnology marshals an extraordinary range of hopes and fears; scientists' own particular concerns with the development of recombinant technology also date from the 1970s (Reiser 2002: 7). They know technology itself is not to 'blame', yet many people cannot help thinking that the new techniques draw out of them a new impetus to social fragmentation in the form of selfishness.[29] The hopes and fears somehow get aligned, so that somewhat utilitarian hopes of medical advance or improved treatments are pitched against fears about damage to society or even damage to humanity in the way they think about themselves as ethical creatures. I have wanted to put the complexity of some of the applications of biotechnology into an arena of interpersonal relations already made complex by the kinds of decisions that ordinary people – with or without the help of the law – make all the time.

This is where relatives have the capacity to surprise us. Divorce rises; the family remains popular. How can this be the case? Although particular families break up, *relationships* often endure. We could even say the family dissolves but the kinship remains.[30] I have already touched on the fact that in Euro-American culture, the body, insofar as its boundaries seem self-evident, can stand as a symbol of the integrated person. Connections between persons are generally thought of as lying outside the body, through all kinds of communication and forms of association. *Kinship*, though, is where Westerners think about connections between bodies themselves.[31] Indeed, if they use the body to think about the uniqueness of the individual, they also use it to talk about the way persons are connected to one another, not through what they share in a general way, as we might speak of all humankind as kin, but through what has been transmitted in particular ways. So they trace specific connections (genealogies) and the network tells them how closely they are related (degrees of relatedness). Modern knowledge of genetics endorses this way of thinking: genes make each individual unique *and* connects it to many immediate – as well as countless more distant – others.

Recombinant DNA, that is, DNA in its characteristic of separable and re-arrangeable segments, invites human intervention. There is a tendency when thinking about genes to stress connection, whether narrowly (the unique individual as the product of the nuclear family) or widely (all of humankind). Recombinant DNA further invites us to ponder the *disconnections*, the ability to take things apart and thus make them potentially parts of fresh constellations. 'Genes aren't us', the ethicist Julian Savulescu was reported as stating in *The Age* (19 June 2002). He went on to say that we are not the sum of our genes and genes do not determine who we are. I suggest that this is true in quite a profound sense that would mimic the possibilities that biotechnology affords them if they did not already antedate it. Ordinary *knowledge* about genetic connection gives a choice; there might be no choice about recognising the kinship constituted in the genetic connection itself (cf Strathern 1999b), but people may or may not make active relationships out of these connections. They may decide to ignore potential links. So fresh connections may or may not ensue: persons can disappear completely from one's life, or never seem to leave it. In valuing *or* devaluing their relationships, relatives thus become aware of the way they are connected *and* disconnected (cf. Edwards and Strathern 2000; Franklin 2003). Recombinant families just make this very visible, showing how cutting off ties leads to making others, or how household arrangements offer innumerable permutations on degrees of disconnection.

So people already act out diverse ways of thinking about themselves: not just as isolates set apart or as members of collectivities or groups but also as beings who value their connections to others, who – when things are going well, that is – manage being at once autonomous and relational.[32] The social relations of kinship, we might say, set that process of management in train.

How to deal with one's attachment to kin while also detaching oneself from them is central to kinship in Western (Euro-American) society. Western kinship regimes take to extremes the idea of bringing up a child to be independent, not only as an independent 'member of society' but also as independent from family and relatives. It does not take an expert to say this; Euro-Americans already know it in the way they act. But in contrast to the huge investment they make in the language and imagery of individuals or groups, they need fresh ways of telling themselves about the complexities and ambiguities of relationships.

There are two outcomes from all this for the way Euro-Americans implement their values. The first is evident in recombinant families and the opportunities for new connections. Divorce reorders kinship. If they take their eyes off the units that are reformed and look instead at the trail of relationships, they find families interconnected in new ways. Divorces link children, that is, children now living in different families are linked through the dissolved marriages of their parents[33]:

If we talk of family in an uncritical way, the creative possibilities inherent in kinship for the structuring of interpersonal relations are obscured.... The study of divorce as a cultural expression of kinship, rather than as a social problem with family, demonstrates the distinctiveness of western patterns of relational organisation ... [and] it offers the prospect of locating distinctively Euro-American patterns of kinship and putting them into comparative perspective.

Simpson 1994: 832

Simpson thus makes the positive suggestion that we should treat these linkages as phenomena in their own right. It is clear that in valuing their relationships, people already do.

The second outcome for the way Euro-Americans implement their values concerns disconnections. In addition to dislocating kinship from families, what about the way in which relationships, as the ongoing activation of social ties, may be dislocated from kinship in the sense of genetic connection? Do not the new 'genetic families', based as they often are on medical data kinspersons share, give new dimensions to individualism (the self-reference of the medical patient)? Dislocating relationships from kinship is of course inherent in donor anonymity and is always the alternative after divorce or separation. Thus Segalen's (2001: 260) recomposition may indeed add to pre-existing family networks, so that, say, biological father and stepfather co-exist and work out a modus vivendi, but in France at least this tends to be especially true of relatively affluent, middle class families. In other sectors of society, recombination can also erase previous unions, usually cutting off ties with the old father where the new father adopts the children and gives them his name. And it can lead to diverse ways in which the new units are viewed. One British instance (Simpson 1994: 834–5)[34] invites us to consider the perspective of the grandparents: the husband's parents speak of having six grandchildren where the wife's parents speak of three; husband and wife would like to see all six of their children, the offspring of four different marriages, treated equally, but the wife's parents only give treats to their own child's children (by two marriages).

We have seen that both the generalised universal 'family of man' and the close domestic family – which probably calls itself 'nuclear', recomposed or otherwise – alike embody notions of exclusion. Those values of exclusion make all the difference between families that defend boundaries and families that emphasise recombinant relationships (so to speak) and thus live out their idea of themselves as overlapping with others. In the former, when kin are cut from one another, it is to extrude one set from outside the circle of the other set, like the hapless Washington grandparents. Cutting thus externalises (the grandparents then have to negotiate access). In the latter case, however, cutting *defines* the conditions under which families overlap, is internal to the ensuing network. If there were no separation, no severance of couples at divorce, there would be no recombination.[35]

Euro-Americans[36] have no difficulty in imagining persons as different combinations of elements – from genes and their environment, to the baby and its nurturers,[37] to someone's relatives and circle of friends – and each such combination bestows an identity made distinct through the person's relations with the world. What biotechnology adds – especially through the ARTs – is the prospect of reading distinct social identities back into the very process of conception (for instance, via gamete donation and its proliferation of social sources).[38] Yet in one sense indigenous (Euro-American) notions of kinship already make persons combinations of other persons. This is not a question of losing one's identity but of specifying it: the fact that everyone is a part of someone else is held to conserve the individuality of each recombination.

∽

THIS IS LESS A CONCLUSION THAN A SHIFT IN REGISTER. BEING PARTS OF others carries its own responsibility; how we (users of biotechnology) take decisions entails how we define those responsibilities. Two debates from

Australia are the impetus here. The first is an academic one, largely in response to the way legal thinking has been influenced by the technology, and is inevitably inconclusive. The second concerns changes in clinical practice that conclusively implement a response to public questions.

In their book, *Are Persons Property?*, the Australian feminist and legal theorists, Davies and Naffine, write about autonomy with reference to notions of self-ownership and about the particular problem that a thoroughly ordinary and everyday phenomenon, the pregnant woman, presents for the law. 'The pregnant woman and foetus are one legal person and that is the woman' (2001: 84). The counter-action, as we well know, is to claim the uniqueness of the fetus, even to the point of claiming that it is a person in its right (Savill 2002: 50). But the law must continue to be equivocal. In their words, the facts of reproduction render incoherent the notions of individualism on which these views are based. The complexities of this situation are compounded by technological interventions that produce embryos outside the body. We return to the issue of ownership, indeed persons as property, in Chapters Five and Six. Here I pursue the observation that biotechnology has provided new ways of conceptualising the individuality of the fetus.[39] If ever we needed new ways of thinking about persons as parts of persons, by contrast, the pregnant woman is a paradigmatic case.

The remark is hardly new. Reassessing 'The mother of the legal person', Savill (2002)[40] notes how close the law can get. When the (British) Law Lords had to take a decision on culpability in an appeal over a fetus killed through injury done to the mother, speakers referred openly to the modern science of human fertilisation and the light it had thrown on the reality of embryological and fetal separateness. This in turn elicited a strong statement that there was nonetheless 'an intimate bond' between a mother and the fetus dependent on her body for its support. Lord Mustill is quoted as saying:

But the relationship was one of bond not identity. The mother and the foetus were two distinct organisms living symbiotically, not a single organism with two aspects.

Savill 2002: 44

The view was not powerful enough to displace the doctrine that the fetus has no legal personality (it lacks full autonomy; as an incomplete human being, it is in corporeal terms *sui generis*.). It also left out the extent to which the maternal body is changed by pregnancy, and indeed becomes in its new state dependent on the fetus for the completion of its developmental trajectory. This is the point at which Savill (2002: 66) quotes Karpin's illuminating suggestion that we conceptualise the maternal body as a 'nexus of relations'. Karpin does not mean:

> a relationship in which mother and fetus . . . are equal partners because that would rely on a basic premise of distinction. The value of a nexus-of-relations perspective is that it makes obsolete a notion of subjectivity that is dependent for its subject status on distinction, separation and defensive opposition to others.
>
> Karpin 1994: 46

I have one disagreement.[41] I do not think we need be afraid of distinctions and separations. In the same volume, Gatens (2002: 168) turns to Spinoza for his understanding that individuals:

> are not 'atoms' or 'monads' but are themselves made up of 'parts' that are in constant interchange with each other . . . [such that] for an individual to endure requires exchange, struggle and cooperation with other individuals, who are also made up of parts.

Spinoza's ethical–political ontology, she remarks, 'facilitates understanding difference as enabling identity and *relations of interdependence as enabling autonomy*' (2002: 169, my emphasis). Biotechnology has introduced into the domain of body management the kinds of separations, cuts and combinations that have always characterised relations between persons.

Yet the fact remains that Euro-Americans do not always talk about relations very clearly. Some of their current dilemmas stem from those areas in which the vocabulary for the interests at stake is exhausted.[42] I have suggested that certain aspects of biotechnology, such as recombinant genetics, offers fresh ways of thinking about social arrangements and indeed about biotechnology's own interventions. Franklin (2003) provides an arresting account of people moving in and out of the discourses of genetics in dealing with kin relations. If so, the virtue is less the novelty of these discourses than their capacity to bring people back *to what they already know*. They already 'know' that mother and fetus are both separable and parts of each other; what is lacking is an adequate language for this kind of relation. This limits the way in which responsibilities are conceptualised. It is as though Euro-Americans could only speak of each as either merged with or external to one another, an exclusive unity or an exclusion of the one from the other's interests. Yet (to put Spinoza's words into another frame) it is their separability that is at the basis of their interdependency. If literal separation is the precondition for recombination in the case of families, then in the case of mother and fetus separation is integral to any relationship between them.[43]

I would repeat that people already know this. But one reason for the shortage of relational idioms is the overdetermination of other idioms. For when it comes to legislation and litigation, a relationship is not (and cannot be) a legal subject in Western (Euro-American) law. This is a problem we shall have to live with. So the arguments remain fascinating but inconclusive.

Other problems are shifted, and the consequences of how people make decisions have evident effect in the conclusions people draw.

Children born of donated gametes, and given the nature of the procedures it is more likely to have been the sperm donor rather than the egg donor who has been completely separated from the results of conception, are now in the position of having to decide whether or not pursue their genetic paternity. Members of Sydney's Donor Conception Support Group are reported as saying: 'They just want to find out who they are. They don't want replacement parents' (*Sydney Morning Herald*, 29 November 2001). Certain donors do not wish even that, the same article goes on, 'I would much prefer them to simply say thank you, enjoy their mothers and fathers and get on with their lives', said one donor who threatened to take legal action if he was identified. Or it may be a mother who makes such a decision on behalf of her child, as in the case of the sperm donor who went to the Family Court in Melbourne to seek access to a two-year-old boy; the Court was told that the child was not being denied a relationship, just 'an active parental relationship' (*Sun Herald*, Sydney, 27 January 2002).[44] Other decisions follow, such as an IVF clinic trying to eliminate anonymous donations altogether from their procedures because of the ethical problems to which they give rise. 'Nowadays, the clinic advises clients to ask a friend or relative to provide sperm', said a nurse (*Sydney Morning Herald*, 29 November 2001).

'Or relative'! A final surprise, then, sprung by relatives, in this case by relatives who – like friends – are willing to donate to kin they know. If one recalls all those early debates about anonymity being needed to protect the nuclear family, saving it equally from intrusive strangers and the shadow of incest, a wheel seems to have turned full circle. Seemingly, that problem has been pushed to one side, and pre-existing kinship comes into its own.[45] Of course, it is not without complications. Edwards (1999; 2000) offers an account, and it is one of the few fully ethnographic accounts, of the way English kinsfolk weigh up such matters. Thompson (2001 : 174) describes a Californian fertility clinic where friends and relatives are involved in gamete donation, and where 'certain bases of kin differentiation are foregrounded and recrafted while other are minimized'. Although this may be so that the intending parents come out 'through legitimate and intact chains of descent as the real parents', my focus is on the separations and recombinations that make this possible. In one case, for example, the surrogate asked to gestate eggs and sperm from a husband–wife pair was the husband's sister. It was not counted as incest. It was a near thing, though, and the sister joked that it was lucky she had her tubes tied because that ensured that none of her own eggs would meet any sperm that might accidentally be transferred with the embryo. A further case Thompson (2001: 187) cites is a co-venture of a kind that came to the fore from the early days of IVF, namely mothers and daughters assisting one another, in this case the daughter providing an egg to be inseminated by her mother's husband. The fact that he was her stepfather helped, but the fact that the egg contained genetic endowment from the daughter's father (mother's former husband) was not mentioned. In this case, the daughter was happy to have helped her mother, but did not like thinking about the spare embryos that were not used and that, outside her mother's body, simply remained the creation of herself and her stepfather.

Yet however painful, casual, taken for granted or requiring great effort it is, relatives can probably handle the complex business of negotiating closeness and distance, separating themselves from this part of procreation in order to associate with that part. Is it because, regardless of what happens in other parts of their lives, kinship has taught them to be adept at managing two kinds of relations at once, not just connections but disconnections as well?

## ACKNOWLEDGEMENTS

Considerable thanks to the Julius Stone Institute and to Helen Irving and the Law Faculty at the University of Sydney for the opportunity to participate in the 2002 Macquarie Bank Lecture series *Biotechnologies: Between Expert Knowledges and Public Values*. The Gender Relations Centre and Department of Anthropology at the Research School of Pacific and Asian Studies, Australian National University, Canberra, also my hosts, provided much further discussion; warm personal thanks to Margaret Jolly and Mark Mosko. I remain grateful to the other authors of *Technologies of Procreation* for their continuing insights; however, I have probably drawn more on Sarah Franklin's (2001 b; 2003) re-conceptualisations than I realise. Janet Dolgin once again provided me with something of a base, as did Alain Pottage. Monica Bonaccorso's study proved very informative, and Maria Carranza gave exceptional help in acquainting me with current affairs in Australia.

2

# Embedded Science

Our picture of science is still heavily impregnated with epistemology – that
is, the 'theory' of knowledge.

John Ziman, 2000: 6

*I*N 2003 THE INTERNATIONAL COUNCIL FOR SCIENCE PREPARED TO
launch what it regarded as one of its most important strategic reviews
ever. This was a review of the responsibilities of science and society. A fascinating phenomenon of the last decade or so has been the international
circulation of the idea that science needs society as much as society needs
science. 'Science and Society' programmes seem to spring up on all sides. In
summoning the combined skills of experts and non-experts alike, such programmes try to make explicit the interdependence of the two. Thus a central
formula in U.K. science policy has recently undergone a shift in that direction: from the Public Understanding of Science to the concept of Science and
Society.[1] The call is for a greater understanding of how society is implicated
in science, and how science might be made accountable to society: a 'new
social contract'.[2] In thinking about what stands for society, how one knows
when it has been engaged, society becomes itself an explicit object of inquiry.
There is considerable interest here for a social anthropology engaged with
what is made explicit and what is left implicit. For anthropologists frequently
claim that much knowledge is embedded in habits and practices that render
it implicit. If the same claim were to be made for Western (Euro-American)
science in its societies of origin, where would one look for a tacit or embedded
science?

Supposing science is already 'in' society, then, where is it? What do I need
to make explicit in order to find examples of its embedding? I am going
to introduce certain knowledge practices. I shall argue that Euro-Americans

already act out ways of putting together knowledge that are 'scientific'. But they do not always make it evident to themselves in such terms, and in this sense the practices are only science in a tacit or implicit manner. Two arenas catch my attention. The first is that of anthropologists prosecuting their discipline although they inhabit a rather arcane and esoteric corner of society in doing so.[3] The second belongs to a part of social life far from arcane, indeed the parts of their lives people often find ordinary, as I expound in the second half of the chapter.

What science do I mean? I mean the science that claims its antecedents in the scientific revolution of the seventeenth century, a precursor to the European Enlightenment. That was the century that witnessed 'self-conscious and large-scale attempts to change belief, and ways of securing belief, about the natural world', when people felt that they were proposing 'new and very important changes in the knowledge of natural reality and in the practices by which legitimate knowledge was to be secured' (Shapin 1996: 5). It laid down ways of thinking that are still very much with us, or (better put) that have spurred numerous other revolutions that keep science at once recognisable and forever changing. One can have a greater or lesser sense of epoch, but that earlier period is at least a starting point for asking about implicit habits of scientific thinking.[4]

'The scientific world is . . . that which we verify' (Osborne 1998, quoting Bachelard). For present purposes, I take 'science' as standing not for one kind of knowledge, nor for that matter – though it would have the greater historical accuracy – for many kinds. Rather, I take it as allowing for twinned or paired or otherwise related but divergent thinking that rests on, among other things, two ways of verifying information. The divergence between invention and discovery is the case in point. One might see this as the difference between verifying hypotheses enacted out through new instruments of knowledge (such as inventing an engine to use the force of compressed steam or a technique to use the behaviour of enzymes in determining gene sequences) and verifying what new observations can yield with respect to what is already known (such as discovering landfalls or micro-organisms, hitherto unnamed or unrecorded but recognisable). The line may be fine, but the law turns this duplex into a critical distinction. In the arena of intellectual property rights, the law considers the distinction as coming from science, and attributes to science different ways of relating to the outcomes.[5] At any rate, such divergence allows ideas to appear alongside of and co-produced with critiques of them, and it creates the possibility of different kinds of knowledge existing in tandem.

The duplex works with fractal effect; the same divergence can be repeated at any scale. So each element of a pair can itself bifurcate, that is, become a pair itself. I do not draw attention to this process, but it makes for constant dovetailing in the narrative that follows.

## ISOLATED KNOWLEDGE

In *The island of the day before*, Eco (1995) has his hero of sorts sail between islands inhabited by people who live by different theories. Thus on one island people are forever on their knees gazing into ponds, for they hold that someone who is not seen cannot be. On the next, the inhabitants exist only by being the subject of narration, talking incessantly to keep one another alive, striving to make each story unique in order to be able to tell one another apart. These islanders have mistaken theories for life. Yet there is another truth behind their predicament that a social anthropologist might appreciate. Eco has to put his people on different islands because otherwise they might have heard about one another's theories and come to hold their own less tenaciously.[6]

One spectacle that the new genetics has brought onto centre stage is the realisation that scientific knowledge is no island. It has been impossible to isolate the knowledge that people assume scientists are accumulating about the working of the human genome. On the contrary, this has been a prime area in which it is thought irresponsible *not* to anticipate possible social repercussions (it attracts many science and society projects). What is interesting is prominence given to knowledge itself. It is not just the implementation of knowledge that is at issue, for example, in the form of protocols to deal with risk or pharmacogenetics ('My very own medicine'[7]), but also the very holding of knowledge as such when that knowledge is derived from the human (that is, some person's) genome. One of the products of genetic knowledge acquired for clinical purposes is widely understood to be information on a whole range of matters about life circumstances of great interest to the person in question. The issue is that many of them could also be of great interest to third parties. In this light, it has become a truism to say that genetic knowledge is frequently regarded as at once full of promise and full of danger.

Following its discussion document, the report of the U.K. Human Genetics Commission (HGC 2002) addresses debate in this area. What might be knowledge for the individual is also given something of a distance as 'personal genetic data', namely, information about other individuals that is personal to them. Several questions that have to do with what kind of information concerning third parties it is permissible to have access to, and to keep, acquire further weight when that includes information about genetic make-up. In its recommendations, the HGC report very quickly moves from its opening premise that personal information is private information to the point that it is not private at all:

Genetic knowledge may bring people into a specific moral relationship with one another. We have therefore proposed the following concept of *genetic solidarity and altruism*, which promotes the common good.

2002: 13, original emphasis

Such interest in relationships is not taken for granted but must be flagged as an explicit value to be taken into account. So although, as the HGC report explains, many of the principles to which it adheres are concerned with safeguarding the individual, 'it is important . . . to see the individual as a member of society' (2002: 2.8).[8] Note the imperative to *recognise* this fact of society. Recognition then produces a moral precept that becomes an awkward problem. Society is concretised as 'community' and then – echoing terms encountered in the previous chapter – revealed in a particularly distinctive form, the family:

We do not lead our lives in isolation, but as members of communities, large and small. We must also think of a family as a micro-community.

2002: 2.10

The problem is evident: how to balance the fact of sharing information that may lead to better medical outcomes with the privacy that an individual expects. The balance is particularly acute when it comes to relations with other family members.[9] Information that one family member has may be important for others, and the 'web of moral responsibilities' that characterises such relations becomes an example of a more general issue of balancing 'social and individual interests'.[10]

The crux is that knowledge personal to one person may also be information that is potentially personal to another, so that revelation could help the third party. Regardless of the entanglement of relations, difficulties are created by conventions in the handling of information as such. Thus, if personal information is considered private, finding out about the genetic make-up of another person becomes an invasion of privacy; if testing for genetic disorders becomes likened to research or invasive surgery, then the worry is intervening when the patient is not someone who will be the beneficiary of the knowledge (2002: 4.54). 'Informed consent' becomes pretty stretched for those trying to deal with what is perceived as the 'ethics' of the case.

It is ironic that what began as an aid to uncovering hereditary diseases – being able to trace kin connections – has turned into a different kind of aid and a different kind of problem. It was once the case that genetic knowledge could only be built up through information known about family members by family members. DNA diagnosis can bypass cumbersome trawls through kin connections, and cuts to the heart of the matter; information about inheritance is bundled up in the individual's own genome. The HGC report dwells on the issues that arise in what it calls family analysis, 'carrying out a test on one person in order to ascertain the significance of a genetic characteristic that is shared with a relative' (2002: 4.54). There is the related question of whether individuals knowing about their own make-up should volunteer their knowledge for the information of others (Finkler 2000), a topic to which the next chapter returns. Relatives are turned from those who are a source of information about genetic connections (as were inferred from lines of descent) into those who need to be told.

Such issues have become the bread and butter concerns of media debates, ethical scrutiny, and the like. I want to suggest there is a bit more here than meets the eye, and that concerns the role we accord knowledge. Can I use the social anthropologist's eye, or voice, or theory, to develop the point? Of course anthropology does not exist on an island, and its theories are not immune to influence from others. And for as many who take the archetypal subject of ethnography to be an island society, many more assume that the entities they study are no more like islands than people are. I shall try to elucidate.

## RELATIONS EVERYWHERE

Perhaps it was no great surprise after all that it was 'relations' that jumped out of the kinship material in Chapter One. And I could present other examples. However, Gell (1998) is particularly helpful in giving us a familiar response to how one understands social anthropology's basic position while doing so in an unfamiliar place. What, he asks, would an anthropological theory of art look like? It would have to look like other anthropological theories, and they all look like theories of social relations, that is, of social interactions.[11] 'The "anthropological theory of art" is a theory of the social relations that obtain in the neighbourhood of works of art' (Gell 1998: 26). An exceptional pronouncement for the world of art perhaps, but totally unexceptional for a social anthropologist, which is exactly the effect for which Gell was striving. Relationships provide a 'relational' context in which to account for the pro-duction and circulation of art, that is, a theory of relations. *But how does that come to be the anthropologist's response? Where on earth do we get a relational view from?*

Relations are at once anthropology's field of enquiry, its problematic, and in the eyes of some a problem for it. The accusation is that it seems impossible to see beyond them (Weiner 1993; Moutu 2003). But why is social anthropology constituted by its relationality? What are the needs to which it is responding? One of these needs appears to have been put in its path by science, and 'science's relation' (see the Introduction to Part I) offers an answer with two aspects to it.

Arguably, the first part of the answer lies in certain nineteenth century roots of social science. The burgeoning of social science was at once made possible by natural science and carried the self-knowledge that the very idea of science could be incorporated into the study of society via certain protocols and methods. Statistical methods were one. Moore (1996: 11) dilates on Foucault's observations here. If the notion of the art of government as a means of managing populations emerged in Europe between the sixteenth and eighteenth centuries, this was also the time when, as a model for government, the family (and patriarchy) disappeared. In its place was a new understanding of internal organisation, to be found, in Foucault's phrase, in statistics as the science of the state.

There is nothing novel in observing that present-day statistical methods developed as a reaction to the opening up of the world to bureaucratic intervention – after the traders, the administrators – and to administrators' need to know about the populations they controlled. The point about statistics is that it rests on the supposition that knowledge is generated by putting distinct pieces of information together and then measuring the degree of their relation to one another. The systematic search for correlations between entities was the result.[12] Descombes epitomises the consequence for social science:

Sociologists inspired by positivism imagine that in order to be scientific they must bow to the rules of what they call the 'naturalist[ic] method': scientific work would then consist of collecting data, preferably quantified, and of seeking correlations between the data.

2000: 39

Such data are understood as individual elements in the same way as persons may be thought of as individuals and society defined as the connections between them (Schlecker and Hirsch 2001: 71). This leads to innumerable issues in the definition of the unit of comparison (Strathern 1991) but is nonetheless held to reflect a scientific approach. Here, then, there is a fairly direct and *explicit* gesture toward the influence of 'science' on the subject.

Correlation may be taken a significant further step in the quest for causal relations. Demonstrating causal relations – verification through predicting outcome – is another hallmark of scientific method. But science, and this became especially true of social science, does not need this step to appreciate the force of correlation. It is an achievement in itself to demonstrate the fit among data from different domains.

Now, regardless of the personal beliefs of practitioners, the material and apprehensible world of the seventeenth century had become conceivable as a self-verifying system (hence the attraction of auto-regulating mechanics and perpetual motion, for example, Crook 2004). If it operated without anyone having to seek a cause beyond it, then it must operate on its own terms. The idea of entities existing on their own terms was replicated in the items that made up the natural – or social – world, that is, the items between which connections were being sought. If an aim was fit between data from different domains, then the very independence of these domains from one another became the prerequisite to determining co-variation or correlation; this became 'Galton's problem' (Jorgensen 1979). Relations were made evident to the extent that the items being related to one another were otherwise autonomous. In short, apparently unique elements in the world could be explained by the way they impacted on or were variously connected to one another, and what science determined and described were the relations between them.[13] Indeed, they were not to be explained by anything beyond one another, and knowledge came from nowhere but the demonstration of interrelationships.

We might see the effort to demonstrate connections through relating hitherto unconnected facts as involving the creation or invention of new kinds of relations, new systems of classification, say, that link phenomena already known in other ways. Such instruments of description turn hypothetical connections into actualised ones, ones that stay stable (Law 1994). However, relating apparently independent entities to one another (inventing the relations that made them connected) is but half of the scientific enterprise. The other half has to do with discovery, uncovering relations that already exist. When it comes to the elucidation of society, perhaps social science's own pre-eminence in this sphere (discovery) meant that associations between this aspect of natural science and the development of social science have tended to remain *implicit*. This is the second part of the answer.

Ziman (2000: 5, original emphasis) observes that there are many forms of knowledge: 'What makes any particular form of it *scientific?*' He sums up the old answer in the phrase 'epistemological naturalism'. Science is a complex system, with various elements interacting, itself a model of such interrelations. Although he hopes for a new (non-epistemological, even possibly 'life-world') model, for present purposes I shall be satisfied to elucidate aspects of the old. By that I mean the science that addresses a world understood in terms of itself. If relating hitherto unconnected facts involves the invention of new kinds of relations, then showing or uncovering how each fact is already part of everything else, already predictable or definable through the internal coherence of relations that already exist, is more like discovery.

The other half of the scientific enterprise, then, is to specify the co-defining elements of an internally coherent system that will furnish a description of every element as part of it – as one might (literally) imagine the periodic table, or the model of DNA – thereby creating the notion of 'orders' of kinds. Knowledge will come from specifying what does, or does not, belong to the system. The system entails its own canons of verification. Science here consists of a circuit of intelligible signs that mutually reinforce one another, a perception of their field of which nineteenth scientists were particularly conscious (Beer 1996). This does not mean the circuit is all-encompassing ('scientific paradigms are never epistemically complete or coherent' [Ziman 2000: 198]), but it does mean that definitions are bound up in one another. Neutrons, electrons, positrons – these terms must be mutually sustaining.[14] Systems of classification appear in a new light, not as the invention of scientists but, when the gaps get filled in, as a means to discovering what is known to exist but is not yet brought to light.

Now this is, so to speak, an approach to the world with which social science was to become familiar (and echoes political economy's critique of classical economics). It came out of a criticism of the first view that, translated into the orbit of social life, saw society as the links between individuals, entities otherwise independent of one another. The criticism is that to understand social relations as existing between individuals is mixing orders of logic. By definition, individuals preclude relations. Relations can only exist between relata – elements of the relation. Far from relations being sought as *connections* among things, here things are already in relation, that is, *co-implicated*, with one another.

The contrast was played out in social anthropology with great force between structural functionalists and structuralists in the middle of the twentieth century.[15] On the one hand, it was supposed, alliance, as found in relations set up through marriage, rested in the connections people created between autonomous social groups defined by independent criteria such as consanguinity or descent. On the other hand, went the objection, the possibility of such connection was already implicated in the very definition of groups as wife-givers and wife-takers to one another. Rather than being created in the effort to make connections, in their co-implication relations are seen to be inherent in the very way in which the entities are classified, a pre-condition of their existence.

Nonetheless, what seemed obvious to students of society could also be elusive as an object of analysis. How is such co-implication to be verified? The pre-condition of relationality becomes elusive if one tries to attribute it to some pre-prexisting mental state or to the collective properties of people and societies. Descombes (2000), taking up Winch's (1958) claim that the mental and the social are 'two different sides of the same coin', sees the antecedents of this claim in Durkheim's efforts to elucidate collective representations:

One cannot ask any longer whether such and such a form of representation (for example the concept of space or of causality) belongs to an individual conscious- ness or a collective consciousness. But one can ask oneself in what social world can people form such a concept. And then reverse the question: what concepts does one have to possess for such a social relation to establish itself?

Descombes, 2000: 39

He ends with the example of property.[16] The concept posits a social relation between holders and non-holders. In this sense the idea of property is a 'col- lective representation', for the idea and the social relation it incarnates are dependent upon one another. The point to draw more generally from the ar- gument is that relations exist 'internally' as elements of a system that is already described by the relations it consists of; it is in this Dumontian sense holistic (self-organising).

The pre-condition of relationality becomes very obvious (self-evident) in one sphere, and this is found in an unusual quarter within anthropology. Radcliffe-Brown and the structural-functionalists, who according to their crit- ics failed to get the point when it came to delineations of descent groups or elements of myth, saw the priority of relations brilliantly when it came to the analysis of kinship terminologies. It was in this context that social anthro- pologists insisted on the analytic term 'person' (rather than individual), for the person was already an element of a social relationship, already a relata, a function of relating. Indeed, it was possible to talk of kinship *systems*, which made up 'a complex unity', or more generally of a *structure*, which constituted 'an arrangement of persons in institutionally controlled or defined relation- ships, such as the relationship of king and subject, or' – the kinship analogy quickly follows – 'that of husband and wife' (Radcliffe-Brown 1952: 53, 11). Paradigmatically, to be a parent implies a relationship with a child. Here is evidence of co-implication: entities in a state of mutual definition.

The relations I have been talking about exist in the systems of knowledge that science has developed. I said that relations remain anthropology's problematic, and problem. Their elucidation takes divergent paths. Explicit comparison with science was made possible by the positivist supposition of a world of discrete entities between which connections were to be made. At the same time, the kind of closed system that kin terminologies suggested to anthropologists, the matrix of mutually defining terms co-implicated with one another, evokes a comparison – that remains largely implicit – with that second set of scientific suppositions, where relations wait to be discovered. But what does the Euro-American observer (including the anthropologist) imagine is produced by such relational exercises?

Viveiros de Castro draws from a contemporary of Durkheim, Tarde,[17] who asks: 'What is society? From our point of view, it can be defined as the reciprocal possession, under extremely varied forms, of everyone [all] by everyone [each]'. Entities are no more nor less than the sum total of their reciprocal inter-possessions. This may come about through striving for connection or from uncovering a prior state of relationality. Either way, I want to fold this supposition into one of Viveiros de Castro's own insights, that the hallmark of modernist philosophy is the 'conversion of ontological questions into epistemological ones' (1999: S79). He writes that Euro-American anthropologists 'persist in thinking that in order to explain a non-Western ontology, we must derive it from (or reduce it to) an epistemology' (1999: S79 [emphasis omitted]), that is, to a concern with representations, with how people make things known to themselves. An example is a nod to natural science from Radcliffe-Brown (1952: 7), 'The basis of science is systemic classification'. Classification is understood as an epistemological matter for the observer (how one organises information), a cognitive matter for the informant (how one understands). From either view, knowledge is both ends and means.

If one asks what fuels epistemological fervour, then one answer could lie in that perpetual motion machine, the tool science has made of the duplex 'relation'.[18] Its two kinds of relations are simultaneously about creating connections (between things) and about the prior co-implication of everything in everything else (things already connected). These two divergent, if related, views of the relation, and thus of modes of relating, capable of summoning whole theoretical positions, are each a potential source of criticism for the other. Positivism and its critiques develop together.[19] They are both – overtly or not – an outcome of scientific thinking insofar as they put 'knowledge' at the forefront of relational endeavour and can imagine different approaches to it.

But what is partly explicit, partly implicit, as far as the discipline of social anthropology is concerned, is wholly implicit when it comes to the second arena, a segment of 'ordinary life', I turn to consider. I have wanted to suggest ways in which scientific thinking is embedded in Euro-American thought without necessarily being recognised *as* scientific. If it (scientific thinking) is indeed carried by the divergent notion of relation outlined here, where else may we find it?

### KINSHIP UNCOVERED

Let me remind you of the question: Why on earth a *relational* view? I have very sketchily said something about the provocative nature of the question for the way social anthropologists prosecute their discipline. The discipline is not the kind of representative (Callon 1986) of 'society' most people would first think of, and I promised another arena where we might find science already 'in' society. Nonetheless, it has been helpful to begin with academic knowledge because of not dissimilar preoccupations that dominate the second arena as well. I refer to what the HGC in the United Kingdom concretised as a micro-community, though to dwell less on the family than on kinship. I refer to how people think about and interact with their relatives.

As a corner of the ordinary everyday world in which Euro-Americans live, kinship is an unexpected candidate only in the way that Gell's art objects are; if art objects are not where you expect to find social relations, kinship is not where you would expect to find science. What we would be looking for is a particular, divergent, notion of relation. I draw here on an earlier exercise, and must be forgiven for refracting Euro-American through English kinship.

On the one hand, the individuality of persons is the first fact of English kinship, that is, out of a relationship (between procreative partners) comes a unique entity of a different order altogether, in whose identity kin relations play only a partial role. Kinship (among other sets of social relations) is thus thought of as something over and above the individual. Kin roles evoke the individual's relational part (Strathern 1992a: 14, 78). English language usage co-opts the term 'connecting' for such relations. The connotations of the term give English kinship its sentimental cast – relatedness predicated on the absorption of difference by commonality and togetherness (Viveiros de Castro 1999: S80) – and posit the connections as linking discrete individuals. But where, on the other hand, would one find the analogue to relations already co-implicated in one another?

We have seen that kinship terms afforded British social anthropology a model of mutually co-defining, co-implicated, elements. Such kinship systems were being examined from all parts of the world, in the majority of cases from well outside the orbit of the scientific revolution. Science hardly invented mutually defining kin reciprocals! Perhaps, though, its habits of thought, *its ways of knowing,* helped fuel the divergent thinking that allowed anthropologists to uncover the phenomenon elsewhere. For, perversely, it is the one characteristic of non–Euro-American kin systems that is often far more developed terminologically than it is in, say, English. English has conceptual reciprocals such as parent–child but, apart from same-sex 'brother' and 'sister', and 'cousin', few terminological ones. On the contrary, something else happens. I suggest that an analogue to the co-implications found in kin classifications elsewhere emerges in a field that, on the face of it, does not appear to be about kinship at all, what the indigenes call *class*.[20]

Nothing is straightforward, of course, and social class (in the indigenous sense) exists not only as an adjunct to kinship but also as a divergent if related domain of action and thought in itself. How class is treated or regarded replicates the same contrast between two types of relations that fuel the acquisition and validation of knowledge. We have seen this at work in systems of classification.[21] So although kinship classification (in the anthropological elucidation of indigenous models) seems to be the place where traditional anthropologists discerned relationality as a matter of *co-implication*, classification in other spheres, such as where anthropologists compare 'societies', could take on the character of *connections* between discrete, individual entities, exemplifying the author's creativity in analysis.[22] This is also my hypothesis about class. I wonder if it might be possible to perceive early modern antecedents in the way class combined with kinship.

First, connections: class reinforced the positivist view of kinship as a network of relations. The metaphors here are those of association, of webs of connection through which individuals moved. I do not know what was going on in the seventeenth century in terms of kinship formation. But in parallel to what we learn about seventeenth century societies for the validation of knowledge (Shapin 1996: 133),[23] the English eighteenth century is full of (kin) relatives validating the status of their association with one another, literally, the 'society' they keep (Handler and Segal 1990). In fact, how one judged scientific facts, what was claimed and what carried authority, rested in part on the scientist's personal connections (Shapin 1994).[24] There was no particular kinship cast to the efforts to establish procedures for vetting scientific information and thus how one was to 'know' it, but there were suppositions about the quality of scientific gentlemen that had definite class overtones: who was admissible as a social acquaintance and whose work thus carried credibility.

For the eighteenth century was the time when, outside the sphere of the court, the middle classes were developing their own rules of social admissibility. Who counted as 'a connection'? What today the English would call relatives were frequently referred to as connections. This was also the time when a crucial distinction emerged between connections and family (Handler and Segal 1990: 32). Handler and Segal argue that the distinction captured that between the man-made or constructed and the natural. *Connections*, on the one hand, were mutable, created, invented in that sense, made socially knowable through strategies of acknowledgement. *The natural*, on the other hand, was found in the certainty of the blood tie, and was open to discovery, where much drama might be made of welcome or unwelcome facts, it being close relations between people already linked who came to be known as 'family'. Yet divergence in the apprehension of relations reappears here too. For seen from the outside, it was the concept of family, a term Johnson's dictionary used for class, tribe or species (Handler and Segal 1990: 32), that also gave evidence for the paradigmatic distinction between naturally individuated units and the connections that can be made between them.[25] I return to some of these points in Chapter Three.

The notion of family had itself been undergoing changes without which it could not have been appropriated in these ways. Across Europe in the seventeenth and eighteenth centuries, families began acquiring an equivocal association with the household, which formerly contained persons both related and unrelated. The principal index had been the 'house' (the original meaning of *familia*). But the urban middle classes had households, not (large) houses. Once the idea of a household was separated from that of the house, it could embrace smaller units of people already related to one another as kin, 'blood relations' (Mitterauer and Sieder 1977: 7–10 passim).[26] People were reclassifying themselves both in respect of their given identities and in respect of the relations they made.

Secondly, co-implications: I suggest that social class provided a second way of thinking about relations. Class smacked of system; it was encompassing, holistic. And it worked on a different meaning of family, principally as the prime determinant of someone's status. The family with this class inflection was so to speak the holistic counterpart to a network of connections between individuals. Class fixed people. Because classes were fixed, immobile (it was individuals who moved), they were totalising; everything about someone's comportment, style, accent and upbringing uncovered his or her class before it uncovered his or her family. Certainly within the middle class, how people lived their lives as family members evinced and created their middle class milieu. At the same time, one was naturally at home in one's own class. There was even for a while an ideology that drew parallels with the way that populations divide naturally (classes perceived as natural systems).

This relational dimension was a phenomenon of which the actors were only too aware, namely the relative position of classes and gradients within classes, down to fine details of discrimination. Ultimately, it was a question of one's standing in relation to one's own *and* other classes that was totalising. Much class activity required co-acknowledgement, that is, protocols delineating who it was with whom one was prepared to be associated and, as idiom had it, possibilities for individuals to rise and fall. However, the relations between classes themselves were a given.

There are points here of interest to contemporary kinship thinking, such as the longstanding impasse between individualism and its critics. The questions, predictably, diverge. Why is relationality so clumsily an object of exhortation (a constant subject for [re]invention)? Why is it not presupposed (only waiting to be discovered)? Why do Euro-Americans have to tell themselves – and we saw the Human Genetics Commission doing just this – that they should *recognise* the extent to which they are related? And why, then, are they surprised when they discover that they are *already* related? Finally, despite the commonalities across Eurasian kinship systems and indeed across Europe, correlated with all kinds of values to do with property, agriculture and so forth, there is a strong feeling that northern European and North American societies and their offshoots have further commonalities. Perhaps we can build up kinship as a case where long ago science became embedded in society, and society in science.

Science did not rise from the sea as an island. Ways to conceptualise its descriptions and claims emerged through borrowings from other domains of life (Ziman 2000). Certainly, we know that nineteenth century evolutionists looked to the connection between individuals (genealogies) to talk about connections (classifications) between non-human creatures and things (Beer 1983). Was there a sense in which kinship fuelled earlier conditions for certain kinds of scientific thinking? May we hazard, in turn, that if science drew on kinship it also changed it?

When Viveiros de Castro speaks of the displacement of ontology by epistemology, he is making a comparative, rather than a historical, statement. I want to add that whatever epistemological foundations lay in Europe's history, today we live out an epistemology of a special kind. We can dub it scientific if we like. It turns kinship into an artefact of knowledge, and at its core is the possibility of knowledges – antithetical, in parallel or in combination – coming from more than one source. And with that comes different ways of verifying connections between persons. In the organisation of such knowledge, Euro-Americans have, we might say, a scientific kinship system.

## CAVEAT

'There was no such thing as the Scientific Revolution'. Shapin has no sooner uttered this phrase than, referring to his work by this title, he adds, 'and this is a book about it' (1996). There was no event in the seventeenth century that went under this name (the phrase was apparently coined in the 1930s),[27] no integrated body of knowledge that could be lumped together as 'science'; and, even more crucially, if one starts looking at what people actually did or said, science was nothing but a whole range of thoughts and practices that had their own local trajectories in the context of a general public that by and large was ignorant, indifferent or sceptical. At the same time, it is clear that the precursors of scientists were working in ways that had effects that have been out of proportion with what was happening then, have gathered momentum ever since and are of intense interest to the present. An anthropologist might put it differently: being unable to see close to what appears very visible from afar is a matter of incommensurate scale.

For there is a question about how to validate my argument. I have been speculating about phenomena for which I can produce almost no evidence of the kind with which social anthropologists commonly deal: facts on the ground, the sustained ethnographic case. It is not the simplifications in this account that are at issue, it is knowing what kind of material would qualify as verifying. Here it may prove impossible to find sufficient historical detail of the appropriate order to substantiate what I am suggesting about the characteristics of Euro-American kin reckoning and the scientific imagination, or indeed about the validity of Euro-American as a cultural configuration in such terms. Insofar as individual and person are phenomena that belong to different orders of description, we could also say that in summoning different ideas about relations they exist at different scales. Concomitantly, data are of a different scale from the models I have been describing.

This is the chaotic puzzle: feet appear to touch the ground, but magnify them to many orders and you will find convolutions and indentations in the surface that repeat themselves at ever greater orders, until it seems that nothing is touching anything. A description of an organism is lost in attention to the molecular characteristics of its genome. What characterises a population will not necessarily characterise an individual component of it, and so forth. These are old maxims, and they are in anthropology too. Neither Durkheim's society nor Lévi-Strauss's structure could be seen in the particulars. The whole point of *Suicide,* as Durkheim expounded his discovery, was that individual reasons did not detract from collective ones; the point of the distinction between statistical and mechanical models, which Lévi-Strauss invented, was that one model could not be refuted by material generated from the other.

There is a further way the anthropologist might put it differently, and the comment comes from Hirsch (personal communication, 2003). People can only act in the world they inhabit, but the impetus to action includes imagined dimensions of it, situations within their apparent grasp and thus culturally feasible. Foucault's (1972: 191–2) discursive formation ('the total set of relations', 'an indefinite field of relations') is about everything that creates the conditions of feasibility. Chapter Three enlarges on the point. In the meanwhile, even supposing that nothing of my speculation remains or that the imagined worlds are not plausible enough, the questions about anthropology's commitment to relations and the different ways in which relatives sort out their connections will not be disappeared so easily. They too are raised again in Chapter Three. A small comment on the role of knowledge in a contemporary facet of kin reckoning provides a conclusion of sorts for this one.

Going back to the genetic information case with which I began is to appreciate that there could be a no more knowledge-intensive technology than testing for genetic connections. Franklin observes:

> what is 'conceivable' about amniocentesis testing, or genetic screening for breast cancer,[28] or paternity testing, is *already built into the* conception of kinship as a hybrid of individual and society, of natural and cultural facts. The dilemma of 'what to make of our genes' derives from the assumption that they make us who we are to begin with.
>
> 2003: 74, original emphasis; footnote added

What is also built into the conception of kinship, I have argued, is the double legacy of scientific knowledge. We can now give a certain precision to this connection. It is already implicated in what I have said about the dependency of scientific knowledge on two ways of conceiving relations (the made and the given, connections and co-implications) and, following from this, two ways of validating knowledge (as invention, discovery).

Perhaps indeed it is not surprising that Euro-Americans see kinship as the site par excellence of relationality, and among anthropologists get suitably intrigued about other people's kinship systems. At least as far as English kinship is concerned, relations inhere in the web of connections people make, their individual networks, for in this they see much that is open to invention, to recognition in the sense of active acknowledgement.[29] The recombined families of Chapter One deliberately foster relations between elements that were once other families. At the same time, relations also inhere in the recognition of (in the sense of uncovering) given capacities, ties and characteristics that already connect persons to others; these relations, open only to discovery, are premised on the demonstration of existing relationship.[30] A clinic could not call on friends and kin to help with gamete donations if the pre-existing tie did not hint at pre-existing obligations, even though in the case of relatives old kin are turned into new kin. Both these modes take knowledge, if I can put it like that, as informative of kinship.

There is much more one could say about the role of knowledge in Euro-American kinship formation. Highly relevant to the present is how notions about biology and genetics, a kind of secondary, explicit absorption of science 'into' society, probably overlays much older absorptions of various kinds, recoverable only as implicit or tacit dimensions of knowledge practices. The genome is available for discovery, but personal information derived from it sends people scurrying to their relatives and connections, as well as to the law in the hopes that regulation can settle all the old questions of who should be in the know. If not, new regulations must be invented. They do so with the inflection we have already noticed; whom one allows into one's circle of acquaintances slides into whom one allows to become acquainted with genetic information about oneself.

## ACKNOWLEDGEMENTS

My thanks to James Weiner and Andrew Moutu for making me see the question that needs asking. Alan Strathern will know why he too is to be thanked. With the title 'Living science', an earlier version was presented at the 2003 ASA Decennial meetings in Manchester, convened under the rubric *Anthropology and Science*. I am grateful to Jeanette Edwards, Penny Harvey and Peter Wade for their generous invitation.

3

༄

# Emergent Properties

Geneaology or issue which they had, Artes which they studied, Actes
which they did. This part of History is named Anthropology.

Richard Harvey 1593, *Philadelphus*. Oxford English Dictionary's
first entry for 'anthropology'

Indeed it would be lost labour to seek for the parentage of all words,
when many probably had none. But there is no such thing;
there is no word which is not ... [the] son of something ...

Richard Trench 1882, *On the study of words*

*A*NTHROPOLOGISTS OFTEN FIND THEMSELVES GRAVITATING TOWARD
debate, public dispute, litigation even, as telling moments in cultural
life. For what may be as interesting as the positions being defended are the
cultural resources people bring to their aid, the narratives, tropes and images
enlisted in the service of the persuasive point. An unusual state of affairs is
rendered familiar or one situation is made vivid through analogy with another;
conviction might lie in appeal to the old, or quite new combinations of ideas
may be conjured up. Of course, what is said in the heat of argument is likely
to be a poor index to what people contemplate in less freighted moments. Yet
an unreliable guide in this regard can turn out to be a fascinating guide in
another respect. If only in order to persuade, the narratives, images, tropes and
analogies must at the least communicate what is possible, and anthropological
interest in such resources is an interest in the possibilities entailed by what
is said or done for what others say or do. It is that possible and potentially
realisable world that anthropologists abstract as culture. This is not an idealist
view, rather, it opens up empirical study to the potentials people make all

the time for themselves (and for others), and thus to the possible worlds that inform their actions in the present one.

In pulling and pushing language for the sake of argument, people may force new properties onto old concepts. Although the arenas in which new properties emerge are not only legion but also often inaccessible to scrutiny, debate and litigation have at least the virtue of being accessible. These two arenas offer some present-day materials for my own exposition, although I present them somewhat warily.[1] However, if I have a question it is about emergent properties and new claims that came from the early modern English-speaking world. This means I also touch on historical materials, although with no pretence of handling them as an historian would. The question is what made the English at this time endow the words 'relation' and 'relative' with the property of kinship, kinship by blood and marriage, that is. I do not answer it, but I do hope to show why it might be interesting to ask.

The reasons begin, and end, in the present. I sandwich the historical issue between recent ones. This tracking back and forth to some extent mimics the way in which kinship in its various guises appears and disappears as a cultural resource for thinking about other things.

I

*Multiple Origins*

I take inspiration from an anthropologist and lawyer who is an observer of the family as it has been faring in U.S. litigation over the last quarter century. American lawmakers concern themselves simultaneously with traditional values *and* with new rules reflecting changing conventions. The families being constructed by the law may either be 'holistic, solidary communities' or be understood as 'collections of autonomous individuals making their own selections, free to choose relationships through bargained negotiation' (Dolgin 2000: 543). Dolgin's argument opens with the opinion of a lawyer who, on behalf of his clients, made it clear that they would always love any child born to them, evoking a traditional moral frame.[2] At the same time, the intending parents were advertising an offer of $50 000 for female gametes (*ova*) chosen for (anticipated) characteristics specified in some detail. The ingredients for creating a child may be obtained in the marketplace, then, although once a baby is part of the family market values should no longer intrude and relationships should take their expected course. Perhaps we must simply see these as dimensions being held in tandem: a new location for individual choice is also a location for expressing enduring values of family solidarity. Incidentally, the advertisement attracted a big response.

Dolgin writes about determinations of parenthood where relationships complicated through gamete donation and surrogacy lead to dispute. Although it is possible to track a path through lawsuits that shows the value Americans put on genetic ties (Dolgin 1990), it is equally possible to show the extent to which the fact and quality of relationship is taken as paramount. Courts have been known to refuse evidence about 'biological' paternity and attend only to familial relationships. One man who discovered that he was not the biological father and tried to sever ties with his son was brought back to the relationship he had already established: if 'a parent–child bond' had been formed then 'a relationship still exists at law' (2000: 531).[3]

So what creates a relation? Although the fact of relationship may be deduced from behaviour between parents and children after birth, legal decisions have also given weight to the possibility of prenatal determinations focused on the birth yet abstracted from the birth process. Claims are based neither on biology nor on behaviour. Rather they are based on a mental condition: the parents' intention. Dolgin describes in detail a case brought in 1998 to the California Court of Appeal.[4] A child had been born from an embryo created from anonymous donors and gestated for a fee by a surrogate; the original couple, Luanne and John Buzzanca, were now divorced and Luanne sought parental status, arguing that she and her former husband were the legal parents. Despite, as Dolgin points out, there being six potential parents (the divorced couple, the surrogate and her husband, and the sperm and egg donors), the trial court had come to the conclusion that in law the child had no parentage.[5] The appellate court overturned this; intention is sufficient cause:

a husband and wife [may] be deemed the lawful parents of a child after a surrogate bears a biologically unrelated child on their behalf.... [A] child is procreated because a medical procedure was initiated and consented to by intended parents.[6]

California Court of Appeal 1998 (72 Cal. Rptr. 2d at 282)

It is the law that validates the relation, deeming what shall be so, but it is the parents' intention that gives it reason.

Recognition of intent is consonant with the emphasis that can be put on choice and the individual subject as decision maker, where 'the law reflects and fosters an ideology of family that prizes autonomous individuality, [viewing] ... the domestic arena in terms once reserved for life in the marketplace' (Dolgin 2000: 542). At the same time, it is made clear that establishing legal parentage would set up obligations. Once so declared, the relationship to the child has consequences, especially economic ones in this case, given that the divorced husband was trying to avoid child support. The state has its own interest in establishing paternity precisely because the relationship carries responsibility; regardless of the ways in which parenthood may be created, the child must still be looked after, and someone must be accountable.

Numerous arguments are going on at the same time, including the place of the market in the making of families and the fact that relationships entail responsibilities. Taken for granted is the role of medical technology, which (after Latour) has lengthened the chains of events, circumstances and personnel it takes to produce parents and children.[7] It feeds people's interests in attaching persons to or detaching them from one another. Indeed, technology would not multiply the number of claimants or the bases on which claims can be made were it not for the way people seize on new openings.[8] The legal decision reported on here has added another possibility. Creativity lies in mental acts, and 'intending' parents emerge with the power to create children.

At this point I jump to another arena altogether, from debate in the law courts to debates among practitioners of science and specifically biomedicine.

I am thinking here of Biagioli's (1998; 2003) study of scientific names, how authors become attached to their works. The International Committee of Medical Journal Editors' (ICMJE) guidelines, speaking for hundreds of English-language journals, now require that each name listed in an article's byline 'must refer to a person who is *fully* responsible for the *entire* article (not just for the task that he/she may have performed)' (Biagioli in prep.: 23, original italics). This is in response to many issues, among them authors not always being aware their names have been appropriated. A series of fraud cases that questioned how responsibility was distributed through multiple authorship fuelled debate (1998: 7–8). Also in the background, recent sociotechnological magnification – the 'increasingly large-scale, collaborative and capital-intensive contexts of [biomedical] research' (1998: 6) – has led to an explosion in authorial naming. Large numbers of names are strung together.

In scientific authorship, as Biagioli describes it, multiple naming has become the norm. Being named carries at once credit and liability; those whose reputation may profit from publicity are also declaring their accountability as far as intellectual content is concerned. At least this is how the ICMJE guidelines attempt to strengthen the concept of authorship, as a declaration of responsibility requiring individuals to choose how they publicly attach themselves to particular projects. But people have protested at the idea that authors should vouch for one another. A 1997 letter to *Science* invokes what could almost be Dolgin's modern family of autonomous subjects[9]: 'If marriage partners are not held liable for the actions of spouses, why should we assume that scientific collaborators are liable?' (quoted by Biagioli 1998: 10).

Others point to pre-existing relationships. Indeed, at the further extreme, one organisation has adopted a no-choice model: all publications emanating from the laboratory have an author default list that contains the names of everyone contributing to the enterprise as a whole.[10]

What Biagioli brings to light, then, are divergent values, not unlike Dolgin's two present day American families. Side by side with a model of individual authorship is one that (like the traditional family) stresses solidarity between all those involved in creating knowledge. For not all scientists agree that authorship should be restricted to intellectual contribution – advocates of a corporate model would include a diversity of scientific workers.[11] So a quite different solution is the proposal to replace 'authorship' altogether, for example by dividing contributor from guarantor. Contributorship would include everyone, differentiated by descriptions of their functions that the reader could assess,[12] whereas others would guarantee that audit controls were in place.

One of the British journals, *British Medical Journal*, that has been interested in just this proposal has also committed itself to offering copyright ownership to its authors (Times Higher Education Supplement 28 January 2000). Today's electronic methods of production and distribution mean that authors can search out audiences before they publish, and in any case may have an independent interest in dissemination. In the U.K. proposals, journals would instead secure a 'license to publish'.[13] This move could be seen either as endorsing or as turning on its head earlier provisions that separated copyright from moral right.[14] Moral rights protect certain relationships between a work and its creator, as in the right to be identified as author[15]; a creator, with a claim on the work's integrity, is thus technically distinguished from an owner claiming economic benefit. Although copyright protects the originality of the authorial composition, ownership of the copyright has often been vested in the publisher. These most recent proposals would universalise the 'author', literary or scientific, as copyright holder. Hence the division between creator of the work and owner of the economic rights remains the same, but the term copyright has shifted across the divide; it now rests in the author, and the journal publisher (or whoever) becomes a license holder. Truly, as Biagioli notes (in prep.), '[T]he kinship between authors and works is a tricky two-way street'.

However, Biagioli is not saying this in relation to intellectual property.[16] On the contrary, the claims to scientific authorship that he discusses are at a tangent to rights (for example, via patents) created by intellectual property law. In science writing there is no dichotomy between property rights which fence off the commons through the fiction of the single author, and the public domain. Scientific authors search for ways to claim accreditation of their work, and these can only come from the public domain; attributions of originality, or monetary gain, could detract from such claims and impede verification. Literary credit is another matter: if individual creativity is central there, that very notion of creativity is the result of historical struggles over intellectual property where (he opines) 'the focus on the individual author as the holder of... property rights misrepresented the long chain of human agency that produced a literary work' (Biagioli 1998: 11).[17] But perhaps there are chains of distribution as well as production. Perhaps, for literary producers at least, the emergent figure of the new copyright holder will keep two dimensions in tandem: a new location for individual originality becomes at the same time a location for a new sense of community. Think of the knowledge and electronic skill with which the author–entrepreneur can now open up original networks of access to his or her products.[18]

I should comment on this leap from one arena to another: from parental suits to scientific authorship. In each, debates turn on the implications of multiplicity. Yet such echoes between the two appear adventitious, trivial, a fleeting effect of phrasing. Surely we could not sustain an analogy long enough to think usefully about the former (parenthood) in terms of the latter (authorship)? The potential parallels in this juxtaposition can, therefore, be interesting for one reason only, because they bring to mind a possibility already realised, an occasion when someone has in fact proferred connections of just this kind. What I have presented is not a worked-out analogy, then, but rather the kinds of raw materials from which analogies are made and the cultural possibilities these contain. My pretend analogy sets the stage for one that was no pretence at all.

## An Analogy

Behind the Buzzanca appeal was a much cited case brought to the California Supreme Court in 1993.[19] One of the judges, in her dissent, analysed the court's clinching argument: it rested on a hidden comparison between reproductive and intellectual creativity. She exposed the analogy in order to dispose of it; in her view it was misleading (and it did not re-emerge as such in the Buzzanca hearing).

Anna Johnson had undertaken to act as a gestational surrogate on behalf of Crispina Calvert and her husband; the embryo came from their own gametes. In the dispute that followed, each woman laid claim to motherhood (the one through birth, the other through genes). The Supreme Court found that the Calverts were the 'genetic, biological and natural' parents. That 'and natural' was determined by one crucial factor, procreative intent.[20] The majority

argued: 'But for [the Calverts'] acted-on intention, the child would not exist'.
They quoted a commentator, who proceeded to make a most dreadful pun:

The mental concept of the child is a controlling factor of its creation, and the
originators of that concept merit full credit *as conceivers.*
California Supreme Court 1993 (851 P.2d at 795) (my emphasis)

The pun I return to. The commentator meant the conceivers of the mental
concept, valuable for fixing in 'the initiating parents of a child', a sense of
their obligations (cf. Morgan 1994: 392).[21] Because the child would not be
born but for the efforts of the intended parents, wrote another commentator,
this meant they were 'the first cause, or the prime movers, of the procreative
relationship'. Justice Kennard, dissenting, seized on this formula: she pointed
out that the originator-of-the-concept rationale is frequently advanced when
justifying protection of intellectual property.

   With this one – among six – reasons for not concurring with the majority view that intention should be the decisive factor, Justice Kennard thereby
exposed these phrases as half an analogy; the other half came from the philosophy of intellectual property which holds (as she put it) that an idea belongs
to its creator because it is a manifestation of the creator's personality or self.
The majority were implying that 'just as a song or invention is protected as
the property of the "originator of the concept'," so too a child should be regarded as belonging to the originator of the concept of the child' (California
Supreme Court 1993: 851 P.2d at 796). But, she argued, there is a problem in
making a comparison with rights to property: the marketplace. Unlike songs
or inventions, rights in children cannot be sold for a consideration or made
freely available; no one can have a property right of any kind (intellectual or
otherwise) in a child because children are not property in the first place.[22]

   Now the comparison is not just with property; it is also with the kinds of
connections that exist between parent and child and between the originator of
a concept and its realisation. Just as well perhaps that the majority judges did
not pursue further the analogy with intellectual property. They might have
run into some of the current controversy (found in information technology
[IT] applications for instance) over idea and expression.[23] If the parallel is
to patenting an 'invention', it cannot be the idea of a child to which claim is
made – that is already in the public domain – but to its embodiment in a new
outcome[24]; whereas if it is a particular expression of the idea, as in a song
subject to copyright, then claim can only be laid to the unique features of the
child itself, and one might have to argue about how much was intended by
the parents' intention and what in any case was copiable about it. Intellectual
property rights would, in fact, bring us back from vague claims about creativity

to the particular child who had been born. Yet vague as the claims were, they obviously made cultural sense.

First, in abstracting parents from the birth, the doctrine of intent allows medical technology to appear as enabling of natural inclinations as it does of biological functions. (The role of the surrogate is not under dispute; it is the 'real' parent about which there is categorical doubt [Strathern 1998].) Second is the value given to abstraction as such, as though ideas hold the immaterial essence of things. (This was contested vigorously by Justice Kennard, who pointed out that but for the gestational surrogacy the child would not exist.) Third and above all is the fact that the analogy between reproductive and intellectual creativity is – as we shall see – not pulled out of thin air.

Of interest to the anthropologist is the possibility of the analogy being articulated at all. That it was put down with serious argument was no slur on the judges' own creativity in implying such a parallel. It had potential, was culturally plausible. People are culturally at home when they can jump across different domains of experience without feeling they have left sense behind. What links the two domains in this case – reproductive and intellectual creativity – is an entirely commonsensical (although not uncontested) view about the originators of things claiming benefit or having responsibility attributed to them; the language of intellectual property rights emphasises the 'naturalness' of an identification between conceiver and conceived. Another link is the warning against confusing identification with economic possession when persons are at stake. The idea of owning children as property appears to go against commonsense, but it does not, I think, go against cultural sense; the warning goes on being given.

Not out of thin air: something is being sustained here that might hold our attention. Old patterns emerge from new convergences, more, it seems, not less, stimulated by the pace of change. Just such a pattern lies in the way, *in the same breath, English-speakers find it possible to talk about practices to do with making kinship and practices to do with making knowledge.*

As in the comparison of spouses and scientific collaborators, one might have supposed that kinship relations would invariably be the source of figurative language for the production of knowledge, not the other way around. Note, for instance, how the term 'paternity' has slipped into regular usage to designate one of the new moral rights that English intellectual property law recognises (protecting an identification between author and work). However, I gave Justice Kennard's opinions space precisely because of the direction of her analogy. She asserted that the arguments being putting forward about parental claims were derived *from* arguments familiar from the law's protection of authorship. This too is not out of thin air; this direction, counterintuitive as it might be, has a history of its own. I shall take up some already much discussed materials in order to thicken the air further. Another stage must be set, and this will be the stage for my historical question.

## II

### Offspring into Property

If one were not alert to the way in which idioms appear and disappear, a hasty glance backward might suggest that paternity was an old established trope. The truth is that only recently has it been incorporated into English copyright law. It is therefore fascinating to consider its fate at the very time when authorial rights in literary works were becoming an arena for debate, that is, in eighteenth century England (see Coombe 1998: 219–20).[25]

When Daniel Defoe protested in 1710, '[A] book is the Author's Property, 'tis the Child of his Inventions, the Brat of his Brain' (quoted in Rose 1993: 39), Rose suggests that he was casting back to familiar sixteenth and seventeenth century metaphors: 'the most common figure [of speech] in the early modern period is paternity: the author as begetter and the book as child'.[26] To ascribe significance in the hindsight of modern property rights, however, would be to pluck a metaphor out of context. Defoe is not talking about an enduring proprietorship[27] but complaining of piracy through unacknowledged printing, which he likens to child-stealing. He is arguing for the protection of the writer's interest in selling his work (e.g., to a printer) for proper remuneration. The author rewarded, property in it passes to the purchaser; the author retains an expectation of acknowledgement. Of those sixteenth and seventeenth century usages, Rose comments:

Inscribed with the notion of likeness more than of property, the paternity metaphor is consonant with the emergence of the individual author in the patriarchal patronage society concerned with blood, lineage, and the dynastic principle that like engenders like.

Rose 1993: 39

Notions of parenthood and parentage had far flung referents, summoning both economic values (the productivity of children) and political ones (the paternalism of the state). Indeed Rose (1993: 40) characterises Defoe's paternity trope as at once harking back to courtly Renaissance ideas of patronage and evoking contemporary middle class domesticity. Authorial *property* rights, by contrast, emerged in a liberal society and with other arguments. The eighteenth century battle bears some re-telling. Pressed into the authors' cause was an old equation between literary property and landed estates from which a living might be made[28]; a new notion was growing at the same time, that such property could refer not only to the material (such as an estate) but also to the immaterial, not only to the book as a physical body but also to a more abstract entity, the composition as a text.[29] Here, far from assisting the new ideas that were developing about authorship, the idiom of paternity seems to have got in the way. It was of course being propelled out of political discourse in general – for liberal theorists of the eighteenth century, to whom property was the basis of political rights, 'the claim that begetting conferred rights was problematical' (Jordanova 1995: 375)[30] – but perhaps there were some local reasons as well.

At the very moment when a creational concept of author was taking shape, that particular kinship idiom, with its emphasis on inheritance and descent, seems to disappear from view. Works might continue to be referred to as offspring, but the vivid vision of paternity fades. Was the image of the book as a father's child altogether too concrete? Children and money again! Rose observes that the metaphor would quickly run into trouble if the idea of begetter and offspring were extended to the marketplace. Who would sell their children for profit?[31] He does not go so far as to claim this ostensible absurdity was the reason for the figure's demise, he simply observes that it would present rhetorical difficulties.[32] But he gives a clue as to what else might have been going on.

Creeping up on new ways of thinking about property were, we have seen, new ways of linking writers to their writing: the emergent owner was not the bookseller but the author, and the emergent book not the volume but the text. As Rose (1993: 89) quotes Blackstone, here defending the argument that duplicates of an author's work make it no less the author's original work in conception: 'Now the identity of a literary composition consists intirely in the sentiment and the language: the same conceptions, cloathed in the same words, must necessarily be the same composition' (from Blackstone's *Commentaries*, 1765–69, emphasis removed). Then there was the claim that the author's right was based on the fact that he created rather than just discovered or planted his land (Rose 1993: 56–7, 116). So could it also be that creeping up on paternal begetting as a figure of speech were fresh possibilities in ideas of conception and creation? But other possibilities perhaps offered somewhat different grounds for identifying the author with his work.

'Conception' (and 'creation' by that time) had long established double connotations, at once procreative and intellectual, and they are still in place: witness the dreadful pun brought into the surrogacy case. We know that by the end of the eighteenth century the view had taken hold that it was the particular form in which (literary) authors gave expression to ideas that belonged to them, and this form was the mark of their unique work.[33] Woodmansee (1994: 36–7) describes how this eighteenth century notion of the author being inspired from within took over from earlier sixteenth and seventeenth century views of the writer as a vehicle inspired by external agencies, human or divine. Recapitulating that earlier relationship in a father–child idiom – the writer fathering his book, just as God fathered the world (Rose 1993: 38, quoting Gilbert and Gubar 1979) – would reinforce the writer's perception of dependency. Did those too-vivid images of dependency need to disappear? Was authorial creativity best separated from enmeshment in relationships?

I can only extrapolate.[34] Perhaps the concreteness of the father–child image had lain partly in the kind or quality of relation it presupposed. Those who used the imagery apparently wanted to claim the kind of possessiveness that parents felt toward their children[35]; did a new rhetoric of conception and creation instead allow one to take the child's view? The author's text was now to embody the author's genius and it was this, as Woodmansee (1994) describes, which made a work unique. Genius lay in style and expression. It was the child's view, we could say, insofar as the father becomes superfluous: the omnipotent heir can create his own world.[36] If there is pride in saying that one will create works that never existed before, then the author does not want the pre-existence of fathers either, for he must be as original as his work.[37] The relationship between author and text could instead be imagined as one of correspondence, a kind of non-generational generation or, as the North London mothers (see Introduction: Part I) might prompt us to reflect, as extensions not only of himself but also of the conceptual world in which his works lodge. Either way, evidence of authorial identity would lie not in lineage or genealogy but in an informational matrix (as might be said these days) where a work encodes information about the producer of it.

If anthropological interest in cultural resources is indeed an interest in the possibilities that people's saying or doing hold for what others say or do, then there is only a certain universe of things anyone can and cannot do. In such a universe, not making connections may be as enabling as making them. Relocation, displacement, making the once present absent, withholding what others are expecting – these can all capacitate the contexts in which people act (Battaglia 1995; 1999). We might see *dropping* an inappropriate kinship metaphor as *part* of a nexus of ideas and concepts that link kinship and knowledge, not apart from it. Can one suggest that the metaphor of paternity was actually edged out by new notions of creativity that were powerful precisely to the extent that the resonances with kinship could be held at a remove? For if 'conception' and 'creation' retain kinship echoes, they seemingly displace the idea of an interpersonal relationship with more immediate but at the same time more abstract evidence of connection: the work itself informs one about the author. Does creation become a kind of procreation without parenthood? If so, this would be consonant not only with the emerging originality of the author but also with the emerging uniqueness of the literary text.

## Information into Knowledge

As we already know, what was happening with the text did not take quite the same route in science. Sixteenth and seventeenth century booksellers originally had authors' names printed in order to point to the person responsible for the contents should they prove seditious or libelous (cf. Biagioli 1998: 3). Indeed Defoe had appealed to the complementarity of punishment and reward (Rose 1993: 38); if he were liable to attack for what was ill judged he should also reap the benefits for what was well performed.

Accountability was then and continues to be important in scientific writing. It is not the form of the presentation over which claims are made but the quality of information about the world that is being communicated, and this has to be verified. Scientific authorship is implicated in a type of text production defined by the responsibility being claimed for its content. Here its value lay – and lies – in how it can stand up to other kinds of information about the world; the author is actually abstracted from it in that sense.[38]

However, the author abstracted from the text is made concretely present elsewhere; he or she has become one of an assembly of authors. For scientific authorship has long been a plural entity, a situation that Foucault originally attributed to the development of the scientific method. If today there are many kinds of names associated with a scientific paper, alongside the citations of other authors of other papers, this is all part of an informational process; the presence of several names does not dilute authorship but strengthens it, as Biagioli remarks, and may do so in part by placing the author within an arena of social relations.[39]

Writing about the problems of trust engendered through the collective character of empirical knowledge-making, Shapin (1994: 359) observes that 'scientific knowledge is produced by and in a network of actors' (emphasis removed). He is talking of the seventeenth century. He asks how verifiability was ascertained, and answers that 'knowledge about people was constitutively implicated in knowledge of things' (1994: 302). What counted as knowledge depended on what people were willing to attest, and the value of their testimony rested in turn on the kind of people they were:[40]

What was understood of gentlemen generally, and what was routine and expected in their social relations, might effectively be appropriated to pattern and justify social relations within the new practice of empirical and experimental science.

Shapin 1994: 123

Texts that circulated with a presumed equality between them, having to hold their own, were also circulating between persons who could vouch for one another. Accountability had to be a social matter; relations linked people who could be relied upon. It was the relations that turned a multiplicity of persons into a social arena of authority.[41]

Relations were also doing something else. It was relations that produced knowledge out of information.[42] If items of information, the categories in terms of which the world could be described, were judged against one another, any fit was simultaneously a relation between them. 'Knowledge' became understood as accountable information, and it was by virtue of being relational that it was accountable. Here we return to the notion outlined in Chapter Two that the concept of 'relation' and its partner 'connection' may well have enabled the kind of secular enquiry fueled by the Enlightenment conviction that the world (nature) is open to scrutiny. Relations are produced through the very activity of understanding when that understanding has to be produced from within,[43] that is, from within the compass of the human mind and without reference to divinity, when things in the world can only be compared with other things on the same earthly plane.[44] What validates one fact are other facts, always provided the connections can be made to hold. And Shapin's seventeenth century experimenters were looking for connections everywhere, always provided the facts could be made to hold.[45]

Let me generalise, for a moment, from a perspective that begins with the perspective of 'science's (kind of) relation' but shifts beyond it. We can recognise the divergence between two modes of relating characteristic of scientific interest: creating connections between things (invention) and elucidating the pre-existing relations that already implicate things in one another (discovery). However, with science's relation in place, other conceptual operations become visible and among them those that give social anthropology some of its operational purchase. 'Anthropology's relation' also encompasses more general features of conceptual relations, ones not tied to the foundational ideas of culture and nature or to the epistemology they generate, that come from conditions of sociality at large. At the same time, in so far as these features are pressed into service by anthropology as a discipline derived from the Enlightenment and the scientific revolution, making knowledge for the purposes of description and analysis remains a contingent context for them.

So what, in this context, are these general features of conceptual relations? One grasps a piece of information as knowledge by being aware of its context or grounds, that is, of how it sustains a relationship to other pieces of information; in short, knowledge is gained through knowledge. As a result, it (knowledge) can also always appear as a linking middle term; it is what we know about this and know about that which has us bring items together. I comment on two significant properties of conceptual relations from this view.[46]

*The notion of relation can be applied to any order of connection*; this is its first property. Hence one can, seemingly, make connections anywhere. For in describing phenomena, the fact of relation instantiates connections in such a way as also to produce instances of itself. At whatever level or order, the demonstration of a relationship, whether by resemblance, cause and effect or contiguity, reinforces the understanding that through relational practices – classification, analysis, comparison – relations can be demonstrated. We could call the relation a self-similar or self-organising construct, a figure whose organisational power is not affected by scale. Without this powerful device one could not, for example, generate new properties out of old and thus allow old ones to emerge from the new. To go back to the seventeenth and eighteenth centuries, perhaps the capacity for making conceptual relations was itself being 'conceptualised' (forming concepts about concepts) under the pressure of systematic enquiry into practices of knowledge-making.[47]

Conceptual relations have a second and quite distinct property: *they require other elements to complete them*. They are relations between what? This makes their connecting functions complex, for the relation always summons entities other than itself, whether – as we have seen elaborated in science's relation – the appearance is that these entities are pre-existing (the relation is between them) or whether they are obviously brought into existence by the relationship (and thus exist within it).[48] One not only perceives relations between things but also perceives things as relations.[49] Yet insofar as 'things' (the terms bound by or containing the relation) are routinely conceptualised apart from the relation, we can (after Wagner 1986) call the relation an organising trope with the second order capacity to organise elements either similar to or dissimilar from itself.[50] Hence the relation as a model of complex phenomena has the power to bring heterogeneous orders or levels of knowledge together while conserving their difference. It allows concrete and abstract knowledge to be manipulated simultaneously. It makes Latour's (1986) two-dimensional inscriptions, the diagrams, charts and tables that have long enabled scientists to superimpose images of different scales and origins, work. Indeed, working as one might say technology works,[51] conceptual relations are part of the machinery of exposition. One cannot point to a relation without bringing about its effect.

The very concept (relation) thus participates in the way we give expression to what we know about it. So relations themselves can appear at once concrete and abstract. They can produce a sense of an embedded or embodied knowledge out of information that would, otherwise, be abstracted from context, float around weightlessly. Or they can seem ethereal or disembodied, hypothetical linkages hovering over the brute facts and realities of information on the ground. However, equally so, conceptual relations are but one part of anthropology's (kind of) relation. Drawn from social life at large, both from the discipline's observations about society and from its interests in people's descriptions of their connections with one another, what ethnography pushes into the foreground are all kinds of interactions. Anthropology's relation also summons what are thought of as interpersonal ties.

On the face of it, the conceptual relations of knowledge-making discussed here might seem at a far remove from the arena of social relations such as those acted out in the families of various sorts that have also appeared in this chapter. As dreadful as the double entendre in 'conceive' is, have I simply conjured another pun (relations at once conceptual and interpersonal)? Not if, as promised, I can articulate the historical question properly.

## Relations into Relations

I have no idea what conceptual relations once connotated[52] or how one should be differentiating the eighteenth from the seventeeth century in this regard. So I am not really certain when, or in what social milieu, to locate the question. But this is it. We can imagine the part that the concept of relation played in the unfolding of understandings about the nature of knowledge. *How then did it come to be applied to kin?* For it would seem that *relation*, already in English a combination of Latin roots, and variously a narrative, reference back to something or comparison, became in the sixteenth and seventeenth centuries applied to ties, whether by blood or marriage, through kinship. Although an early entry of 1502 for a kin relation in the Oxford English Dictionary suggests that I might be overstating the case, I note that *relative* (the substantive) does not become applied to kinsmen until the mid seventeenth century, also true of the verb *relate*, by contrast with a plethora of fourteenth and fifteenth century usages for relation, relative and relate in the sense of logical or conceptual connection.

It was not alone; several terms to do with knowledge practices on the one hand and on the other kinship practices were seemingly in flux.[53] In many instances it was a case of adding new properties to old, so that existing terms acquired double meanings. I point to two such clusters, of which the digressions on copyrighting and on the verification of scientific findings have already given an indication.

One cluster refers to propagation, and the oldest candidate here is the very term *conceive* and its correlates, *concept* and *conception*. To create offspring and to form an idea: this double sense of conceive had been recorded since the 1300s.[54] But there is also *generate, reproduce, create* and *issue*, and some of these terms only doubled their reference much later. Thus *creation* was used in the fourteenth century for begetting and with divine connotations of causing to come into being; it was first recorded as applying to an intellectual product or form in the late sixteenth – early seventeenth century. This was in the sense of summoning through the imagination as well as in the then more established legal sense of constitute. Other doubles also emerged in the early modern period. Consider the second cluster, dominated in my own mind by the term *relation*, which includes *connection* and *affinity*. *Affinity* seems to have been a relationship by marriage or an alliance between consociates before it became, in the sixteenth century, a term for structural resemblance (between languages) or causal connection. Conversely, *connection* itself, which appears in the seventeenth century, seems to have referred to the joining of words and ideas by logical process before it came in the eighteenth to designate the joining of persons through marriage or (more rarely) consanguinity.[55] Of more recent coinage, connection nonetheless followed the same sequence as relation and relative.

The clusters are connected. The one elides mental conceptions and procreative acts; the other elides the kinds of connections these produce. Elucidating the nature of mental conceptions was one of philosophy's contributions to the new knowledges of the time, whereas the relationship between procreation and kinship fed into emergent formulations of nature and culture. But that is in prospect; there is something to be explained in retrospect.

If these were originally puns and conjunctions allowed by the English language and the way it created verbal connections,[56] then they must also have been allowed by English kinship in the way it set up connections between persons.[57] Was the attention to knowledge-making that we associate with the new sciences also refashioning the way people represented their relations to one another? What was the nature of those relations? What was entailed in having 'relation' introduce into thinking about kin an intellectualised sense of connection? And embedded there, did it acquire further properties? For, once introduced into kinship, 'the relation' could be borrowed back again.

Listen now to this deliberate analogy, addressed to the elucidation of knowledge processes. How we know kinsfolk and how we know things are drawn together in a parallel with all the force of serious explication. In his *Essay concerning human understanding* (1690), Locke conjured up the image of two cassowaries on display in St. James's Park, London. Cassowaries are large, flightless birds from Papua New Guinea and South East Asia, and to Londoners they seemed quite enigmatic, eluding immediate classification. However, the philosopher wanted to illustrate the logical circumstance whereby a relation could be perceived clearly even though the precise nature of the entities themselves might be in doubt. He offered a parallel with this strange bird, its enigmatic identity (not his phrase) contrasting with the clearly perceived relationship between the pair: they were dam and chick.[58] The one was the offspring of the other. The parent–child relation, a matter of kinship, illustrated how one could, as a matter of knowledge, conceive relations between entities.

We might assume that all at issue here were relations between concepts, as between the concepts of parent and offspring. But not only did Locke draw on the concrete act of propagation (it was 'the notion that one laid the egg out of which the other was hatched' [Locke 1690: 237] that gave the idea of relationship), the avian connection had been preceded by several references to human kinship and to interpersonal relations.

Kinship makes evident one very notable property of the relation: the tie that invisibly links kin is both embodied in each (kins)person and can be understood as separate from them. Thus in talking about the way in which the act of comparison (bringing items into relationship) is a clarifying exercise, Locke argued that 'in comparing two men, in reference to one common parent, it is very easy to frame the idea of brothers, without yet having the perfect idea of a man' (1690: 236). What he was comparing were the two kinds of relations. Throughout his disquisition on the relation, he took kin relationships as immediately accessible exemplars of logical relations. Thus he gave as examples correlative terms obvious to everyone: 'father and son, husband and wife'. The argument is building up for a consideration of that 'most comprehensive relation, wherein all things that do or can exist are concerned; and that is the relation of cause and effect . . . [from which comes] the two fountains of all our knowledge, sensation and reflection' (1690: 237).

In making the comparisons, Locke linked a conceptual relation between entities to a procreative relation between hen and chick as though both usages were as thoroughly sedimented in the English language. Only with hindsight do we note that between the two it was relation as applied to the kin connection that was the relative novelty. So, for all that the conceptual notion of relation can be borrowed back so effectively from the domain of kin relations, the historical question remains: how did it come to be applied to kinspersons in the first place?

The reader already knows that this is not the occasion for an answer. But recent technological developments have perhaps added to the reasons that make the question worth asking. Although kinship and knowledge provide figurative or metaphorical resources for one another, borrowed back and forth, the historical direction in which the concept of 'relation' expanded – from knowledge-making to kinship connection – would seem to have left traces in a certain persistent asymmetry. Not only for this reason but also perhaps including this reason, 'knowledge' holds the privileged position.

## III

### Kinship and Knowledge

Anthropology's relation echoes and is echoed in the way people crossover between conceptual and interpersonal ways of relating. The remainder of this chapter offers some Euro-American examples. They return to the specific case of knowledge and kinship that characterises the 'scientific kinship system' I claimed in Chapter Two. But I return to this point with the additional information about the apparent directional drift in the English language, in which fresh conceptualisations of the world seemingly worked their way into the apprehension of relations between (kins)persons. In discussing people's interpretations, it pursues an argument about the role of analogies as common vehicles for such manoevres and about what becomes explicit or remains implicit crossovers.

Analogies are not relations of cause and effect; concepts do not – pace the Calverts and Buzzancas – procreate. They get carried by people across domains, often because there is some argument to pursue. Analogies are relations of resemblance; that does not mean their fancifulness is idle. On the contrary, much of culture is a fabrication of resemblances, a making sense through indicative continuities, just as one text points to another text.[59] This is true whether analogies are pressed into the service of innovation or into the service of keeping values intact. It follows that appreciating the power of a parallel between conceptual and familial relations does not depend on demonstrating the direct derivation of one from the other. It is conceivable, for example, that the terms 'relation' and 'relative' migrated into kinship from their more general usage, at the time, for associates, persons connected through mutual acknowledgment. Like the circle of scientists, the circle of persons who publicly recognised one another (as associates) possibly anticipated some of the class overtones of kinship so evident by Jane Austen's time. However, even the usage of relation (relative appears only rarely with this connotation) for non-kin associates was itself fairly recent; its application to the mode by which persons are mutually connected through knowledge and circumstance, and for the aggregate of such associations, apparently comes from the seventeenth century.

The point is that once narratives, tropes and images are lodged in a particular context or domain, they are capable of summoning other contexts whether or not they were derived directly from them. If the spectrum I have just conjured falls broadly into a set of parallels between knowledge and kinship, it would seem that since early modern times English-speakers have kept these domains in tandem. Each has had its own developmental trajectory, but each seems still to offer people the power of drawing the other into itself. Needless to say, they do not work on one another to quite the same effect; they are not entirely symmetrical. Here we must to consider how terms come to be naturalised in their new domains. Their metaphorical status laid aside, the potential for analogy may be submerged.

Familial and procreative language in philosophy and science have long been naturalised to refer not only to classificatory schema but also to non-human processes of reproduction. In any case the evidence is that some of these terms were widely used in, for instance, natural historical and anatomical writings *before* they became applicable to human relations, one such term being 'reproduction' itself (cf. Jordanova 1995: 372). But then no one blinks an eye at referring to mother and daughter cells either. Such terms have a technical job to do in defining certain states or processes or connections between concepts, and any figurative recall will seem for the most part irrelevant. Beer asks us to consider this description of the planets:

When we contemplate the constituents of the planetary system from the point of view which this relation affords us, it is no longer mere analogy which strikes us, no longer a general resemblance among [the planets]. . . . The resemblance is now perceived as a true *family likeness*; they are bound up in one chain – interwoven in one web of mutual relation.

Chambers 1844: 11–12, from John Herschel's 1833<br>Treatise on Astronomy in Lardener's Cyclopaedia,<br>quoted in Beer 1983: 169, original emphasis

Herschel wanted to displace a weak sense of analogy between planetary bodies (they look alike) with a strong sense of the webs of affinity between them (their orbits are calibrated in respect of one another). The first relation in this passage is a mathematical deduction between distances from the sun and revolutions around it, whereas the second sounds as though it could have acquired resonances of kinship.[60] But equally well, he could simply be reinforcing the usage that had become habitual in science. A family is an assemblage of objects, and all he was insisting on was their necessary or systemic connection.[61] It did not have to be expressly as kinship that such ideas were embedded in knowledge practices.

Ideas about knowledge embedded in kinship practices were another matter altogether; they were there *as* knowledge. This was nothing novel. The question is what inflection early modern ideas about intellectual procreation and conceptual reations might have added. Was new impetus given to the legal axiom that between mother and father only the mother is known with certainty? Note the part that relations played in this axiom. The father had a relationship to his child because of his (certain) relationship to the mother;[62] if one relation had been brought into being through another relation,[63] is that not also about how knowledge was being argued (one piece of information validated through another piece of information)? However, the analogy here is mine.[64] In folk terms, all one needed to say was that the father was related to the child because his relationship to the mother was known, at once declared and acknowledged. In short, knowledge was already a *part* of the way in which Euro-Americans reckoned they were related to one another; that is still the case.

For English-speakers, a peculiarity of knowing in kinship terms is that information about origins is already grasped as knowledge. Parentage implies relatedness; facts about birth imply parentage, and people who find things out about their ancestry, and thus about their relations with others, acquire identity by that very discovery. The information constitutes what they know about themselves.[65]

One fact about being a kinsperson, then, is that information about kin is not something that can be selected or rejected *as information* (cf Strathern 1999). Information already bestows identity. Let me expand the point. Because kinship identity is realised within a field of relationships, knowing about one's kin is also knowing about oneself. One has no option over the relationships; any subsequent selection or rejection implies selecting or rejecting those who are already one's relatives or else revealed not to be relatives at all. Hence, information can only be screened out at the invidious cost of appearing to choose ('oh, I don't want to know about them').[66] Whether what one discovers is the basis for deciding never to see certain people again or for welcoming them into the home, the information is already, so to speak, knowledge, that is, already embedded in the way one acts toward these others. This leads to a sense in which we may say that knowledge creates relationships: relationships come into being when the knowledge does. As a proposition about kin, it can be taken quite literally.

So what room does that leave for figurative manoevres? As long as the domains ('kinship', 'knowledge') are kept separate, perhaps through associations and connotations that do not seem to bear in immediately on each other, the potential for analogy remains present. And as long as they are separate, the one endows the other with its own distinct properties, bringing a different sense of reality with it.

An example running through this account is that either knowledge or kinship can make the other appear relatively concrete or relatively abstract. As we have seen in the borrowings back, a reference to kinship can give fresh concreteness to the abstract perception of relations in the way Locke appears to have intended – as did, and do, the all too solid questions about children, money and property. Or to the contrary kinship may appear to be rendered too abstract for some people's comfort. Jordanova's documentation of changing terms for procreation in eighteenth century England affords an example. *Reproduction* came to be applied to human beings, displacing the earlier term *generation*. Reproduction 'abstracts the [procreative] process from the bodies and persons involved, whether they are parents or offspring' (1995: 372). Indeed, its abstract sense of forming or creating or bringing into existence was only applied to human procreation under some protest. By contrast with *generation*, reproduction was held to disregard mankind's privileged genealogy. Indeed, the very point was that it encompassed the entire organic world; extending it to human beings was a new way of organising knowledge about the world. For John Wesley, she observes, the term was thus a denial of human kinship with God for it levelled man with – in his words – nettles or onions.

It would be wrong, then, to infer that knowledge invariably offers abstraction, kinship concreteness. Rather, what is going to appear abstract and what is going to appear concrete will depend on the argument of the moment. It will also depend on the way in which objects of knowledge acquire status and certainty. Abstractions lead to fresh reifications and in the process may well acquire, so to speak, new bodies. When the text is detached from the book as a material body (the bound volume), it is turned into an immaterial but nonetheless recognisable thing over which rights can be owned. The perception of a 'thing' in which rights may be held can be a stimulus to fresh concretization or corporealization. Should we be surprised that it is also in the eighteenth century that the very term *corpus* subsequently became attached to the idea of a collection or gathering together of works?

The asymmetry is another issue. To say that knowledge is a part of contemporary kinship in a way that kinship is not a part of knowledge, my general point here, reminds us of the relation and its direction of expansion. My interest in the early modern material has been, all along, its pointers to practices of making knowledge. Recall the explicitness with which the practitioners of the new science set about their task, as explicit as their latter day counterparts writing for scientific journals have to be. What I do not know is how we might or might not, historically speaking, align creating knowledge with creating kinship.

Let me conclude with a situation in which anthropologists do know something about kinship practices. It returns us to present-day arguments, to practices stimulated by the so-called new reproductive technologies and to the arena of litigation. We might read the situation either as a move toward greater abstraction – a new form of relatedness without relatives – or as a move toward greater concreteness, where value is recovered for kinship substance, indeed where one might say that kinship is being turned back from knowledge into information. In this context, there are moments when the domains of kinship practice and knowledge practice cannot be kept separate, and analogy again becomes impossible.

## The Informational Family

It is generally assumed that parents have an interest in their children's health and that doctors will inform parents about it. In 1992, an American, Donna Safer sued (against the estate of) her father's physician for not having informed her of her parent's condition. She had been diagnosed with the same cancer that her father had died from, twenty-eight years earlier, when she was ten. Her complaint was that had she known she might have been able to take precautionary measures. The New Jersey trial court concluded that a doctor had no legal duty to warn the child of a patient of a genetic risk. It was said that the harm was already within the non-patient child (Dolgin 2000: 556). The appeals court disagreed and said that there was an obligation to inform in instances of genetic disorders 'where [given the nature of the technology] the individual or group at risk is easily identified.' It went on:

[T]he duty [is appropriately] seen as owed not only to the patient himself... [but] extends beyond the interests of a patient to members of the immediate family of the patient who may be adversely affected by a breach of that duty.

quoted by Dolgin 2000: 557.

Of the diverse cases considered by Dolgin, this she takes as the most radical. It compels her to identify an emergent phenomenon, the 'genetic family'.

Warning parents about a child's genetic condition is one thing. That simply reflects social and legal understandings of the parent–child relationship, granting parents the right to know and decide what their child should know. Otherwise, family members have as much right to confidentiality as anyone. The reverse case[67] not only removes the doctrine of patient confidentiality among adults but also imposes an obligation on third parties to warn family members about the medical condition of other family members. Dolgin sees this both as undermining individual privacy and as treating family members as an undifferentiated group.[68] In my view, it could also be doing something else.

When knowledge is knowledge of genetic makeup, there is no option as to the ensuing facts of relationship. But although information about origins automatically becomes knowledge for the person, under other circumstances, as here concerning the health of individual family members, it can revert to information again. This is true insofar as it becomes similar to other kinds of information about the world acquired from outside sources. Indeed, and this is what Dolgin stresses, nothing else need be known about the relationship between parent and child than the fact that the body of one held or holds information that could be useful to the other.

A kinship system that has a propensity to base relatedness on what can be *known* about people's connections to one another was bound to be intensely interested in the new certainties afforded by genetic testing. What could be more concrete than heredity evident in every body cell? The genetic family, that is, the family whose members are proved or presumed to be genetically related, is at once held together by the substance people ascribe to genes and by the information these genes supposedly contain. What is newly important about the genetic tie is that it gives family members information about one another.

The concreteness of the gene has the potential to displace other concretivities. Like finding direct evidence of inspiration from within a literary work, genes offer direct knowledge of heredity unmediated by parentage, a possibility that has been appreciated for some time (Wexler 1992). Yet, in practice, personal knowledge of a family's genetic history is the route by which people may start enquiring into their own susceptibilities or find out more about afflictions already on them, and on the basis of personal knowledge persuade doctors to give them 'genetic tests' (Finkler 2000). So why is Dolgin so struck by the novel properties of what she calls the genetic family, at least as it is legally constructed through cases such as Donna Safer's? Relatives have become like their genes; value lies in the information they carry, and what strikes her in this regard is the substitutability of persons for one another. What is lost is the concretivity of specific relationships.

'Genes suggest nothing about social relationships. They are simply data. As such they neither represent nor demand particular *moral* links among the people they describe' (Dolgin 2000: 544, her emphasis). In fact, Dolgin has also argued (personal communication) that the genetic family challenges the presumption that the law can safeguard modern families – so-called families of choice – as units of love, solidarity and lasting commitment. The construct of the genetic family precludes choice and is indifferent to the character of family life. Thus the genetic family is *neither* America's 'traditional' family with its hierarchy or community in which members find their place by reference to one another (privacy belonged to the familial whole represented by its patriarchal head [her term]) *nor* its 'modern' family consciously held together through autonomous choice, where the unit of value was the unique individual (and privacy accorded individual members within it). 'Within the genetic family, any unit (any person) or combination of units can exist without reference to any others ... [and] the unit of value ... is the whole (itself variously defined) as well as the parts (insofar as they mirror the whole and each other)' (Dolgin 2000: 558). As to privacy: information about any one member of the family is merged with information about them all.[69] In short:

The links connecting Donna to her father – or any member of a genetic family to any other – are a-moral links that neither define nor depend upon the scope and meaning of social relationships among the parties.

Dolgin 2000: 561.

This fractal vision assumes a family within which, as repositories of information, persons are replicas of one another.[70] Relatedness without relatives one might say.[71]

You might think this is rather much to derive from a court case. However, we do know something about contemporary kinship practices. And, among many other possibilities, the genetic family is also being lived outside the American courtroom. Indeed it may be re-lived as an extended family. The positive aspect of having breast cancer was for one woman in Finkler's (2000: 98) study her 'relationship with the extended family. I'm stuck with this. It's nice to know that I'm back in the family.' Genetic information that appears to extract relatedness from relationships can equally encourage people to seek out far flung connections that may or may not be turned back into active relationships. The point is that they do not have to be.

'In contemporary society people have tended to become separated from kin, if not from their immediate family, and family and kinship have taken on an amorphous cast, for multiple reasons, the most obvious being geographic dispersal'. Finkler's (2000: 206) general observations on the American family follow with the specific comment that notions of genetic inheritance may move it together again. She was reporting on a study of women either diagnosed as having a hereditary disease or with a (family) history of one and their search for information from relatives with whom they might have long been out of close contact.[72] But the re-corporealization of the family, if I may call it that,[73] comes with this astringent proviso:

interaction with family and kin may no longer be required in order for people to recognize relatedness and connection. . . . To the sense that one forms part of a family chiefly because one shares the same genes, requiring no social participation nor sense of responsibility to those who are related except to provide blood samples for testing purposes, removes the moral context of family relations.

Finkler 2000: 206

More than this, Finkler's expectation that people would blame their ancestors for passing on 'faulty' genes was upturned; the women she interviewed said their families were not accountable for their affliction. Genes are amoral entities.[74] For there is a sense in which they are equally a-relational: 'they are another kind of thing, a thing-in-itself where no trope can be admitted' (Haraway 1997: 134). The genes' location in kinship becomes all the more fascinating.

The routines of family life have usually meant that relationships without responsibilities tend to fade away. A truism about *knowledge* can keep them in view: the genes that carry the data informing you what you are at the very same time comprise the mechanisms that have the potential to bring about what you are. This looks like a reworking of an old theme, the constitutive nature of kinship knowledge. But to find kinship knowledge in the gene is, so to speak, to find it in itself. Knowledge and kinship become momentarily inseparable. They are not analogues of one another; even more so than Herschel's planets, resemblance dissolves into an identity. Only an 'extraneous' factor could prise them apart again. And Justice Kennard's winkling out of the analogy between conceivers of ideas and conceivers of children introduces just such a factor. It was property ownership that showed them to be different: in this context, property opens up new comparisons. Thus one can say, as a point of deliberate comparison, that knowledge may be regarded as belonging to persons in the same way as they might imagine their genes belonging to them.

Indeed, in the background to Donna Safer's suit for the wrong done to her by the withholding of genetic information lies increasing nervousness about setting precedents for ownership, as Dolgin (2000: 550–1) describes. Two issues, among many others, concern commentators in the United States. On the one hand, legal instruments (such as statutes) that define genetic information as the property of those to whom it pertains do so with concerns about individual privacy in mind. On the other hand, the very idea that people should claim property in genetic information is vigorously opposed by sections of the biotechnology industry; they see the imposition of ownership rules on genetic information as likely to require a record-keeping regime that would inhibit research and provide a context for litigation, as well as interfere with profits. Commentators have been as inventive as those concerned with authorship.[75] It has been proposed in the United States that ownership should be replaced by the doctrine of informed consent. Informed consent rules grant people the right to *know* about the uses to which others will put information about their genes.

Another analogy follows. Like the division proposed in the United Kingdom between license to publish and copyright, this could divide the owners of rights to exploit the information (who would enjoy the economic benefit of, say, developing technology) from the persons giving informed consent (who would enjoy a kind of moral right, an identification with their genes and a potential safeguard to their genetic privacy). For the latter, and it is a cultural commonplace, what seems supremely at issue in gene information is that this core bit of kinship should be accessed *as* knowledge for, belonging to and about themselves.

I STARTED WITH SOME OBSERVATIONS ABOUT CULTURAL RESOURCES. Kinship practices and knowledge practices comprise fields that have, since early modern times, provided figurative ammunition for each other. The complex possibilities established by terms such as 'conception' had long been in place, whereas others – of which I have singled out 'relation' – appear to have been formed at this time. As far as the latter is concerned, and as far as the evidence goes, one usage (in the context of knowledge, namely, conceptual relations) had historical priority over the other (interpersonal relations). Recall, again, that the term 'relation' already denoted intellectual practice – narration, referring back to something, making a comparison – before it became applied to social ties and specifically to ties of blood and marriage. This was the period when the relation in its conceptual sense was to be given a long chain of effects in new practices of knowledge-making.

Over time, analogies between domains may be submerged, revived and submerged again. I ended by pointing to a recent social phenomenon, the genetic family, which gives a new literalism to understandings about knowledge, and where knowledge about persons also appears as knowledge about the world. Kinship identity can be imagined as embodied in an informational code and information can be imagined as a kinship substance. It is as though the analogies between knowledge and kinship were compacted into one another.

But that elision is brought into being by a concatenation of circumstances that certainly do not exhaust everything one might want to say about either knowledge or kinship. I noted that property started up fresh analogies. Let me briefly go back to the beginning, and to a different fate for ideas about genetic substance.

The U.S. women who hoped, in response to the advertisement, to sell their eggs for $50,000 were prepared to convert one kind of substance (genetic material) into another (money), and were not looking for any enduring sense of connection. In another part of the same world, the United Kingdom, where by law that conversion is not possible, egg donors do different kinds of conversions. One potential conversion is into connections but connections created outside a premise of kinship. Here new separations emerge as well. If one starts not with kin, people whom one knows, but with people whom one does *not* know, fresh scope for relational reasoning also emerges.

In meeting various egg donors in Britain, Konrad was struck by the extremely vague and amorphous way in which they talked about the connection between donors and recipients; she suggests that it is out of the very condition of anonymous diffuseness that people conceive relations of a kind (Konrad 1998: 652). 'As ova substance is disseminated in multiple directions to multiple numbers of recipients... donors and recipients are partaking collectively in an exchange order of non-genealogical relatedness' (1998: 655). In this process, substance may be leached of 'biological' significance (the eggs are 'not like a physical thing that have come from my body', quoted at 1998: 651). What signifies is being the origin of a process that another carries forward. Here women's conservation of privacy is important;[76] they aim to help others whom they do not know and largely do not want to know. The wish to assist 'a someone' contains the essence of their own agency, an extension of themselves that takes effect across a disperse universe of unidentified others.

Konrad thus describes persons forming themselves through an extensional relatedness via multiple persons who are separated from them by being neither locatable nor nameable.[77] Ova donors need effect no specific transaction in order to value their action. 'What appears as the agency of these donors does so as the value of multiple and untraceable circulations of persons and body parts anonymized as (an)other's action, as a generalized, diffuse relatedness' (1998: 661). This relatedness may not have relatives, but it does have signifying others. Women as would-be mothers: the donors see their situations (the situations of both donors and recipients) as parallel.

Reaching out to an audience of multiple recipients sounds not so far removed from the aspirations of authors. But unlike authorial identity, at least of the scientific kind, the basis for these particular donors' relations with the women they saw themselves as helping was that their accountability would have no forward effect: their gesture contained its own definition of responsibility (to help a someone). The relations did not translate into interaction. The eggs did not need a name.[78] Hence it seemed possible to leave quite undefined whether or not what they were giving away was something they felt they owned. Konrad (1998: 651) quoted one among apparently several women who said, 'I don't think the eggs are mine, they're not something physical that they're my eggs. I don't even think of them as eggs'. In other words, the parallelism rests on what is also an unbridgeable gulf between them: in this sense, donors and recipients are in a relation of analogy.

Many of the British women's feelings have no doubt been echoed on the American side (cf. Ragoné 1994 on similar expressions in surrogacy arrangements), and I am not labouring after a contrast. All I do is underline the obvious, that there are always new domains with which to make connections and thus new material for analogies.

In the prevailing (Euro-American) view, technology and its scientific basis has had a tremendously inventive impact in creating new material. It is intriguing, then, to realise the way in which some analogies have been locked together for centuries. We cannot know out of the present flux where kinship and knowledge are going to end up; we can know something of past circumstances. The expansion of the term relation is a case in point. So I come back to wanting to ask about kin connections between English-speakers in early modern times. To what kinship practices did the new concept of relation speak; what emergent problems or possibilities in social interaction might its properties have addressed? From the perspective of kinship, anthropologically speaking, the sciences of the time come to look rather interesting.

### ACKNOWLEDGEMENTS

Initially presented as the 2000 Robert and Maurine Rothschild Lecture to the Department of History of Science, Harvard University, as 'Emergent properties: new technologies, new persons, new claims'. My thanks to the Chair and to the Department both for their invitation and for their many comments, especially Mario Biagioli and Peter Galison. 'Emergent properties' continues an essay on 'The Relation' (1995); I thank Annelise Riles for insisting on my not forgetting it. The project owes much to many colleagues, notably Debbora Battaglia, Barbara Bodenhorn, Janet Carsten, Jeanette Edwards, Sarah Franklin, Frances Price, Heléna Ragoné. I also record here the lasting stimulus of a Wenner Gren conference organised by Sarah Franklin and Susan McKinnon on *New Directions in Kinship* to which parts of this were presented. Paul Connerton gave the earlier manuscript adroit scrutiny, as did Susan Drucker-Brown, Joyce Evans and, on several points, Eric Hirsch and Annelise Riles. My debts to Janet Dolgin and Mario Biagioli for papers not published at the time should be evident. Finally Patricia Fara's subsequent comments have afforded a glimpse into discussions among historians that could help locate some of the observations here.

PART TWO

# THE ARITHMETIC OF OWNERSHIP

# Introduction: The Arithmetic of Ownership

*I* HAVE BEEN DEALING WITH THE IMPETUS TO KINSHIP THINKING provided by technologies that have confronted people with unprecedented explictness about relations where knowledge holds a key role. The people in question are heirs to the scientific revolution. Habits of knowledge already embedded (for Euro-Americans) in everyday practices are made visible, and then made visible again in regulation or legislation. That is what the Human Genetics Commission (HGC) was so concerned about.

Now the HGC documents mentioned in Part I largely confine children to specific chapters; children are treated first and foremost as minors, persons too young to give independent consent to medical treatment. Yet in another sense, the whole exercise is about children, that is, about offspring and what it means to be heirs of another kind, to a genetic inheritance. There would much less concern about human genetics if genetic information were not regarded as revealing inherited characteristics. The HGC generalises this when it says that one of the identifying features of genetic information is that it 'is not only information about the individual person, but about his or her biological relations' (HGC 2000: 7). However, although the text refers generally to issues that arise for family members, it is only in the context of children as young persons that it also deals explicitly with children as offspring.

Part II introduces materials from peoples who may be intensely interested in their origins through their parents precisely because of the kind of offspring that connection makes them into, a concern they carry all their life. In Euro-American kinship thinking these days, the genetic source is a kind of tracer that spells out – counts out – the respective contributions of different kinds of parents and points to how many there are according to the nature of their contributions (several generations may be involved). But once the parental contributions have combined in the individual child, the child's multiple origins become a matter largely personal to it, largely private in the eyes of third parties outside the family. However, there are places, and my examples come from the Pacific, where the multiplication of distinct parental origins forms a set of crucial and enduring social resources. It matters how people count the number and *kinds* of parents they have and even – as recounted in the final chapter – the number of offspring.

Arithmetic of this kind turns out to be germane to the sources of creativity that people can claim and to the way they assert claims over their own and other people's offspring. When these positions are found in the doubling and quadrupling of what an older anthropology would have called kinship roles, we begin to see why kinship 'systems' are more than just complicated to describe; they are also uncovered as complex phenomena in themselves (Mosko and Damon in press). From one point of view, the chapters in this second part of the book simply illustrate the point. From another, they invite us to see how we might use the tool described in Part I, the ability to handle two kinds of relations at once, the duplex relation.[1]

The duplex works in a (Euro-American) world simultaneously perceptible from different viewpoints. Switching back and forth between what appears given and what appears constructed, or between categories and individuals, offers positions that anticipate each other. These are understood to be viewpoints on one world.[2] To adopt Riles' striking phrase for the way internationalist networks and personal relationships sit side by side, the duplex produces 'the same form seen twice' (Riles 2000: 69; also 115–6). The form is that of the relation. Yet suppose we encountered not a doubled world but worlds that could be counted in different ways? What of our duplex then?

### CONCEPTION BY INTENT

Hairsbreadths in vocabulary seem to separate what could so easily seem similar propositions. This is what Bamford (2004) found when she thought she knew what Kamea people in the Papua New Guinea Highlands meant in asserting that brothers and sisters were 'one blood'. The idiom of blood sounds familiar. Yet in truth it is not the vocabulary that discriminates but what of the world it refers to. They were not talking about descent or physiology; the familiar phrase refers to a vision of connection quite foreign to English-speakers, and quite narrow, namely the shared experience of having once been 'contained' in a single woman's womb. Again, I introduce a vignette to set the scene.

One of the questions Kamea ask themselves is why girls grow faster than boys. They have a ready answer: because of the thoughts in the girls' heads! It is nothing less than their intention to marry that makes them mature. In a wonderful reprise of imagining we have heard it all being followed by surprise that actually we have not, 'Women think only of men and getting married', she quotes Kamea saying; 'this is what makes them grow quickly' (Bamford 2004: 296). Intent to marry accompanies intent to conceive, an echo of the (Amazonian) Wari' tenet that to become kin is to desire kin (Vilaça 2002: 352–3). In this case, intent is fuelled by the food that a prospective groom's family gives the family of his betrothed as a prelude to bridewealth. These people 'constitute her capacity to act as a "container" [become pregnant] and, in doing so, engender her identity as a reproductively mature female' (Bamford 2004: 297). Where, that is, who food comes from is quite critical: it is the groom's kin who in this way create the mother. The groom in turn is made into a father whose constitutive act is to continue the flow of food and other gifts to his wife's kin. The child may not come up in spots if he fails in his duty but will indubitably remain stunted, all skin and bone.

Although the body registers the effects of people's actions, one of Bamford's arguments is that the body is not a vehicle that renders substance, let alone procreative substance, the linking material of kinship. That takes other forms. For example, what is in their heads affects men too. Men prize their connections with their fathers and fathers' fathers and point to their inheritance of land as proof. A man's land claims depend crucially on knowledge, to be precise knowledge of where his ancestors have cultivated, in order that he may cultivate there (claims not activated through labour will eventually disappear). In fact, men and women engender their own modes of relating, a woman's children (especially girls) tracing lateral ties through one-blood connections and a man's children (especially boys) seeing themselves as part of a lineal succession. The modes are so divergent that the anthropologist refers to the momentum of Kamea social life as an intersection of 'two distinct relational forms' (Bamford 2004: 302).

In this vignette lies just the kind of material that would fuel continuing Euro-American sterotypes about the personalised, face-to-face character of small scale communities. I hope the observations about the conceptual role of intent and the significance of knowledge will have offered at least preliminary pause.

## LEAVING 'KNOWLEDGE' TO ONE SIDE

Scientific knowledge gives Euro-Americans a way of being truthful about the nature of the world. Indeed, it is literally a practice of verification. The ability to occupy two positions at once, key to the relational tool I have introduced, is no more than a tool or a facility, and exists alongside diverse attempts to co-opt it. All we can say is that a social anthropology made possible by the way relationality is developed for the epistemological ends of investigation and enquiry also finds itself practising its own forms of relationality. Part I spelled out anthropology's dual interest in conceptual and interpersonal relations, in investigating relations between concepts and relations between persons. Anthropology does not have to summon a nature–culture divide (science's relation) in order to do so. But it does summon knowledge-making practices.

Spelling out the anthropological usefulness of the tool spurs me to reflect on Part II and thus on Chapters Four to Six in a particular way. (And the rendition might draw the pieces together, even bestow some value on their original independence.) At the outset, Chapter Four opens with a set of stereotypes about Euro-Americans inhabiting technology where others – here Pacific Islanders (from New Ireland) – apparently inhabit communities. Chapter Six ends with an internationalist example of just such thinking being applied to new legislative attempts in the Pacific, which will in turn drive new political and economic interests. This is knowledge put to work, I might add, a means rather than an end.

In pressing its dual interests into a source of knowledge for itself, anthropology may seemingly find arenas of social life that correspond to one or other side of the duplex. One aspect of society appears a more apposite exemplar than another. So the two kinds of relations frequently emerge as though they could be distributed across different forms of association, institutions, societies even. That is one way in which Euro-American knowledge practices work. They allocate values or insights or facilities to different places (other people may strive to make them appear in the same place), rather as the ancient Greeks distributed virtues and vices among the gods. Chapter Five offers an example of Euro-American human rights discourse pitting categorical against interpersonal relations. But if we gave ear to Gell's (1999a: 35) admonishment, that a woman is mother to a child not through her physical presence or acts but as a term in a relation, we must take the view that persons do not exist independently of concepts of them. We ought in turn to be astonished to find kinship become associated with interpersonal relations as *against* the categorical or conceptual relations of society – or of property, McKinnon (2001) reminds us – in the anthropological tradition. I am afraid this is almost how Chapter Four proceeds, using Euro-American intellectual property regimes and Melanesian memorial practices as foils for one another. Why this might be marginally tenable as a comparison emerges at the end of Chapter Six. Between these forays into epistemology is a narrative of a different sort.

Science's relation and, with its own reach, anthropology's relation, afford an immense resource to a society whose project rests on knowledge of the world. I further remarked that if anthropology's relation does not have to summon a nature–culture divide, it does summon knowledge practices, by which I meant the kind of knowledge-making that informs epistemology.[3] But anthropology (among other routes to insight!) also forces us to observe that not all projects are knowledge-projects in this sense. Does that bring it up short? Or can anthropology use its tool to ask *what a non-epistemic version of the relation would look like?*

There is nothing arcane about this: we have just encountered legislation pressing into service a contrast between techno-industrial and communal rights. The Model Law for the Pacific Islands (described in Chapter Six) is based on an assumption about the inappropriateness of an intellectual property rights (IPR) regime formed in a technology-conscious, industrial-political economy for the kind of protection Pacific Islanders might seek for their cultural resources, understood as their inheritance. It has required various fact-finding missions. Importantly, the aim was not to understand more about the nature of those Pacific Island communities; rather, it was to set up an instrument that would give these communities formal recognition in the legal process.

Here I draw on Riles' (2003) work a second time. In thinking about different genres of legal knowledge, she distinguishes between instruments whose existence is defined by the ends to which they are put and representations that are to be analysed for their meanings and thus for what they express. In fact, she argues that the law's expressive genre makes objects such as 'communities' by producing significations about them; at the same time, in instrumental genre, it creates documents and verdicts that do not represent but instantiate (say) a community's rights. In her words, the expressive and the instrumental are sequential responses to one another. If we take thus take knowledge of the world (epistemology) as representation, an end in itself, an immediate analogy would suggest that non-epistemic knowledge will be found when instrumental means come to the fore. As we shall see, this is not the only conclusion.

My attention is drawn to the law, as a domain of Euro-American institutional life, for the very reason that it treats knowledge as means as well as ends. Any illumination it brings of the world may be displaced by its instrumental value in setting up the protocols and boundaries that direct people's actions. Here, it is treating knowledge in a non-epistemic manner. Now the law's great strength is its deployment of categorical or conceptual relations. Thus IPR regimes attempt to give categorical value to the products of people's activities through the concept of property. Frequently, however, it declares little interest in interpersonal relations. People as subjects in law must be dealt with categorically too, as in the conceptual definition of who are entitled to call themselves members of a rights-holding community. More than that, the law insists on a separation between legal (conceptual) and personal (interpersonal) matters. A human rights commentary on this very point is mentioned at the end of Chapter Five, and a forceful criticism appears in Chapter Six from the Australian legal writers whom we also met in the first. Indeed the separation, on which the law insists, frequently puts the distinction in concrete terms that finds very general resonance: Euro-Americans like to tell themselves that they distinguish *property* from *persons*.

However, when it comes to relations, it is apparent that this non-epistemic apprehension of knowledge deals with only part of the conceptual–interpersonal duplex and indeed sets up barriers between the two kinds. In this context, as its criticisms of human rights discourse shows, anthropology's relation can only work by bringing in evidence from beyond the law in a kind of counter-balancing or compensatory fashion. The challenge is whether the (anthropologists') duplex as such, with both kinds of relations in view, can also point to non-epistemic phenomena. Here it is fortuitous that my attention was drawn to the law in the arena where it deals at once with knowledge and with property, namely intellectual property rights. For the global dissemination of IPR thinking, as culminates in protocols such as the Pacific Islands Model Law, conveys in its wake all kinds of questions about persons and property. This brings us face to face with cosmologies that include claims of considerable interest to the law (property) but rest more widely on concepts of ownership.

Ownership is of passionate concern to Euro-Americans. Indeed the short disquisition on ownership in Chapter Four could have been written with Tarde in mind (see Chapter Two). But it is also a very useful translation, in a way property is not, for certain ways in which people (including people not in this tradition) perceive their claims over one another. Perhaps there is a candidate here for non-epistemic relations of both kinds. The argument requires bringing in non–Euro-American material, primarily from Melanesia.

Riles observes that expressive and instrumental forms of legal knowledge act in concert with each other. But there is knowledge, including knowledge available to the law, that lies beyond this pair. Ownership involves descriptions and representations of the world yet is not itself a project of description or a representation. And it would require qualification (e.g., property ownership) to render it instrumental. Ideas about ownership thus offer a possible axis for comparison with ways of thought that lie outside the Enlightenment orbit – and with those that lie within to which Enlightenment thinking can give only clumsy guidance.

Pursuing ownership may thus throw light on the fact that, despite constant assertions to the contrary, for Euro-Americans the question of whether persons are property will not die. The conundrum, which the law seems to have settled and yet not quite, unsettles assumed ways of knowing about the world. For it unsettles axioms of agency (subject–object and person–thing) derived from the relational nexus based on nature–culture, biology–society, discovery–invention and so forth. Thus we find all over again, and the book opened with this very concern, biotechnology raising in people's minds new questions about persons (including bodies and body parts) being owned.

In broaching Euro-American anxieties on this score with materials drawn altogether from elsewhere, we encounter other interests that compel people to combine and separate conceptual and interpersonal relations. This includes an interest in propagation, that is, in creativity and procreation, where – as Kamea assume – nothing is finished at birth, and the determination of who is an offspring of whom has to be worked upon. Kinship emerges as a prime field in which claims are made over persons as categories. If these are relations in the first place neither expressive nor instrumental, they are non-epistemic by virtue of the fact that kinds of knowledge cease to be a principal reference point.

### THE ARITHMETIC OF OWNERSHIP

Chapter Four dwells at some length on intellectual property rights and on the kind of investment that Euro-American people make in their ownership. If invention shows the creativity of individuals, it must be marked off from the discovery of natural facts that were always there for anyone to come across.

One reason to reproduce this piece is that it immediately summons an instrumental application of knowledge. The categorical distinction between invention and discovery becomes far less significant as offering divergent ways of verifying the nature of the world than it becomes, in IPR, a legal tool for adjudicating between rights. Hirsch (2004: 184) highlights Rabinow's (1996b) famous question of a U.S. scientist, 'Who invented PCR [polymerase chain reaction]?', to which the reply came, 'Conception, development and application are all scientific issues – invention is a question for the patent lawyers'. This brings Euro-American moderns closer to their New Ireland counterparts than the reverse. Moreover, what for a moment looks like a contrast between the categorical distinctions of Euro-American patent law and New Ireland rituals of procreation – the one producing things out of things, the other persons out of persons – dissolves. Euro-Americans also aim to produce creative scientists who can claim ownership, adding the magic of individualism to invention, whereas New Irelanders aim to produce images of persons as concepts or categories whose form they wish to own.

It is the anthropologist who puts these people and their ideas together. But the anthropologist also hopes to recognise her duplex in the hands of others.

The two-sided relation emerges in the way people try to make conceptual artefacts, and specifically categories, out of social relations. Here 'people' becomes inclusive, as the chapter stresses what lies in common between those of a 'Euro-American' background and those who hail from 'Melanesia'. Of course they are not the same. New Ireland carvers think they are reproducing what was always there, whereas Euro-American experimenters think they innovate. Nonetheless, the extended 'as if' analogy that drives the chapter, 'suppose a type of New Ireland mortuary sculpture (Malanggan) were a patentable form of technology', is meant to bring these circumstances together.

Ownership pinpoints differences of interest (Hayden 2003). Patents are about the ownership of rights to exploit an idea, whereas copyright is an ownership right over the form in which ideas are expressed against the interests that other people might have. What New Irelanders own, and to some extent distribute to other persons, is the concept or image of a (particular) deceased person. The image is a categorical rendering of the person that is capable of being communicated to others, and thereby so to speak interpersonally reworked. As we shall see, the rendering of the image (as a sculpture or mask for example) involves knowledge in its execution and in people's recognition of its features. Perhaps we could call the knowledge non-epistemic. For it is clear that Malanggan 'knowledge' is transmitted not in order for people to know about 'the world' or improve upon it but in order to capture power (Wagner 1975), to confer title. The persuasive effect of the work is accomplished if it simply summons a presence that is, aesthetically speaking, memorable.

Chapter One did not pause on the intriguing title of Davies and Naffine's book, *Are persons property?* (2001). The same question is asked in Papua New Guinea, and is answered by law and custom in different ways. Chapter Five, taking us further along the path of ownership, thus opens with a court case from Papua New Guinea concerning claims over a woman being given away, it would seem, as though she were property. The image of her as bones (literally, a skull) in a netbag, seems to compound the indignity. But this echo of Euro-American interest in body parts leads us to unpack the Melanesian fabrication along lines hinted in Chapter Four. The image of a person is an image of a relationship.

An image reifies (categorises) a relationship by presenting the whole person as seen from view of their claimant/relative. In this sense we can talk of ownership: people may own the (whole) concept of the person as a relative. The specific relationship that they summon or elicit from the person is that (whole) person in relation to them. We can also talk of relations or relationships as the subject of politico-ritual interest much as the individual person in Western jurisprudence is a subject in law. However, when they come to take action, persons become agents in that they must choose which of several potential relationships is to be acted upon. It is relationships, not knowledge, people describe as compelling action. As a consequence, persons may appear either as singular (whole, categorically available for possession by others) or as plural (partible, an agent enmeshed in a multitude of agents).

Euro-American property thinking points to different premises. Ideas about bodies and body parts suggest, by contrast, that it is possible to have property in a part but not the whole. Other habits of thought are also contextualised, such as the equation of kinship with tradition, and the antinomy tradition and modernity. Chapter Four ended with a comment on whether people think they are pursuing the new or the old: here we have legal rhetoric pitting the new against the old. Finally, it is probably superfluous to add that anthropology's relation is held in place by the way the narrative is constructed. The analysis thus elucidates an interplay between categorical and interpersonal relations in the manner in which a bride-to-be was regarded by her kin, and regarded herself. Neither view substituted for the other.

Several themes found in earlier chapters are encountered again in Chapter Six. It starts off a vein similar to Chapter Three with a comment on rhetoric, in this case in terms of (culturally salient) issues that are brought to bear on the law but are not part of it. It also echoes the discussion about 'how many' authors make up an author. Where Chapter Four draws inspiration from European legal thinking about patents, here copyright takes centre stage. Above all it continues the argument of Chapter Five about categorical claims on persons. In opening up the Malanggan case again, it pursues the issue of non-epistemic relations, in both senses of non-epistemic (on the one hand a type of knowledge and on the other hand not about knowledge at all). This leads to the question voiced by Kalinoe and Simet, namely what if anything is intellectual about the ownership of rights to designs or other intangibles that could be glossed as knowledge? *Intellectual* may not be the right epithet for immaterial effects such as images, and I query the significance of their location in the mind.

Chapter Six is confrontational about one question of ownership. It does not make up a query about whether persons can be property but takes the query directly from the work of academic lawyers. A contrast presented by IPR proves illuminating insofar as it emerges that Euro-American legal thinking allows that persons can only own (rights over) what is embedded in an object understood as a 'thing'. This logic lies behind the arithmetic of ownership. Melanesian people, and the examples are from areas where images of the person or relationship are found in ornaments and emblems, compute claims over the person in the form of categorical ownership. Here, ornaments, and other emblems, such as land or paintings, may be regarded as the 'bodies' of those who thus 'own' him or her, as the body itself can. Persons are in this manner embodied in others. The Kamea mother-to-be, whose contours are transformed as she consumes the bridewealth food (girls are fed copious quantities) would find this familiar.

But then perhaps the North London mother would not find dissonant an analogy that jumps out of this last chapter. The analogy is between her experience of her child as an extension both of herself and of the world and those Euro-American views of property that see it as at once enhancing the person and attaching him or her to this (same) world. Indeed, filtering the discussion of knowledge through property yields another dividend. It uncovers a condition of subjectivity under which knowledge comes to have value as an end rather than a means, that is, assumes an epistemological character: the duty to know oneself.[4] For it would be too narrow to read simple instrumentalism back into the mother's compulsion to improve her parenting of her child (even her relationship with it, to take Adrian Mole[5] as our guide). The scientific impetus to improvement, including self-improvement, demands that the world is understood first. Instrumental value can be found at any order of injunction (you need to understand the world as it is because you never know when you are going to need the knowledge; research is justified by future use even if none is evident now, and so on). But this is only possible because the (one) world is regarded as infinitely open to exploration. And that premise is re-iterated over and again.

In what way do the two sides of the anthropology's relation work for Melanesian ownership? In the making of a conceptual link between kin, the person (the particular relationship) becomes categorised, reified, claimable; in the enactment claims are then re-embedded in a nexus of interpersonal relationships with particular histories to them. Thus the Murik or Omie child appears now with a singular identity and now with multiple identities. The two aspects to relating are also found in the contrast between observing rules and bestowing nurture. Together, the three chapters in Part II suggest how the respective facilities in linking concepts and linking persons work off against each other in situations where people are concerned with their origins, and with the origins of powers as they conceptualise them. The details of the way these Melanesian persons divide themselves from one another, where Euro-American constructs suppose people adding themselves to one another, throws some light on the kinds of calculations made about the ownership of (pro)creative potential.

∽

THE ANTHROPOLOGISTS' RELATION IS A TOOL, A DUPLEX FASHIONED BY the social world in which they (and everyone else) live, by the way people switch between conceptual and interpersonal relations in their dealings with one another. This fashioning lay behind their early forays into kinship systems long before relations between nature and culture became debated. And this social world includes but goes beyond the Euro-American, and indeed non–Euro-American kinship gave the tool much of its cutting edge.

Yet in anthropological hands, the duplex has a major limitation. It becomes an epistemological artefact. For all that it allows one to ask about non-epistemic relations, its limitation is (obviously) the form that the duplex takes, the relation. For although it is good at elucidating the other side of things, especially in the case of societies outside the orbit of those developed by the Enlightenment and the scientific revolution, things indeed remain 'other', that is, seen always *in relation to* the vantage point of the moment. This is the trick of the Euro-American 'one world', and a final surprise that should be no surprise. What happens to the duplex when anthropologists find they can count worlds in different ways is, precisely, nothing. In short, the relation will not disappear.

By this I mean that the duplex whose form is the relation translates everything into itself. So it is impossible with this tool to comprehend different worlds other than in relation to one another. The hard-won feminist message, that male only makes sense in relation to female, was a significant challenge to essentialism or positivism; but when it comes to the 'two distinct relational forms' of Kamea gender, the limit is that we can *only* see these as correlates of each other. In the way kin become embodied in kin, the viewpoints of son and sister's son, hazarded in Chapter Six as a counterpart to the multiple worlds of human-animal interactions in Amazonia, appear already related.

The edge of this tool is simultaneously its power. Whatever one declares about incommensurability or asymmetry, the elements of anthropological narrative will re-arrange themselves in relation to one another. So it will forever translate diverse and multiple worlds into versions of – perspectives on – the same world. We just need to know that.

### ACKNOWLEDGEMENT

My debt to Eduardo Viveiros de Castro should be evident throughout the book, but no more so than here; Chapter Six provides some exemplification. His three nano-essays on kinship and magic (in prep.) take everything a notch further.

# 4

～

# The Patent and the Malanggan

The Malanggan exists at no specific time or place, but moves through time
and place, like a thunderstorm.

Alfred Gell, 1998: 226

*T*HE PERCEPTION THAT TECHNOLOGY IS EVERYWHERE – WITHIN AND
around us – comes from, among other places, the way modern people
describe themselves. They (moderns of the Euro-American sort) run together
all kinds of devices, examples of ingenuity and aids to living as though they had
a total existence more powerful than any particular contraption could hold
by itself. The conglomerate is glued together by two major assumptions. In
everyday parlance, 'technology' points to what is contemporary and innovative
about modernity; it also points to the creative inventiveness that brings itself
into being. A substantial corpus of intellectual property rights, for instance,
concerns itself with the producers of contraptions when the producers can
also show that they were the original innovators and inventors. I wish to
take advantage of the prevalent disourse of technology and the increasingly
prevalent discourse of intellectual property to describe a part of our world not
ordinarily brought within the range of these constructs. It creates an interesting
context for a question. What is strange about technology that Euro-Americans
should so insist on their familiarity with it? My toolkit is a couple of textbooks
on intellectual property rights (IPR), an art catalogue from an exhibition of
wooden sculptures and some anthropological reflections on enchantment.

## INTRODUCING THE BODY

New Ireland, off the coast of Papua New Guinea, is famous for its intricately
carved and coloured sculptures called *Malanggan*. Indeed the possibilities of

their travelling beyond these islands is written into the technology. They are by and large both portable and durable, while in the minds of the producers they are also supremely ephemeral. Malanggan are produced to be discarded. Created with great care they may be displayed for no more than a few days, hours even, before they have to be destroyed or thrown away. One mode of destruction is to put them into the hands of European traders: they are one of the most collectible types of art object from any ethnographic region of the world.

Malanggan come from northern New Ireland where they circulate across several distinct language groups.[1] We may imagine them as bodies, although the body appears in many different shapes and forms. The most familiar (most portable) take on the shapes of human and animal beings, a mask, say, with the general appearance of a head, made up of numerous smaller figures, snakes, birds, fish, parrot wings.[2] Its purpose is to contain the life force of a deceased person; New Irelanders say it provides the deceased with 'body' or 'skin' now that their other body no longer exists.[3] Present bodies may at once substitute for absent bodies (New Ireland exegesis) and (exegesis mine) may be presented as composed of other bodies, as a head is composed of birds and fish. It is an open question whether we should see the smaller bodies as inside the larger or as attached to its surface; from either perspective, visually speaking, images are composed of images. So what kind of space for dwelling is being created here?

Imagining entities 'containing' entities is one way of making notions of habitation and dwelling concrete. But of course such a strategy literalises[4] the basic phenomenological understanding that one cannot describe the world as it appears to people without describing the character of people's being, which makes the world what it is.[5] It follows that people are as much within it as the world is within them. Alongside this formulation comes the question: rather than being surprised that there is anything special about inhabiting technology, why do Euro-Americans think technology requires special techniques of habitation, and thus why in effect do they *distance* it from themselves?[6] From that point of view, different cultural perceptions of worlds within worlds start to become interesting. This mask is not the dead person's spirit, it is a skin or body for that person's spirit. The spirit is about to become an ancestor, and the body is carved into a form recognisable as ancestral to the person's clan. A transient container for ancestral power to be, it is also contained by ancestral power. So what is so special about the working of this power that it must be placed within a body before it can be released? Why, like Euro-Americans thinking about technology, do New Irelanders go to such lengths to *separate* themselves – the contained by contrast with container – from what they see as otherwise enveloping them? We shall come back to this.

No doubt Euro-American observers would comment on the technical skill that goes into making Malanggan.[7] They might also be tempted to read the animal motifs as referring to nature, apposite for Euro-American sensibilities, which would place seemingly non-modern peoples closer to their environment than themselves because they lack the intervening devices of high technology. However, for New Irelanders that cannot be what the birds and the fish are about. These people would no more think that they were in nature or nature in them[8] than they would think there was some kind of opposition between nature and the application of knowledge that Euro-Americans call technology.

## ENCHANTMENT

Exactly this distinction is, on the other hand, thoroughly embedded in Euro-American ways of thinking and is reinvented over and again, just as one of its partners, the distinction between the social and the biological, is constantly reinvented (Pottage 1998: 741)

Consider how 'technology' inhabits the English language. By pointing to a substantive entity, it gathers numerous things together under the one rubric so that English-speakers show to themselves the products of technology everywhere and distinguish them from other products. In common parlance, a dishwasher is an artefact of a technological world in a way the kitchen sink simply is not. Technology, in the culturally pervasive sense in which it inhabits this language, does not just reify effort or production; it reifies, gives tangible form to, a creativity regarded as rejuvenating. So technology embodies more than the recognition of the techniques of human handiwork; it is evidence of the continually creative mind that seeks to enlarge society's capacities.[9] Moreover, it mobilises agents whose efforts are socially extended, not just as a tool extends human effort but as innovations substitute for old travails (the dishwasher purportedly releasing the washer-upper for other ways of spending time, an altogether friendlier image than Gell's [1998] devastating depiction of landmines as the dispersed agency of a military commander). Put these together and we have enumerated some of the values attendant on that particular kind of creativity Euro-Americans recognise in an invention. For, of all the products of human creativity, inventions are defined by the power that technology has to give them life. Thinking about its foundation in inventiveness, we might say that technology lives among us in an enchanted state.

Here I take liberties with Gell's (1999b: chapter 5) disquisition on the enchantment of technology. The enchantment of technology lies in 'the power that technical processes have of casting a spell over us' (1999b: 163),[10] the way artefacts are construed as having come into being, and thus what makes us marvel at the very ability to translate an idea into an invention and an invention into a device that works. Power seems to end up in the artefacts themselves, harnessing the human energy they augment.[11] Above all, they are physical manifestations of the technical virtuosity and creativity of the maker. In an industrial world such makers may be known through trademarks that weave their own spells (Coombe 1998), but they may equally well be lost in anonymity. These nameless inventors *could* be named but, importantly, when they are not known they can reflect back a diffuse or generalised aura of capacity, enhancing people's sense that they are all heirs to a collective creativity.[12]

Enchantment lies in a further dimension, the enlargement of social agency. And here we encounter the technology *of* enchantment. An essential technique for creating an enchanted space is separation. I said that rather than being surprised that there is anything special about inhabiting technology, the interesting questions are about how one distances it. An obvious way is by dividing technology from other aspects of life. The magico-purificatory effect of conceptual separation (Latour 1993) suggests there is something special about the inventiveness of human agency; access to technology is in turn prized as extending such general capacities for the individual. How does the purificatory divide work? If Technology inhabits the English language as a substantive entity, it can also evoke other entities in opposition: sometimes Society,[13] sometimes Nature. When it is nature that is counterposed, technology and society may roll together as jointly enlarging the sphere of human endeavour at nature's expense. Nature puts technology at a distance from its own world. Thus whatever is categorised as nature simultaneously provides a measure of the effectiveness of the technology; it reflects degrees of human activity. Moreover, the magic of zero-sum logic makes measurement appear to work automatically: the more human activity there is, the less untouched nature or fewer natural processes there must be in the world. You can see it in every medical advance or diminished bird count. Nature in this sense is the ultimate envelope, containing technology and society within.

There are many ways in which English-speakers in particular and Euro-Americans in general make all this obvious to themselves.[14] I note one; Euro-Americans may claim for their culture the special capacity of globalisation, the ability that their information technology (IT) gives them to be in several places at once,[15] a spatially unmatched reach of efficacy. The world shrinking through communications and the retreat of untouched (natural) spaces are measures of it. Euro-Americans may even describe themselves as inhabiting a space enabled by technology that they alone are capable of making. In this authorial claim, by a kind of reverse logic that assumes people without the adjuncts of IT must live in a less expanded world, they may assume that other peoples do a different kind of inhabiting. Think of all their stereotypes of societies as communities. Take, for example, the people of Papua New Guinea. Perhaps Papua New Guineans have no idea of nature, but surely they have ideas of community, localities that stay put and a kind of dwelling that together yield stable identities, roots and all the rest of it?

### RETURN TO NEW IRELAND – 1

The stereotype would be misleading for New Ireland. This is not only because of the frequency of contact with European navigators, traders and labour recruiters over the past 150 to 200 years[16] but also because they have long had their own ways of moving around, and in a dimension at once spatial, temporal and virtual. Living people are never in just one place. And any one person lives within a stream of persons who move from place to place over time, remembered in some detail. Here the techniques of constructing Malanggan bodies start assuming the characteristics of a technology.

Malanggan do not only take the form of masks; they may be poles, friezes or standing displays.[17] Nor do they only appear at death, although all Malanggan involve the embodiment of deceased persons.[18] What is constant is that such artefacts are briefly displayed for the duration of ceremonies – days, hours – before being deliberately disposed of. The life force of the dead person is then released from its container. But, as Gell remarked (1998: 226), we might as well say the life of the person, for what is held momentarily in one place is an identity composed of the person's associations with many others, whether through the garden lands that they worked or through the groups into which they and their relatives have married. Moreover, the identity in question is not only of the deceased but also of the living owner of the Malanggan who has had it made in a particular way. The owner will produce the designs to which his membership in a clan or a localised unit of the clan entitles him.[19] But designs also travel, just as people do.

Malanggan are manufactured in such a way as to suggest multiple identities. Lincoln (1987) shows a Malanggan (catalogue number 40) composed of chickens and a frigate bird holding the tail of a snake that undulates through stylised foliage, as the catalogue description has it. In another constellation of elements (catalogue number 13) one sees clearly distinguishable snakes and birds – including chickens – and foliage garlands topped by a hornbill. Variation is necessary if people are not to trespass on one another's designs, and no two figures are identical. In certain Malanggan traditions, acceptable variation may involve as little as two or three centimetres of carving (Gunn 1987: 81). Motifs travel between these figures, then, and each new Malanggan is a composite of elements drawn from other Malanggan. It is a place that gathers places from elsewhere to itself, a person (to which Malangan are likened) who gathers the interests of other persons into him- or herself.[20]

The social space being modelled here is one of movement over time and distance.[21] For at death a person's attachments are still scattered in several locations.

> The gardens and plantations of the deceased, scattered here and there, are still in production, their wealth is held by various exchange-partners, their houses are still standing. . . . The process of making the carving coincides with the [subsequent] process of reorganisation and adjustment. . . .
>
> Gell 1998: 225

At the same time the social space is a virtual one in which the deceased is enveloped in the larger persona of clan connections. The clan is an always present environment.[22] If, however, we say that there is a sense in which a person inhabits a clan and the clan inhabits the person, then we must include those relationships beyond the clan that clanship also brings. Everyone has active relationships with other groups, and a living person's actions are oriented in diverse directions. Gathering these in, Malanggan have been spoken of as bringing together an otherwise dispersed agency.[23]

The crucial point about the destruction of the mortuary Malanggan is that the gathered agency of the deceased has then to be redispersed, whether to revitalise old relationships in new form or to return the deceased's powers in a more general way to the clan.[24] When a figure is assembled, it may recapitulate figures created for past clan members, then, containing elements that have travelled down the generations, whereas other motifs may have travelled across local groups so that elements also come from figures originating elsewhere.[25] The dimensions are of both time and space, and here we stumble across what can only be called a *technology of enchantment*. For the figures are constructed in such a way as to bring together in one place simultaneous reference to the past, present and future.

The moment when the Malanggan is discarded is also the moment at which it or its components may be dispersed to others, the moment people from other localities looking at the sculpture pay for the ability to reproduce the parts of the designs at some time in the future. Küchler (1992: 101–2) argues that Malanggan designs anticipate this; they are planned with the future owners in mind. The past has already become the future. So what is the technology that weaves such enchantment?

There are two distinct axes to Malaggan as carved figures. Overlaying the wooden three-dimensional framework with its carved motifs is a two-dimensional surface integrated through the painted designs.

> The carved planes refer to the exchange history of the sculptured image, or its 'outer' or 'public' identity, whereas the painted pattern signifies the present ownership of the image, or its 'inner' identity. . . . [These] together constitute what is called the 'skin' (or *tak*) of the sculpture'.
>
> Küchler 1992: 101

Strategic relationships between groups, above all through marriage, are created by ties of 'skin'. The container of the life force is also a map on which participants in a Malanggan ceremony inscribe their anticipated alliances. For the present owners already know who will want to make claims on the designs, and the Malanggan is carved in such a way as to acknowledge the owners-to-be.[26] The carved container as a repository of social effectiveness (Gell's phrase) through time is then covered by the painted 'inside' of current relationships now rendered on the 'outside'. Enchantment is achieved through the technique by which the form simultaneously extends into past and future while holding it all at a single moment in time and space. It is not just that the present encapsulates the past; the future is projected as a remembering of the present. For while the new relationships move into operation straight away, it will be many years before the motifs reappear in daylight; then they will emerge as components dispersed among other Malanggan. They will be brought to life in new sculptures *looking back* to this moment of acquisition. The conjunction of paint and carving does that: each form carries the other into and away from the present.

What the future owners receive is, they say, 'knowledge' of the Malanggan (along with the re-arrangements of social relations that gives them land rights and so forth). That knowledge makes them effective in the future, and this is what turns Malanggan into a kind of technology. To use a phrase from Sykes (2000; cf Küchler 1992: 101 also), they are transmitters or conduits, rather than memorials or representations. They do not just work to make things work or extend people's reach; a Malanggan converts existing relationships into virtual ones, matter into energy, and living into ancestral agency, heralding the reversal of these transformations at a future stage in the reproductive cycle. The technico-ritual process of carving and painting does not produce *things* as we might think of artistic works; as a thing, the body is not allowed to remain in existence. Rather, like technology, which combines knowledge, material form and effectiveness, the reproduction of the Malanggan body makes it possible to capture, condense and then release power back into the world.[27]

One might remark that this happens in social life all the time: we gather the past into our various projects, and then find ways of seeking to influence the future. There is, however, a mode of presenting Euro-American technology that weaves something of a comparable enchantment, enough to make people feel that something momentous might be going on. This is where patents come in.

## PATENTING TECHNOLOGY

If the very concept of technology creates a field of artefacts and expectations, the law – as we encountered in Chapter One – runs in parallel: it upholds as a generic category the industrial application of new ideas, so that all such applications come to seem to be examples of human creativity.[28] How? Through patents. Patents are part of international intellectual property law, which makes:

a vital contribution to mankind's storehouse of technical information. Eighty percent of the existing technical knowledge in the world is estimated to be available in the patent literature, organized in an internationally recognized classification system.

Tassy and Dambrine 1997: 196

The idea of being able to patent something has a double power. First, the patenting procedure requires a body; the initating idea has to be manifest or embodied in some artefact or device, a concrete invention that 'contains' the idea, while what the patent protects is the idea itself, the creative impetus, minimally an inventive step. Second, patents do not just recognise creativity and originality; they transform creativity into usable knowledge by at once attaching it to and detaching it from the inventor.

That transformative power appeals to the imagination. Indeed, intellectual property systems as a whole have been written about in lyrical terms as though they were part of a *technology of enchantment*. One writer refers to genetic resources brought under the spell of intellectual property rights (Khalil 1995: 232); another confessed that intellectual property has always seemed 'the Carmen of commercial law' – 'a subject with charm, personality and a force of character' (Phillips in Phillips and Firth 1990: vii). And of all IPR protocols, the patent is paradigmatic, '*the* form of intellectual property *par excellence*' (Bainbridge 1999: 7, my emphasis), for 'intellectual property law reserves a very special and powerful mode of protection for inventions' (1999: 317). That mode is a property right that takes the form of monopoly: the patent attaches the invention exclusively to the inventor. In doing so it also detaches it in the form of knowledge: the patent agreement compels the inventor to yield information to the world about how to re-create the artefact. Patents simultaneously produce private property and public(ly available) information.[29]

As part and parcel of the industrialising project of the West, intellectual property regimes nowadays exert international pressure on countries such as Papua New Guinea currently considering the implementation of copyright and patent legislation (in response to World Intellectual Property Organisation [WIPO] and under the aegis of Trade-Related Aspects of Intellectual Property Rights [TRIPS]). In Britain, specifically, patents began taking their present form at the time of the industrial revolution, with the aim among others of encouraging the development of ideas leading to innovation. They grant a monopoly over the benefits to be gained from an invention, provided it is new and provided the details are put in the public domain. The philosophy is that inventions in the long run should contribute to a general good. In the interim, however, benefit is chanelled through the patent holder who is at liberty to control access to it for a set period (until the patent expires).

Any one invention must build on numerous others:[30]

all inventions can be regarded as being comprised of units of information [information is composed of information]. Under this view, that which appears to our eyes to be an 'invention', a creation of something new, is no more than a synthesis [a composite] of known bits of information, not really an invention at all.[31]

Phillips and Firth 1990: 21, after Pendleton

Behind these many inventions are of course numerous others involved in the long process of development. At the point of patenting, an invention becomes a place or passage point at which diverse expertise, all the knowledge that went into creating it, is gathered together and condensed into a single entity (cf Strathern 1996). In turn, precisely because it must meet the specification of being an industrially applicable device, it is through its technological application that the effect of that expertise is extended and dispersed, typically in the form of a manufactured product. Patenting procedures speed up this gathering and dispersal.

I deliberately echo the New Ireland analysis. The fabrication of Malanggan results in a form that condenses a whole history of interactions and in the process makes it possible to channel clan powers – the clan and its relationships with others – for future benefit; we might say that the patent results in a *form* – the potency of information made product – through which technological power is also channelled to the future. Depending on the point in the reproductive cycle, Malanggan transform living and ancestral agency, the one into the other. Patents imply a more linear series of conversions, intangible ideas into enforceable property rights. In the place of the enveloping clan with its ancestral potency, at once inside and outside everyone, English-speakers instead accord nature a similar regenerative and recursive potential. Indeed patenting is part of a process that continues to regenerate nature as fast as it appears to consume it. A kind of technology within technology, patents thereby augment *the enchantment of technology*.

First, patents perpetuate the very concept of nature. If technology in general creates nature as a world of materials waiting to be used or of natural processes that carry on without human intervention, then the law creates a domain of nature in a very specific sense. For the general rationale is that patents cannot apply to any interpretation or manipulation of natural processes that does not require the specific input of human know-how, resulting in things that did not previously exist. Invention modifies nature; discovery does not. So objections to patents may be dismissed as the result of 'technical misunderstandings which arise from a wilful refusal to understand the difference between discovery and invention' (Pottage 1998: 750). The rubric is that nature cannot be patented. Ipso facto, anything patentable is already out of the realm of nature. If it can be used as an exclusionary mechanism, the issue then becomes what does or does not count as nature. Many patents deal with refinements of other inventions already in the made world, and there are numerous grounds on which applications for patents may be refused, for example over the degree of innovation that an inventor has brought to materials already worked upon or over how realistic industrial exploitation may be. But excluding anything that exists 'naturally' is a touchstone of patent law that has come into particular prominence with recent developments in biotechnology. '[M]erely to find a hitherto unknown substance which exists in nature is not to make an invention' (Phillips and Firth 1990: 35). Conversely, Bainbridge (1999: 368) quotes Justice Whitford in 1987 (apropos recombinant DNA technology), 'you cannot patent a discovery, but if on the basis of that discovery you can tell people how it can be usefully employed than a patent of invention may result'. Nature is redefined, re-invented, over and again by such exclusions.

Second, there is the matter of knowledge about the natural world. Instead of thinking of nature as an axiomatic measure of human endeavour, one may regard it as a source of technological innovation added to as fast as it is taken away. As fast as information is made product, new sources of information about the world are uncovered. And they necessarily point to fresh understandings of natural elements or processes until these are transformed by human ingenuity and lifted out of the natural realm.[32] So nature continues to grow in scope. The more it grows, the more it can be consumed, and the more it is consumed through a patent regime, the more knowledge about it is likely to expand.

Yet why do Euro-Americans sometimes accuse scientists of 'patenting nature'? In biotechnology, the manifestation of nature they dwell on is 'life itself' (Franklin 2001). So along with objections to patenting human beings or individuals go living things and life (Strathern 1999a: 171–2; Strathern 1998: 744). Yet the very act of patenting seems to reaffirm a strong divide between nature, which cannot be patented, and artefacts, which can. What could be more explicit than the legal exclusion of plants or animal varieties or biological processes (Walden 1995: 182, apropos the European Patent Convention 1973), not to speak of the human body (in the EC 1998 Biotechnology Directive)? So why do people talk as though nature, or life, were being patented? One does not have to look very far for an answer. Patent confers ownership, and there is a long history of Euro-American suspicion over what people do to one another through asserting ownership.

Patent ownership confers the right to enjoy benefits that arise from the owner's investment in the invention. As with all intellectual property rights, the right is held as private property; although others can seek release of the information (e.g., under license), the owner regulates access. But it is not always clear what the property contains. An often voiced concern is about *what is being gathered into the patent.* Let me note several distinct concerns.

The first concern has been touched on: truncating the network of scientists behind the invention into those who claim the final inventive step that leads to a patentable product. The second concern is the breadth of the patent: how much is being claimed over future processes or products is a matter of current controversy. The third concern is that there is too much modification of what people see as the order of things, and it is here that appeals to nature emerge.

When people claim that property ownership has inappropriately extracted items from that world, they go behind the decision as to whether something is an invention to query the process by which the invention came into being in the first place, back to the moment when all the elements were still unmodified (cf Pottage 1998: 753). To assert that 'nature' is being 'patented' is to draw up political or ethical lines in order to curb the extended agency of human interference. Indeed, criticism of property rights may go hand in hand with the disenchantment of technology; it is alleged that the separation between technology and nature has been breached because patents that properly apply to technology are now being applied to nature. The phrase *patenting nature* is part of the politics of disenchantment.

The fourth concern is a very old one. To assert ownership by way of patent inevitably engages with a long Euro-American debate over private property, historically regarded as carved out of what would otherwise be available to all. This may be nature or it may be other human artefacts and knowledge. Critics of current practices have reintroduced the language of enclosing the commons. Phillips and Firth (1990: 21–2) continue their comment on each invention as a permutation of previous inventions as follows:

Correlative to this view, is the asumption that, if each unit of information is a community resource, part of the common heritage of mankind, no edifice constructed from such communal blocks should be able to constitute a privately-owned invention. [They then add:] The modern intellectual property lawyer finds it difficult to accept this, unless he can persuade himself that there is no difference between a palace and the pile of bricks from which it is built.

What is claimed for society (common heritage) is then claimed for nature:

[T]he patentability of discoveries would result in man's expropriation of nature itself, and it is difficult to justify the expropriation by one of what is already the natural legacy of all.

Phillips and Firth 1990: 35

Expropriation implies an exclusion of, the owner's separation from, others. Ownership works as a kind of extended agency, an extension of a person's capacity, personal or corporate, with a reach as far as products will travel. If what is owned has the legal character of private property, then technology, in the legal form of a patent as the right to exploit it, is so to speak folded within the individual owner.

This is textbook stuff. Here I have a suggestion. In relation to 'inhabiting', the concept of 'containment' conveys the sense in which parts of our social lives seem to be lived within others, figures within figures, knowledge composed of (other) knowledge. With the inflection of dwelling, it implies more than the kind of fit with the world that makes it comfortable and familiar; it points to an existential orientation toward it. Euro-Americans take momentary refuge in nature or in technology, either of which seems at once around and part of them, or else in all the dwelling places afforded by notions of community or locality. But there is a further candidate for habitation, nothing to do with environment or community, that allows Euro-Americans to dwell in a thoroughly taken-for-granted world, an envelope that allows them to live within themselves.

I take my candidate from the way self-acknowledged Euro-American moderns become attached to a world they see full of useful and beautiful things. It is a world they imagine that people desire to appropriate, whether they think of private individuals in exclusive possession of property or of the common people in open possession of its bounty. Ownership. What is not owned exists either to be owned as some future resource not yet exploited or else is notionally owned by humankind in general, including the generations to come. Ownership envelops all. Is ownership a mode of habitation? The manner in which Euro-Americans attach things to themselves makes them at home in the world – whether contained by technology or by nature – from which they think of such things as coming. Ownership is a kind of second skin to these two containers, a world through which people are infinitely interconnected through the inclusions and exclusions of property relations, and in which possession is taken to be at once a natural drive and the just reward of creativity. Property – in rights, in profits – seems comfortably within everyone's grasp, subject only to the limitations of unequal endowment.

It would, I think, be an enchanted world, created not least by the magico-purificatory divide at the heart of property relations, the cultural sleight of hand that suggests that just as things are intrinsically separate from persons so too things intrisically separate persons from one another. Principles of ownership carry their own exclusions and separations. The stereotype is that we would have to go to other cultures to escape that particular enchantment.

### RETURN TO NEW IRELAND – 2

For a third time, the stereotype would be misleading for New Ireland. There is much that can be translated as ownership.

We saw that agency or energy located in numerous social places had to be gathered into one place, focused in the carved and painted Malanggan figures and then redispersed. However, that is only half of the story. Every gathering together, every recombining of motifs out of motifs, involves a specific claim of title. It is not possible to incorporate designs without permission. That is because only certain people have the right to use the knowledge associated with particular Malanggan.

On the one hand, the authorisation to display the image is vested exclusively in the sponsoring clan or local group; on the other hand, expertise is required to carve the figure, and owners of Malanggan must commission an expert carver. Sponsors own not so much rights to the designs as rights to their reproduction, and the subjects of reproduction are images retained as memories. It is the right to make bodies, to make material and to give physical form to images, that is transferred across the generations and across groups. Transfer is sealed by payment. Now if Malanggan can be considered technology, in the captivating effect of the skill required to reproduce the figure at all, we might be tempted to see the *enchantment of technology*. The skill in question is as much intellectual as manual and requires the work of both owner and carver.

When Malanggan are displayed, the new owner takes away the sighting of the form to which he has acquired rights and which he then holds as a memory for what may be as long as a generation. This means that the would-be sponsor (the owner) of a new Malanggan carving will have glimpsed the image long before it is to be reproduced.[33] He must now describe the image in detail to an expert carver, who in turn conceives the new form in his own mind, an inspiration assisted by magic or by dreaming. What is dazzling to the Euro-American is the ability of the carver to produce a form from a description held by another person (the owner) as the memory of a Malanggan seen years earlier. What one suspects[34] is dazzling to New Irelanders is the way the resulting body emerges from two bodies.

I earlier asked why New Irelanders distance themselves from what they regard as enveloping them. Perhaps one answer lies in the enchantment of this particular technology, the way artefacts are construed as having come into being. Reproduction requires two persons, and they have to be socially distinct. The techniques by which new Malanggan come into being work only because of the successful joining of quite *separate* efforts (the work of remembering and the work of carving).[35] Indeed, it is important that the form emerging from the clan repertoire is only like its original in some respects; axiomatically, Malanggan do not duplicate one another (cf Küchler 1987: 244), any more than human offspring duplicate one or other parent alone. (We might say that the 'ancestral' Malanggan body is the child's image of the parent body.) What is contained within the 'skin' (body) of the Malanggan must be kept distinct from the container: social difference is conserved at the very point at which the deceased also merges with the ancestors. Similarly, between sponsor and carver, it has to be the work of joining that makes the reproduction a unique and amazing process. Work is perceived to be at the heart of Malanggan (Sykes personal communication; Lincoln 1987: 33).

Now the mode in which these rights are claimed has long prompted comparisons with intellectual property and specifically with copyright. Some figures are made with an outstretched tongue said to have the function of 'threatening all offenders against the owner's copyright' (Heintze 1987: 53). 'Copyright' is of course the ethnographer's gloss.

One could therefore think of the whole figure as an artistic work subject to copyright, a kind of literary text replete with (permitted) quotations from other texts but itself an original form of expression. However, let us take the analogy step by step. What is gained is the right to reproduce the design. And what circulate in transactions are 'not objects, but the images they embody' (Küchler 1988: 629; Harrison 1992: 234).[36] At issue is not the identical text, the form of expression that is key to Euro-American concepts of copyright, but the idea behind it:

For when the license [for a Malanggan] is sold, not the figure itself but the *description of* the form and associated rites are made available to the purchaser.

Bodrogi 1987: 21, my emphasis

When a Malanggan appears, others may challenge the owner's right to reproduce a particular design, and Gunn (1987: 81, 83) speaks of people having to 'defend copyright held by another subclan' or of the process of transference being subject to public inspection for 'breaches of copyright'. Yet the challenge comes from those who hold a memory or idea of the image they claim is theirs, not from being able to compare its expression or realisation in material form. The carving no longer exists. Moreover, the owner of the supposed copyright cannot necessarily give permission for others to make copies. He can dispose of the copyright, like property, but in many circumstances another can only make a copy by acquiring the copyright itself. And then:

With the sale of the copyright the earlier owner is deprived of all rights to make the type [now] sold.[37]

Bodrogi 1987: 21

Finally, the design is not copied as such; rather, it is lodged in the memory as an image to be recalled at a later date.[38] Indeed, in respect of certain elements of the Malanggan, we may note that claimants' rights exist only *until* the moment of their realisation in material form, the point at which they are transferred to others; people own them most securely as memories still to be realised. Reproduced, not replicated: the analogy with copyright does not seem to go far enough.

If we did indeed think of the Malanggan not only as art or text but also as a piece of technology, then we might refer to the rights in question as being guaranteed by something closer to a patent.[39] Some differences are clear. A patent grants a monopoly to exploit an idea (embodied in some artefact), and is held by one owner at a time; others obtain the idea or artefact through license or purchase. By contrast, use of Malanggan is (usually) effected only by those who simultaneously own the 'patent' rights insofar as one cannot display the product, the embodied image, without having acquired ownership of the idea as well. However, in one respect a Malanggan bears resemblance to an invention under patent.

Such an invention gathers together expertise (all the knowledge that went into making it) and then through its application disperses the effect of that expertise (through products widely available). And that gathering together is done for a set period: a patent is made to expire.[40] In the interim, it has condensed multiple agencies into itself, reproducing them in the names of the new owners. Moreover, the unique item with its particular combination of motifs is the effective materialisation essential for transfer to the next generation; the conceptual template held by the heirs is not extinguished but neither can it be activated without being embodied in a specific Malanggan form. Of course in the case of expiring patents it is the owner's rights that are extinguished after so many years, and the invention goes on being used, whereas New Irelanders extinguish the particular invention (the individual Malanggan), and the rights go on being conserved. Nonetheless, we might conclude that Malanggan not only are like a technology in some of their effects but also are like the very patents taken out to protect the application of technology, at once a description of transferable rights and a specification of how they are to be materialised.

Patent applications in the United Kingdom run at some 27 000 a year, perhaps 7 000 of these being granted, with some 180 000 renewals (Bainbridge 1999: 336–7). This gives the order of recent patents, with upward of some two million, it has been calculated, lying expired in the Patent Office.[41] The reason Malanggan are one of the best represented and collectible type of art object, some 5 000 now housed within the museums of the world,[42] is precisely because their function as unique habitations for energy and power will have long expired. The rights to reproduction remain active until the image has been properly reproduced, but then it (the image) comes to lodge in a new version whose powers are animated by a new generation.[43] This is technology in a state of perpetual transferral.

NEW IRELANDERS, SAYS SYKES (2000), CLAIM MALANGGAN AS A distinctive feature of their modern and customary cultural life. Imperfect as the analogy with technology is, it draws attention to the way in which artefacts such as Malanggan work their effects on people and to the knowledge that is held to be embedded within them. And impossible as the analogy with patenting is, the comparison perhaps enables us to grasp some of the imaginative and ideological potential of Euro-American intellectual property concepts, one of the many forms modern rationalities take (Rabinow 1996a).

The recombination of elements of information, the amalgamation of new and existing forms, the minute variations that may be sufficient to demonstrate crucial intervention, channelling past knowledge to future effect, a limited period of efficacy: all this could as well describe a Malanggan as it describes a patent. Yet there is a gulf of ideological proportions between them. Moderns of New Ireland persuasion think of Malanggan neither as inventions (application of technology),[44] nor as describing the original inventive step (patents). Indeed, individuals are only regarded as producing original images under certain somewhat risky circumstances. The overriding doctrine is that artefacts are acquired not created; therefore, the routes of acquisition are a crucial source of their value. Concomitantly, it is not the protection of new forms that New Ireland people seek but the right to reproduce what others have reproduced before them. This representation of their efforts is as much a *mis*representation (Harrison 2000) as are the equally dogmatic assertions by English-speakers of originality and innovation as the basis of technological advance. The Euro-American doctrine is encapsulated in the very notion of patent rights. These point to inventions as artefacts created not acquired, and what is protected is not a right to reproduce the original invention but the right to prevent others from freely reproducing the capacity that the invention has created.

We have seen how the concept of nature upholds this legal doctrine; it underwrites the distinction between discovery (of things in nature) and invention (abstracted from nature through human ingenuity). And it may do so to the point of absurdity. In talking about attempts to patent a cell line and similar biotechnological innovations, Pottage criticises the way this 'banal doctrinal distinction' (1998: 750) is used to put down political or ethical objections. His own objections to the 'endless permutations of "nature" and "artefact"' (1998: 753) are twofold. First, the distinctions are brought in to truncate arguments concerning the political or ethical implications of what is or is not commodifiable. 'Political oppositions are not a function of [cannot be dismissed as] doctrinal confusion' (1998: 753). Legal doctrine takes, as the basis for decision-making, linguistic and categorical distinctions rather than what is happening to whatever we might want to call nature. Second, there are situations in which it is increasingly obscure just how an invention is to be identified. '[T]he production of an immortal cell line demands little more of the "inventor" than the mastery of a routine scientific technique. The "inventive" process seems merely to transcribe a natural code into a new medium' (1998: 752, note omitted). In his view, biotechnology has rendered transparent or implausible the very distinctions that bind the patent law upon which biotechnology so crucially relies (1998: 745).

The question of 'man's expropriation of nature ... [as] expropriation by one of what is already the natural legacy of all' (Phillips and Firth 1990: 35) is open to debate. But there is a further question in the way the problem is taken care of in the distinction between technology and nature, invention and discovery, and the rest; patent law in effect defines what has *already* been expropriated, that is, is no longer nature. Now New Irelanders remake people out of people, so to speak, bodies out of bodies, and the competition is over claims to ancestral power, that is, making claims to what is already specifically identified as theirs. Patent-holders, on the other hand, deal with people in terms of property claims, and instead make their devices out of things, materials and knowledge ultimately part of a 'commons' belonging to everyone and no one.

When they think of the commons as a natural resource, Euro-Americans may imagine it as a domain free from people's inventiveness, and ideally perhaps even empty of people altogether; at the same time when they think of dwelling, this is the location they often bring to mind, and they would also like to think of the commons as a world that people 'naturally' possess and in which people find their 'natural' habititation. It is this flexibility, we could say, making people apparently now relevant and now not relevant to one's perspective (on the world) that has been so enabling of technological innovation in the West (Eric Hirsch personal communication). But I have deliberately ended with an image of nature as a resource – the commons – that points to human interest in it. Is not part of our feeling comfortable with technology, dwelling 'with' it, the fact that it gives us things we can own and thus take possession of for ourselves? Disquiet when those proprietory extensions of the person seem inappropriate is part of being at home with the techniques and relations of ownership.

New Irelanders have been on the receiving end not just of colonial exports or of intellectual property rights legislation but of the very divide between technology and inhabiting that the convenors of a conference in 2000 called *Inhabiting Technology* have problematised. The New Irelanders serve as a reminder of the political and ethical debates that surround resource extraction, the extension of property regimes and so forth. But too often a Euro-American will re-invent the divide between technology and inhabiting by investing such peoples with the qualities that his or her own ideas about technology would give to nature. I have tried instead to make these people and their ideas present in a different way, by emphasing the very many points on which we might draw parallels in order to heighten those where we cannot.

## ACKNOWLEDGEMENTS

First presented at a conference organised in 2000 by Mike Featherstone, Scott Lash and Philip Dodd jointly for the Institute of Contemporary Arts (ICA), in the journal *Theory, Culture and Society*, and the U.K. Economic and Social Research Council (ESRC) *Virtual Society?* programme, called *Inhabiting Technology*, at the Institute of Contemporary Arts, London. It was written in response to the conference theme of how we 'dwell in' technology. It is not original. I bring together the expertise of several anthropologists dispersed over a range of studies, especially Susanne Küchler on whose work I draw extensively, although probably rather lopsidedly (see her subsequent volume, 2002), and my portrait of Malanggan is a composite of features from different ethnographic areas, following only one track among many analytical possibilities. Principal thanks are due to Karen Sykes and the results of her own investigations in New Ireland. I am very grateful for permission to draw on unpublished material (I follow Sykes' spelling). Terence Hay-Edie, who had been exploring other enchanted worlds, is also due thanks. The stimulus of the conference at the ICA is self-evident; thanks too to members of the Summer Institute on World Arts at the University of East Anglia for several comments.

# 5

# Losing (out on) Intellectual Resources

When their 'transplant' was terminated, the 'root people' on one side felt
that the other side had violated their divine relationship

John Muke, paraphrased in Dorney 1997

## I

'*L*IVING MEN OR WOMEN SHOULD NOT BE ALLOWED TO BE DEALT WITH
as [a] part of compensation payment under any circumstances'. The
custom is 'repugnant to the general principles of humanity' (PNGLR 1997:
150, 151). Thus said Judge Injia in handing down his verdict on, as it was called in
the local headlines, the 'Compo girl case'. This was at the Mt. Hagen National
Court in 1997; it concerned people from the Minj part of the Wahgi region,
in the Western Highlands of Papua New Guinea.[1]

The case offers an interesting comment on the role played by legal technique
in the fabrication of persons and things. In some respects it rehearses issues
that have long troubled anthropologists describing marriage arrangements.
They include the extent to which an equation between women and wealth renders women 'thing'-like, the locus classicus being bridewealth (bride-price)
payments, which feeds an epistemological anxiety, the extent to which anthropological analysis in turn treats its subjects as less than subjects, where
the locus classicus is 'the exchange of women'.[2] With these issues in the background, I note the role played in this case by the reference to human rights.
That role assisted in the fabrication of persons;[3] the antithesis between persons
and things was never far away.

This is an instance in which it might assist analysis to project a Euro-
American distinction between person and thing onto the Papua New Guinean

111

material, although the techniques of fabrication will be of a politico-ritual rather than legal nature, and the distinction does not work quite as Euro-Americans might expect. It will at least allow comparison between the reference to human rights and certain Papua New Guinean formulations. The vernacular I evoke here is common to ways of thinking and acting found in many parts of the country, including Minj. Rendering this material as like rather than unlike the kinds of Euro-American assumptions that lie behind human rights language serves to highlight a significant resource. This is an intellectual resource, modes of thinking that help us think. It would be a pity to lose possible ways of thinking about the manner in which people make claims on others simply because vernaculars seem local and strange.

## The Terms of an Agreement

A compensation payment for a man's death was agreed between clans from two Minj tribal groups, Tangilka and Konumbuka. Muke belonged to the same Tangilka patriclan as the dead man, Willingal, and was later called on to give evidence. Willingal had been killed by police; he was said to have been the bodyguard of a wanted man, a fact disputed by his kin. The final settlement comprised 24 pigs, K20 000 money, and a woman who was to be sent to the aggrieved clan in marriage.[4] The aggrieved in this case were not the clan of the dead man (from Tangilka); on the contrary, it is they who were being asked for compensation. The demands came from his mother's clan in Konumbuka. The rationale was that the deceased's patriclan had not protected their 'child' (sister's child) properly. This had two components, a particular accusation that they had been indirectly responsible by causing the police to come onto their land, and the more general point that they had failed in their care of him. It was a loss to both sets of kin, each of whom had a duty of care that, although carried out in different ways, they owed the other. The two sides came to an agreement and a daughter of Willingal, Miriam, emerged as the obvious bride for the Konumbuka.

The settlement would have gone ahead but for a legal intervention. A human rights NGO (non-governmental organisation) based in Port Moresby, Individual and Community Rights Advocacy Forum (ICRAF), sought orders from the court to enforce Miriam's constitutional rights.[5] Gewertz and Errington (1999: 125) sum up ICRAF's grounds: 'regardless of local custom, trading in women could not be allowed because it was violation of fundamental human rights'. As reported in the national press (*Post Courier* 11 February 1997; *National* 12 February 1997), Justice Injia ordered the two tribes to refrain from enforcing their custom. He commented on the sometimes too-hasty evaluation of customs on the part of external agencies, including modern courts, but observed that the issue was a constitutional one in another sense, involving the precedence of national law over customary practices. It is Gewertz and Errington's (1999: 133) view that the judge was quite self-conscious about the role played by the professional 'middle class' in promoting the reasonableness of modern morality.

Chapter Four referred to New Ireland modernity; here we can listen in on a conversation about how to be modern, and the lineaments we have met before (Chapter One). Modern morality and its entailments provided the terms of a lively debate that we have, remarkably, on record. The conversation took place at the Mt. Hagen Lodge hotel on the eve of the preliminary court hearing the year before (Gewertz and Errington 1999: 123). Apart from the two anthropologists, the others were professional Papua New Guineans: the lawyer employed by ICRAF to argue for Miriam's protective custody, and the priest into whose care the lawyer hoped she would be placed, as well as the hotel proprietor, who had her own strong views, and her nephew. Talk turned to the kind of person modern Papua New Guineans should be. Above all these were imagined as agents, subjects and individuals who could and should exercise choice.

The small party was divided over the question of what kind of person was appropriately bound by what sort of standard, standards 'based on ancestral precedent or on a more universalistic vision of human rights' (1999: 133). The lawyer and priest ceded that many customs were 'good' but deplored 'bad' customs that went against human rights and, in the priest's view, against Christian teaching; the proprietor and her nephew thought that such compensation payments were for the general good of the community and helped keep peace. Traditional culture was 'needed' by Papua New Guineans in poor rural areas and urban squatter settlements; it gave people something meaningful in their lives. The conversation included a discussion of bridewealth, which the propietor defended as cementing matches that brought benefits to clans, whereas her nephew observed that with money as the medium of exchange women became like commodities (1999: 127). All took the modernist view that one could choose between customs, so that rational evaluation by the 'educated and modern' made it possible to apply human rights issues to a local context. Miriam in turn should not be constrained by customs that took away her own ability to choose, not only choice of marriage partner[6] but of future education and lifestyle. Her exercise of agency was at stake.

The cultural rationale for the benefits to clans was spelled out in the affidavit that Muke prepared. Women are regarded as moving along the same channels through which wealth flows. They create ties between groups because the children they bear become consanguineal connections for the descendants. At the same time their work and fertility bring benefit primarily to the husband's rather than their own (father's, brother's) clan. It is appropriate that payments include 'compensation' for the 'loss' that the woman's natal clan suffers. The spouse's clan does not take away something that the natal clan could have enjoyed for themselves – only when female reproductive powers are transferred in marriage can the natal clan enjoy them, that is, when they are realised through the offspring the woman bears – but the ongoing flow of nurture and blessing through gifts, and ancestral (spiritual) support, must be recognised. So one clan will indemnify another first for a bride and then for the children the woman bears. When blood is shed, these ties are severed, and that in itself is an injury. The patrilineal kin who had been the ones to benefit immediately from the deceased's existence must find recompense for the maternal kin, who had vicariously enjoyed the embodiment of their fertility in the member of another clan. The aggrieved Konombuka demanded that a return for the original woman, an ancestress of Willingal, be sent in back in marriage; Miriam was to be part of a 'head payment' (mortuary gifts owed to maternal kin).

The judge could see no objection to payment as such, and said that customary compensation practices involving 'money, pigs and other valuable personal items', that is things, were no problem; however, when the payment takes 'the form of young single women', that is a person, that is another matter (PNGLR 1997: 130; *National* 12 February 1997). One concern was the degree of agency Miriam had been allowed: how voluntarily had she agreed to the settlement? The judge concluded that Miriam was coerced into giving her consent, finding for ICRAF on all counts.

Let me point out three aspects of the judge's conclusions. First, the judge paid considerable attention to understanding the background to the compensation settlement, helped by Muke's extensive and detailed affidavit. Second, nonetheless, '[n]o matter how painful it may be to the small ethnic society concerned, such bad custom must give way to the dictates of our modern national laws' (PNGLR 1997: 153; quoted in *The Independent* [PNG] 14 February 1997). Third, the judge invoked a universalism enshrined in the Papua New Guinea Constitution. This particular compensation payment for the life of a human being was inconsistent with the national constitution and repugnant to the principles of humanity. Running through all of this was the distinction I shall designate as between Tradition and Modernity.

## Tradition and Modernity

Whatever might have happened in the past, the enactment of this custom was now to be judged against a modern constitution that protected women's rights. Invoking a line between the categories *tradition* and *modernity* echoes the strategy seen in Chapter Four, which Pottage (1998) has described in the case of *nature* and *culture* used so adventitiously in the pursuit of patenting claims. Documenting what does or does not count as modern in contemporary practices is like documenting what does or does not count as human intervention (culture) in discriminating invention from discovery.

The analogy with patenting procedure is again helpful. If the determination is that nature is intact, then it is left alone; proprietory claims cannot be made. In the case of tradition, if custom can be proved, then it too is left intact; it is seen to have its own rationale. But if the investigation of nature has required the intervention of obvious human artifice, then what is discovered, by virtue of the attendant inventions, no longer belongs simply to the realm of nature. Similarly, if tradition has already been modified by modernity, then it cannot be appealed to in any simple way.[7] Miriam's affidavit included the fact that she thought the Wahgi custom of head pay marriages had fallen into disuse since the arrival of missionaries; this had been reported in the *Post Courier* at the beginning (9 May 1996) and was repeated again now (11 February, 1997). In fact, the judge found the custom was still extant. However, and perhaps he was thinking of Miriam's aspirations for education and employment, relevant in his eyes was the fact that the framers of the constitution 'were thinking about a modern [Papua New Guinea]'. In other words, tradition was not seen to be intact; it was already open to invasion by modern values, which clearly opened the way to a modern interpretation of customs as either 'good' or 'bad'.[8]

Custom as opposed to individual choice, tradition as opposed to modernity: these categorical distinctions are implicated in one another, while each pair also derives conviction from the other. As we have seen, Justice Injia upheld the value of custom in certain arenas, acknowledging its function within the community, and thus recognising the force of tradition; at the same time, treating these issues as a bundle made it possible to put them all to one side together. Other things were also being bundled away.

Out of sight was any need to determine the kind of *obligations* in which someone such as Miriam finds herself enmeshed. Obvious examples are the obligations entailed in having kinsfolk. It is as though kinship can simply be bundled up and disposed of as part of tradition. And it is in putting such considerations to one side that an intellectual resource becomes lost to view: people's reflections on the fact of relationship and on what happens when kin ties between people become translated into expectations about acts and behaviour (see Banks 2001). Rendering kinship – anywhere – as part of tradition is an old Euro-Americanism.

Now in the context of patent applications, Pottage raised the question of what precisely is to count as human intervention. When a technology becomes routinised, what is inventive about it? Given the extent to which the apprehension of natural facts is mediated by multiple layers of social representation, we might he says always ask what is 'natural' about the terrain that natural science has carved out for itself (1998: 753). More to the point, through the litigations and disputes that accompany patenting in the field of biotechnology, what is to count as nature and what is to count as artefact becomes itself an artefact of political and legal decision making. Concomitantly, in the context of modernising customs, we might raise the question of what is to count as modern. But whereas Pottage pointed to advances in biotechnology that have effectively challenged if not yet dissolved the lines along which various distinctions have been drawn, it would seem that here (in modernising customs) distinctions remain rampant, and kinship gets caught up in them.

This chapter attempts to extricate kinship and the question of obligations from the antithesis between tradition and modernity (Jolly 1996). Shades of *Antigone* (cf. Fox 1993): divine duty (to a brother) as opposed to civic duty (to the king), and an echo of an element in Muke's seminar paper, reported in the newspaper account of his affidavit, which falls unusually on English-hearing ears, namely his reference to divinity. The mother's clan, he said, 'had always exercised their divine curative powers' in helping the dead man prosper; they had not been the cause of Willingal's death as they might have been through the power of the curse that they also wielded (PNGLR 1997: 132; Dorney 1997). In this conflict of duties, the ramifications of kinship, divine or not, fell foul of the state's view of itself as protecting the modern virtues. The modern individual person as subject and agent was uppermost in the judicial mind.

## II

To continue a theme of Chapter Three, issues may be lost from view; issues may also be pushed from view. It is interesting to observe what it is that legal processes (choose to) step over rather than pick up, fabrication by default one might say. The vexed question of body ownership is a case in point.

Despite the difference between the cynical pragmatism of Anglo-American law and the French legal tradition for which the body is the inalienable foundation of legal individualism (Pottage 1998: 745), under neither regime can persons – including Injia's 'living men or women' – be owned as property. Problems arise with embodiment and the (Euro-American) symbolism that equates the person with the individual body. The scandal of slavery was that it involved trafficking in the *whole* body also understood to be the whole person.

Labour was bought and sold but so too was autonomy of action, depriving the person of agency.[9]

How is the Euro-American notion of wholeness or entirety fabricated in this context? The body seems to be taken as entire in the double sense of being a complete functioning (or once functioning) organism, and being of a piece with the individual person as subject and agent. There are equivocations. Although, once animation has departed, a corpse may be treated as a whole body, no one would think of regarding it as a whole person, yet there are occasions when dead and living bodies have to be treated in the same way.

The image of the whole body produces a second image: the body that is not whole. There are an increasing number of circumstances under which it seems desirable to argue that whole bodies and part bodies should not be treated alike. (One argument put forward at the time of the 1998 European Directive on Biotechnology, concerned with the patenting of biological material, including human body parts, suggested that parts could be rendered patentable provided they could no longer be ascribed to specific individuals.) However, the general situation over body parts seems at present entirely equivocal. Some of this equivocation is discussed in the U.K. Nuffield Council on Bioethics' Report (1995) on ethical and legal issues concerning the donation of body tissue, organs or reproductive material, and I shall draw briefly on this.

Reminiscent of the way the plea and judgment in Miriam's case avoided opening up questions about kinship obligation, it points out the lengths U.K. legal and ethical thinking takes to avoid adjudicating on whether it is appropriate to talk of ownership over or property in body parts. Resort to a scheme of consents (to removal, disposal and such) bypasses the problem. Yet the issue of the kinds of interests one has in one's own body and its parts, or of other people's bodies, and the circumstances under which these could amount to a property interest, is there in the background.

Distinctions that appear to occlude that background question also point to it. Primary here is the difference between treating the human body as a 'thing' and treating it if not as a 'person' then at least as pertaining to persons. The same difference is not quite replicated in (propped up by) *the possibility of treating body parts separately from the whole body*. People have in mind detachable organs and tissue. One effect of the Euro-American division between persons and things is to promote property rights (between persons with respect to things) as the paradigmatic exemplification of ownership, so that when one talks of property ownership one implies that rights are being exercised over or in relation to some thing or other. The more entities approximate to things, the more legitimate ownership appears. And perhaps one effect of unanswered questions about whether or not body parts constitute property is the realisation that detachment must be fabricated conceptually as well as physically.

What about other forms of ownership? I shall suggest that the question of obligation in the Papua New Guinean case offers a situation where we may, experimentally, talk of the ownership of persons. The Papua New Guinean material also suggests that there too parts are treated separately from wholes, although these connect to 'persons' and 'things' in very different ways. We can at least ask of it a comparable question about fabrication: how are parts and wholes construed in the first place?

## Body Ownership

The following notes come from the Nuffield report (1995), which has the virtue of being a coherent and straighforward account intended for the layman. It plays a rhetorical role in my argument by hammering home certain Euro-American presumptions about body parts. We can read it as a treatise on the making of things. Persons do not really appear; indeed it is obviously possible to discuss body ownership without explicitly bringing personhood into the picture at all.[10]

English law at the time of the report was silent on whether someone could claim a property right in tissue taken from them. Emphasising the lack of legal direction in this area (there was simply no case law on which it could draw), the report suggested that a likely approach would be on the basis of whether or not consent to removal had been given. Where tissue was removed in the course of treatment, consent to treatment would imply abandonment of claim. Where tissue was donated, any claim would reflect the terms of the donation. The question of ownership, it says, is thus avoided. The view that common law recognises no right of property in a body is attributed to tradition (the 'traditional view'), and avoiding the issue of ownership seems analogous to not interfering in tradition, keeping it intact. Thus the legal instrument of consent can deal with changing (modern) circumstances (such as the hitherto unimagined circulation of body parts) without challenging the traditional view in common law that one cannot have property in the human body. The traditional view was presumably formulated with the idea of the body as a whole entity.[11]

Detachable body parts alter the circumstances. The report is concerned with the extent to which ownership may or may not entail property rights, and here it draws on several legal contexts for comparative evidence.[12] Thus it points out that the issue of property has been avoided in the case of gametes: the Human Fertilisation and Embryology (HFE) Act (1990) requires donors of gametes and embryos to consent to any storage or usage of them. 'By adopting a scheme of consents . . . [the HFE Act] avoids vesting any property claim in the donor . . . *circumventing the need to resolve questions of property and ownership'* (Nuffield Council 1995: 68, 69; my emphasis). Nonetheless, the report argues, the solution conceals 'a property approach' in that it contemplates that the control of gametes and embryos rests with the donor until that moment. It observes that the U.K. Human Tissue Act 1961 and others (e.g., Human Organ Transplants Act 1989) allow that tissue can be removed as an unconditional gift, that is, it becomes free of all claims. This does not tell us whether or not the gift is a gift of property.[13] Finally, the report (Nuffield Council 1995: 68) gives a hypothetical example of how various concepts might work together.

1. The patient consents to an operation which involves removal of her appendix; 2. by her consent she abandons claims to it; 3. on removal it acquires the status of a *res* (thing) in possession of the hospital prior to disposal; 4. in response to a request from the patient for it to be returned, the hospital gives it to her as a gift; 5. the appendix then becomes the property of the patient.

Commentators have argued that, once it is removed, living tissue axiomatically 'becomes the property of the person from whom it is removed'; removal itself does not entail intention to abandon. How so? Seemingly, tissue becomes (eligible for consideration as) 'property' because *by its very detachment* it is made into a legal thing (*res*). What makes such a 'thing'? The converse holds. It seems to become (eligible for consideration as) a thing because *proprietory rights* can be exercised over it.

The tissue may well, in fact, be abandoned or donated, but these imply a prior coming into existence of a *res* and the exercise of rights over it. Indeed such an analysis is logically essential . . . even if the resulting property (i.e. a person's assertion of a property right over a new *res*), exists merely for a moment (a *scintilla temporis*).

                                                      Nuffield Council 1995: 69.

If this argument is accepted, then the appendix would have remained the patient's property had she not by implication waived rights to it. However, this is not the end of argument. Another view has it that tissue at the time of its removal is *res nullius*, that is, a thing but belonging to no one until brought under dominion ('the traditional legal example is the wild animal or plant', i.e. nature); the tissue then becomes the property of the one who removed it or subsequently acquired possession of it. The person from whom it is removed has no claim.[14] As for the claims of those who detach or use tissue, it is unclear as to whether, for example, anatomical specimens can be appropriated as property: 'it is probable that the user of tissue acquires at least the right to possess, and probably a right of ownership over [it]' (1995: 77, 81). Indeed the Nuffield report concludes that there is an overall lack of clarity in English law. Yet no one, it adds, could say that University College London does not 'own' Bentham's skeleton. However, it is that part of Bentham that is his skeleton, not Bentham as such, that University College London is considered owning. The body part is owned as a thing ('skeleton') not as a whole person ('Bentham'). Indeed we have seen that one way in which it becomes a thing is by being owned.

If this were not the case we might otherwise wonder about the odd tenacity of the term *part*. After all, why is the detached and now freestanding entity thought of as a part?

Perhaps what is being fabricated is precisely the possibility of considering detachable parts of the body as things to which claims of ownership may be laid. Owning the whole person is legally unthinkable; owning the whole body is prohibited. In a wonderfully illogical but perfectly sensible way, at the very juncture when through detachment it could be regarded as having ceased to be a part of the body, the tissue or organ is reconstituted neither as a whole entity in itself nor as an intrinsic part of a previous whole. Colloquially, it is, somehow, a freestanding 'part'. So what is kept alive in this nomenclature is the process of detachment itself; it would seem that for as long as its detachability from the person remains evident, it can be thought of as a 'thing' – but not to the lengths of a 'whole thing'. One interpretation could be that the designation (part) refers to an essential incompleteness; the tissue or organ exists only in being destined for other human beings. Another could be that to conceptualise it as a whole entity would point too emphatically to an independent existence, on the market say, and thus to a thing that could easily become a commodity.

## Whole Persons: Things

The Papua New Guinean material offers rather different shifts of perspective. It is based on a synthesis of anthropological analyses (as the Nuffield report is a synthesis) and applies in the first place to societies of the Papua New Guinea Highlands, with my own inflection from Mt. Hagen that abuts the Minj area, and secondarily to Melanesia at large. It suggests a situation in which it might be appropriate to imagine people owning people. This is also the situation in which persons appear as things, although *thing* here has to be understood as a fabrication lying outside a property context.[15] Persons are owned as things through a politico-ritual fabrication[16] that presents the person being claimed by another as singular, entire and *whole*. In other words, it is the whole not the part that is thing-like.

So what kind of thing is being imagined? I understand the techniques of much public (including ritual) activity of Highlands cultures as making relations visible, presenting them as objects of people's attention. Wealth items of the kind that flow in compensation payments objectify relationships by giving them the form of things that can be displayed, such as money, pigs and other valuable items. The same relationships may also be activated through persons; relations become visible in the positions by which persons divide themselves from one another, as mother's kin may divide from father's kin and the one confront the other with its claims. It is persons who emerge as partible, a point to which I return in the next section. In their multiple roles, persons are always half hidden from one another. In contrast, a form presented to be seen must be seen as a whole image is seen; an image can only ever be a whole thing.[17] By form I refer to the contours, bulk, colour, gender of entities, in short, the aspects of 'body'.

From this perspective people may be reified, just as wealth and similar items may be personified.[18] For instance, men are reified, or self-reify, when presenting themselves in decorations that make them an explicit object of attention. Ritual intervention heightens one of the regular processes of social life in which the singularity of the person is manifest. The conditions under which people appear as things are also the conditions under which they appear as whole and singular entities.

This is, we may say, the singularity not of individualism but of relationism. In order to appear in another's eyes as someone of whom the other takes account, the person appears oriented to that particular relationship. So the person who stands for (objectifies) that relationship is in effect eliminating all others in favour of the one. Thus someone may be presented as an initiate (in relation to a senior generation), a bride (about to meet a groom), a clansman (of this group rather than another), with his or her multiple identities eclipsed by the one of the moment. We could call that eclipse an abstraction or detachment. The person is abstracted from all other social contexts in order to exist, however momentarily, in one alone, like assuming a particular role or taking on a category position. Whereas the process of detachment itself belongs to the partitioning of persons, the image presents an already completed thing. It is the visible moment when an initiate, a bride or a clansman, in appearing in 'one' form, in him or herself appears whole and entire. And the person appears whole and entire from the perspective of a specific other. It is to her husband's clan that a prospective wife exists as a bride. This is the image of the woman that they have, so to speak, created. They own it.

If I say, to experiment with Euro-American constructs, that persons may be owned when they appear as things, I can also say they are things because of their capacity to be seen by others as an embodiment of one particular relationship, that is, because they are owned. Let us pursue these Melanesian fabrications of things with reference to other Euro-American constructs; I digress briefly on intellectual property and commodification.

In an inspired rendering of ritual as a kind of intellectual property, Harrison proposes that 'a useful way of viewing intellectual property is that it is the ownership, not of things but of classes of things, of their images or typifications' (1992: 235).[19] But – to continue the analogy with legal processes – let me transpose that insight from ownership of ritual to one of the effects of ritual as a practice of intervention. If we ask what is owned of the person made visible – the image that has been created – then we might want to say it is *the idea or concept* of the relationship that they embody. When a male initiate steps forward all decked out in his transformed body, a new member of a clan, his clansmen own so to speak the concept of this person as a male clansman. He has to look, act and behave like one. His clanmates acknowledge him by claiming him; they see in him, at that moment, the embodiment of a concept. What they own is that concept or image of him manifest as his 'body', and they own it as they own themselves.[20] In Harrison's terms, the image as a typification is constructed of generic and universal elements, anyone in this role will look like this. That is what ritual requires the particular initiate to act out.

Leach (2002: 728) comments on male initiation practices among a people from outside the Highlands, Nekgini speakers from Reite, Madang Province, which are predicated on the fact that a man is nurtured on his land:

The work of the father and his kin, and of the lands upon which they nurture children, is to produce potential from which form can be made. There is nothing mystical about this process, as that form is one which is given by the set of relationships into which that potential person is propelled. The boy is this man's nephew and not another's, this set of cross-cousin's joking-partner, not another's.

The father's affines (his wife's kin and their spirits) give form to the appearance of the boys at initiation as a result of the kind of nurture they bestow. (The boys' substance comes from their father's land.) Now the importance of initiation being carried out among the particular persons who give the initiate's social presence its particular form depends on there also being a sense in which they bring into being the universal or generic (sister's son). In Reite, it might be truer to say affine's sister's husband's son. Through their actions they reify this specific man as at once *their* sister's son and as their *sister's son*. The latter is an abstraction, an image, an idea. The same ritual can be performed for any boy precisely because each is an instantiation of a sister's son.

And through the intervention of the compensation agreement, something very similar was to have been Miriam's lot. Members of her clan claimed dispositional control over their sisters and daughters, whereas the clan to which she would be joined through the marriage had claims on her as a prospective wife and mother. (This was complicated in her case by the fact that she had been brought up by her maternal kin, from a part of the same tribe into which she was now to marry, and that at her father's death they assumed they had rights of bestowal over her.) The moment at which Miriam was detached from all her other relationships and appeared as the single and whole embodiment of the *concept* of reciprocation between clans was the moment at which we could talk of both sides both enjoying ownership in her.

This allowed people to draw on multiple rationales for the overall gift, comprising homicide compensation for the secondary cause of death, mortuary payments to maternal kin ('head pay') and reasons to do with past marriages between the groups. At one point Muke insisted that, as an element in the overall payment, this last was the principal rubric that applied to Miriam; she was not being sold as part of a homicide compensation but returned as part of life cycle payments.

The general conditions of a mortuary payment were relevant. A clan sending out its women in marriage contributes to the prosperity of other clans; through its offshhoots – a sister's child is called a 'transplant'[21] – maternal kin expand their own spheres of influence. So if these progeny prosper through their guardianship then, in turn, as we have seen, death injures them. When their transplant was killed, observed Muke in his affidavit, the 'root people' on one side felt that the other side had violated their divine relationship. In local idiom, the deceased's 'bones' or 'head' (male wealth) should be sent back by the patriclan to the maternal clan that had in its lifetime overseen its welfare. Such wealth, the head pay, is regarded as regenerative for the future. But if kin request that an actual granddaughter of the woman be returned, then they are thinking of how their groups have intermarried in the past. They look for a 'skull in a netbag', that is the strength or value (bones) of a woman's progeny in and within the form of another woman (the netbag or womb), as O'Hanlon and Frankland (1986) describe (see also Muke; PNGLR 1997: 132). A woman who marries under the rubric of a skull in a netbag, as Miriam was doing, is meeting obligations set up by previous marriages.

What kinds of body parts are these 'bones' and 'womb'? I suggest that the bones are not conceptualised as parts but rather as wholes; they are the whole body made manifest from the perspective of the claimants. That is, the wealth they see from the hand of the donors is equated with the claims they have (in the image of strong bones); they own the person in the form of the bones (wealth) they can expect in return.[22] And it was not any, generic, woman (womb) who would satisfy the need for the maternal kin to recover what it had given in the past. A particular relationship was singled out: she should be someone standing in the relation of granddaughter[23] to the actual woman earlier sent in marriage. This is the importance of each side owning 'a granddaughter', embodied in Miriam, that the one could give and the other receive.

A thing created through commodification also embodies a concept; its value must be specifiable in abstract terms against equivalent items. Recall the Mt. Hagen Lodge conversation, which included a discussion of bridewealth (Gewertz and Errington 1999: 127). The proprietor's nephew had observed that with money as the medium of exchange women became like commodities: money made women equal to anything and everything one might want to buy in a way they were not in the past. They became not just equal to things but substitutable one for another (cf. Demian 2001). This is the process that Minnegal and Dwyer (1997: 55) described when people turn from exchanging to selling pigs (my emphasis, omitting theirs).

A pig is brought to an exchange not as a pig per se but *as a particular* pig. Its particular constellation of attributes, and its history, make it not only appropriate but, in a real sense, the only appropriate offering. Where pigs are sold, by contrast, attributes such as size, sex and colour may influence the going price but no longer bear upon the appropriateness of the particular pig to the intended transaction. A pig is suitable for sale simply [i.e. universally] because it is a pig. *Thus it seems that the idea of 'pig' itself has become reified.* The boundary between 'pig' as a category and other things has become more salient in guiding social action than the differences between particular pigs.

Note that the thing created through commodification carries with it categorical information about itself and does not require contextualisation beyond its evaluation in relation to similar entities. This is how initiates may be compared to one another, as are brides over the generations during which clans have intermarried. Unlike a commodity, however, although a person may be presented as a thing with generic and universal attributes, far from being detached from its social origins each image points precisely to the source of its creation. Moreover, sisters' sons may all be alike in the form and conventions by which they display their tie to their mother's brothers, but substitutability is likely to be hedged around with restrictive rules. There will be conditions about 'classificatory' equivalents, that is, who qualifies as a stand in – which mother's brothers will count what persons as sister's sons. Ownership applies only if certain relational preconditions are met.

These two digressions bring us to the question of what rights ownership brings, presaged in the previous chapter. What entitlements flow from the ownership of an image? In the case of ritual as performance, one may well be able to imagine reproductive rights such as copyright, as Harrison suggests. The entitlement to perform a ritual, or produce a song or dance, anticipates the particular realisation of a conceptual entity. Certain people may lay claim to the knowledge involved or to rights of sponsorship or performance; these may or may not be entitlements that can be transferred to others. In the case of persons, compensation or other forms of reciprocation are designed to provide an abstract equivalent to the value once embodied in a now absent other. The claims of Miriam's father's mother's kin included the fact that they had been deprived of a reproductive opportunity, not as a matter of the continuing existence of the deceased person but of their continuing relationship through him to others. However, the question of deciding what might or might not count as rights does not take us very far.

Consider, rather, the question of what public intervention, legal or ritual, creates. Having set up the possibility of persons being owned, as thought–objects and as things, I am forced to the conclusion that it is in the very activation of ownership *as* a question of rights and claims that an intervention of a kind has already taken place.

Euro-American understandings of property ownership invariably entail the ownership of rights; one owns not the thing as such but rights in respect to other persons in relation to the thing. Yet rights is an awkward idiom for the ideas of ownership to which I have been referring, where ownership seems a question of expanding or augmenting identity, an entitlement that allows those – and no others – who claim ownership to re-state their own identity (maternal kin to the sister's or daughter's child). People readily enough assert claims attendant on such connections, staking them out in a manner that looks like claiming rights, but as an intervention – as an action – mobilising claims shifts the perspective the actors have on one another. Here we need to remind ourselves of the difference between wholes and parts. If it is plausible to suggest that what is owned is an image of a person (a concept), then only an entirety can be owned; rights and claims set up a different social field altogether and one in which nothing seems entire. The dispute over Miriam shows this.

## Part-Persons: Agents

There is no simple sense in which one can translate 'body part' into the Melanesian vernaculars I have been presenting; at the same time, the notion touches at such provocative points on the way *persons* might be partitioned that the comparison is inviting to pursue.

I talked, with particular reference to the Papua New Guinea Highlands, of the presentation of persons as whole forms or bodies. Objectified from the perspective of others, the person (the thing–image) is in a specific and thus singular relationship to them. But whole bodies are, in another sense, part-persons. From a second perspective that these other persons have, what they see is divided substance. For in addition to being singular, persons can also be plural. Because the whole person is detached from other relations, taken together these relationships compose the person as an entity with a multiple or plural character. This produces another perspective on the body.

The body's health and sickness are regarded as the outcome of an amalgam of *actions* on the part of multiple others. In this sense it is an assemblage of parts, not as limbs or organs or tissue but as paternal and maternal substances: bone and flesh or blood and semen. Or at least that is the rationale given to various transactions. Indeed, the very possibility of compensating persons for the pain they have suffered (the blood of childbirth), for nurture they have bestowed (mother's breast milk) or for injury they have endured (damage to the body) fabricates a view of the body as partible. Through their actions, including giving or withholding blessings or curses, people bestow bodily energy on one another. As a result, a person's substance may be thought of as body that is a part of other bodies. Who pays and who receives delimits the claims. Thus the mother's clan claim the child because they are due wealth for it; the father's clan claim the child because they are able to pay wealth for it. Each side, in 'growing' the child for the other, reproduces itself not just through the child but through each other.

We can, then, imagine the person as distributed or dispersed (Gell 1998) across a spectrum of relationships, belonging to diverse groupings. Yet although these relationships converge on the one person (rendering the person a composite of diverse ties), the ties as such are dispersed, and can never be gathered together in anything but that person. They do not form a further whole of which the person is a part, as Euro-Americans like to imagine the individual as part of society. If we construe these relations as 'parts', then the only entity they can be part of is a person.

The shift in perspective is created by taking action. For at the moment when claims or rights are activated, the singular person (the abstract thing–image) is then seen to have many social origins, to be a partible entity combining in itself many particular concrete histories. The point at which a claim is translated into a gift or the carrying out of a duty is the point at which the one relationship is (re)perceived to be one among many. The person has other possible destinies.

Let me explicate further. As soon as ownership is realised in the activation of claims, persons have to deal with one another as agents. And as soon as relationships are realised in the activation of ownership, people divide themselves off from one another. What the mother's brothers thought they owned as a product of their own nurture or protection now appears to have been the result of nurture at others' hands as well, spirit as well as flesh, semen as well as blood. This is because when action is taken or when wealth is mobilised or when someone seeks to meet an obligation, decisions have to be made, and these bring into the foregound all those other relationships that demand taking action, sending wealth or meeting obligations. Realisation creates its own moment in time, even if no more than a *scintilla temporis*. Taking action is itself an intervention in that an abstract category now becomes a particular entity in a history of particulars. Perhaps the very idea of right or entitlement or claim is usefully thought of as ownership in an already activated form. Here what they own, and I take my cue from an observation by Kalinoe (personal communication), is how persons 'belong' to one another.

In the Minj compensation settlement, there were many strands of relationships, past events and old debts being brought together in what would be the one transaction it was hoped would answer them all. But that one transaction was in turn to be composed of items of wealth collected by many contributors, where each would find himself faced with other, competing, demands on his resources. Choices had to be made, eliminating one from multiple ways of acting. If acting requires choosing between alternatives, these are basically choices between relations – and thus invariably invoke prior relations. Here one arrives at a local understanding of agency. *Agency is evinced in the ability of persons to (actively) orient themselves or to align themselves with particular relationships,*[24] however foregone a conclusion that decision may seem to be. This is not the same as free choice (indeed someone may have few options in the matter) and does not translate directly into the kinds of acts of choice by which the modern person can be recognised.

Kinship is necessarily predicated on prior relations, on the fact of relationship. Muke's (1996) analysis of the Minj case pinpointed the crux of the matter: kinship on trial. It was not just the clans on trial but a whole set of suppositions summed up in the term kinship – the nature of relationships as a matter of people's conduct and obligations toward one another. Thus Miriam was quoted as saying that she initially agreed to the compensation settlement out of concern for her younger sisters and other clanswomen who might be asked if she refused (Gewertz and Errington 1999: 125–6). In her affidavit, as rendered by judge, she stated that she was willing to be part of her father's head pay, but not willing to marry immediately or to marry just anyone. She felt pressured into probably having to make a quick match, and the payment process left her feeling humiliated in the eyes of others, 'ashamed at being used as a form of compensation' (Gewertz and Errington 1999: 130, quoting the judge's summing up). Indeed, at her first interview with the press (Palme 9 May 1996), she was reported as being upset and shocked by the decision. (The same reporter also pointed out the power imbalance between the two sides: the Tangilka were scattered by warfare over the district; the Konombuka, who had taken some of them in, was one of the biggest tribes in the area.) Whatever one might think about Miriam's predicament and whatever pressure she was under, the observer is left with the fact of relationship. The question is how to take into account the obligations they entail. As Muke implied, what does one do – what action is to be taken – about the fact that one clan is in perpetual spiritual debt to another for the welfare of its progeny?

A set of very particular claims lay behind Miriam's selection. She was already well known to her father's maternal kin and had in fact been living with them since her mother was sent there for safety during previous fighting while her father, Willingal, stayed back with his paternal clansmen. In fact, this family – Willingal's two wives and five children – had been one of several Tangilka living there as refugees and had as yet paid no 'rent' to their hosts. Moreover, Miriam's father's mother's clan had sent many wives to her father's clan who had borne many sons to strengthen it, while few women had come in return. These were all perceived as putting the one clan into the other's debt. Miriam's marriage would help adjust the imbalance. In short, from this perspective the case concerning Miriam and her maternal and paternal kinsfolk is all about the nature of obligations and how people meet debts. The claims that bear in on the actors as immediate reasons for their actions are based on the fact of their relationships with one another. It is because of these relationships that they have to act.

The National Court judge took this on board in his response. Yet it was the degree of obligation to which he apparently objected. Justice Injia found that obliging a woman to be part of a head payment was an infringement of her constitutional rights. For example, her right to equality of treatment was violated because the custom only targeted eligible women and not men (cf. Dorney 14 February 1997). Moroever, he opined, although an open request placed an obligation on any of a clan's girls, the closer the relationship the greater the pressure.

How, then, does the final verdict of this careful and sympathetic judge avoid the fact of relationship? Once again the tradition versus modernity rubric comes into play. Pitching the issue of obligation in terms of obligations *between groups*, tribes and clans, has the effect of invoking a community whose interests seemed 'against' those of the individual. In focusing on the way in which groups bring pressure to bear on individual women, this judicial opinion rehearses a familiar position. Obligations start looking like communal and thus cultural constraints, and cultural constraints somehow belong to the domain of tradition and custom. Yet when Miriam herself talked she had in mind specific individual kin, 'living men and women', of whom she was thinking. She was after all an agent in this herself.[25] In an interview with the Port Moresby *Post Courier* (20 February 1997), Miriam said she was fearful about the way her clanspeople would interpret 'the law' (the judgement given a few days earlier). She said that she wanted her people to really understand the court's decision: her worry was that '[h]er people think the court has given her "freedom" from a traditional obligation and this could take away her tribal support'.

So Miriam also resorts to the notion of tradition. It is an open question whether she was referring to cultural constraint or to the exercise of her own agency. Whichever it was, the latter was not going to be heard. To acknowledge claims as obligations in the context of kinship looks to modern eyes as perpetuating dependency, control and coercion. Human rights discourse – grounded in equality between individuals – sweeps all this away. Muke's question was whether it were also to sweep away kinship as such.

## III

I have taken the Euro-American duo, person and thing, as far as it will go for the kinds of Papuan New Guinean materials presented here. Persons turn out to be most thing-like (embodying a concept) when they are regarded as unitary, whole and abstracted from all social contexts but one, and most person-like (partible) when they find themselves engaged across a plethora of relationships in multiple contexts. Under the first rubric I have wondered whether it is apposite to refer to persons as owned; the second leads to claims and rights, and here a person in orienting him- or herself toward specific relationships can act only for him- or herself. In the former circumstance, what is owned is a concept or image of the person, made visible (reified) through the body. This is an ownership that augments the owner's status, as Miriam's grandmother's clan increased its sense of itself through the fertility it bestowed on another. Her offspring, such as Willingal, their sister's child, would appear to them in that singular and ideational form as an exemplar of a 'sister's child'. In the latter circumstance, when the fact of relationship – that a person is always a composite, a part of a plurality – is translated into action, this makes visible the obligations and expectations through which kin in belonging to one another are bound to and divided off from one another. Action includes acknowledging debts to be discharged, including in turn debts owed for life.

Miriam's case invites us to think again about legal interventions that appeal to human rights. We may think of human rights fitting an anonymous entity abstracted from all social contexts bar one (common humanity) or else, to the contrary, as investing the subject with the dignity of choice (between multiple options). But what about the nature of obligation as it inheres in human interactions, the expectations of dependency in the sense revived by MacIntyre (1999)? Human rights discourse, at least as invoked by Justice Injia, the NGO and journalists in this case, would seem to have no place for the fact of relationship.

## Decontextualisation

Something similar but not identical to this criticism has been voiced by anthropologists commenting on human rights interventions. Wilson (1997a; cf Rapport 1998) strongly advocates greater anthropological application in the arena, an intellectual resource that he suggests is under-used.[26] He would like to see a comparative study of human rights focussed on the ways transnational discourse materialises in specific contexts.

In order to address human rights violations, Wilson argues, the anthropologist does not have to choose between copying the supra-local universalism of legalistic declarations and giving in to a relativity that deems that any local representation is as good as any other.[27] Focus should be on the middle ground between the local and supra-local. Anthropology, he states, is well suited to judge the appropriateness of particular accounts of abuse, to pay attention to historical and biographical cicumstances, to assess concrete examples according to the context in which they occur. It could show how people engage in human rights narratives from their own vantage points.

Rapport (1998) reviews Wilson's insistence that we live in a 'post-cultural' world in which human rights belong to global governance. This is a polity that 'posits individuals as ontologically prior to the cultural milieux which they create' (Rapport 1998: 386). It is individuals who animate and transform cultures: individual actors are 'the anthropological concrete' (after Augé 1995) who can adopt or reject cultural personae. 'In short, the liberal polity which is to be globalised is one which publicly respects the rights of the individual citizen to his own civil freedoms *against* cultural prejudices' (Rapport 1998: 386 original emphasis). In this view identities at once come together and remain distinct, and one can investigate human rights without entering into universalisms. It does not mean having to harmonise different moralities:

All one expects is a common respect for the procedural institutions of the polity which seek to balance, in an *ad hoc*, concrete, case-by-case fashion, the competing demands of diverse perspectives while not serving the exclusive interests of any one.

Rapport, after Rorty, 1998: 385

The manner of intervention would thus acquire its own significance: procedural rules become the candidates for universal application. If human rights are understood as political procedure (human rights as a 'transnational juridical process'), then culture becomes 'an optional resource', one to be employed by individual actors on a global stage who are free to create identities for themselves (Rapport 1998: 387, 388; Weiner 1999). It is a modernist position of course to imagine that one can choose. Much of the rhetorical justification for Culture is in fact cast in terms of allowing people the 'right' to practice their customs as they always have done; conversely, critiques of conservatism perceive cultures as blindly clinging to practices modern sensitivities find repugnant.

Wilson wants to build a theory about the operation of rights. Legal right based on equality before the law implies the subject being stripped of social circumstance, as when descriptions of victims abstract them from their family and class background (1997: 146). Yet, he argues, although human rights discourse models itself on legal discourse it does not have to. His plea is for anthropologists to address themselves to specific interventions and thus provide the crucial local contexts in which decisions are taken. Contextualisation is a familiar and powerful intellectual resource. Thus an anthropologist might readily observe of Miriam's case that there was bound to be more to the two clans' actions than the acting out of tradition, custom or culture. Explicating the ramifications of indebtedness that lay between the people to whom Miriam was related affords just the kind of socio-historical contextualisation, the middle ground, that Wilson regards anthropologists being in a prime position to supply.

Yet are we limited to fabricating that middle ground from the intersections of the local and supra- or trans-local global? A contextual analysis is insufficient if it simply supplies supplementary circumstances for an action, reasons at a remove. I see more interest in fabricating a middle ground as its own order of phenomenon. Pace Augé, I would return to the foundational anthropological concretivity: relations. And thus I give weight to what Wilson slips into the following (1997: 15, my emphasis):

> If human rights reports strip events free of actors' consciousness and social contexts, then part of the anthropologist's brief is to restore the richness of subjectivities and chart the complex *fields of social relations*, contradictory values and the emotional accompaniment to macro-structures that human rights accounts often exclude.

For the next sentence gives it way again when he states that social relations are what trace local connection to macro global processes. It is clear that he is thinking of relationships as mainly supplying the context that has been taken away. Yet, in my view, to regard relations of indebtedness, as in Miriam's case, a matter of context or background is to tell only part of the story.[28] The relationships between the two clans were carried by persons themselves involved in very particular sets of relations to one another. In the spirit of Jolly's (1996) advocacy apropos Vanuatu, my own plea would be that we have to treat social relationships as a complex (complex as in complexity) field of its own. This will give us another perspective altogether.

We certainly do not have to go on re-inventing the contrast between tradition and modernity. There are other intellectual resources at hand. If we consider the notion that culture is carried by persons, a Papua New Guinean might say that persons are also carried by other persons. Individuals do not interact 'with' culture – they interact with persons with whom they have relationships. Although it may be consciously in accord with cultural values that they follow this or that path, much of the motivation to act comes from the claims binding them to others. There is therefore a non-optional aspect to the relationships into which people are locked, producing a situation in which, once brought into being, the very fact of relationship becomes a condition prior ('ontologically prior') to action.

Miriam's case may offer local examples but they are examples of a thoroughly trans-local social fact. People are nowhere free to create relationships. This is true both because every relationship has a momentum and character of its own, that is, must take the form of a (specifiable) relation and thereby embody a particular image of itself, and because each relationship involves other parties, at a minimum in sustaining the relationship. To put words into Miriam's mouth that one might want to put into anyone's mouth, perhaps she would like to be able to fulfill her obligations.

## Intellectual Resources

Wilson's criticism was provoked by the de-contextualisation he saw in human rights reporting. Anthropological expertise in re-contextualisation could, in this view, redress the imbalance, a scholarly intervention with the potential of being an activist one as well. However, there are resources that lie beyond anthropological procedures.

The problem with human rights reporting is not so much detachment from context, a logical impossibility, but the removal of an entity from one context into another. The victim is redescribed in the kind of bare detail similar to a presumption of (human) equality before the law, the new social context being the universe of others who have suffered human rights abuse. The criticism is that, in avoiding personal detail, human rights reporting can lose everything one would want to know about a person's circumstances, career, family. These are all part of that person's 'life', and Wilson observes that it is often that life which has been put at risk or abused. Only the particularity of circumstances would define what an entitlement or right could mean in those specific conditions under which people live. Yet, in my view, we shall not get very far with understanding the deficit only as a deficit in cultural understanding. It is a deficit in social analysis. Personal detail is, as Wilson in effect notes and we may now add, *inter*personal detail. We would be losing (out on) an intellectual resource not to take into account the diverse ways in which persons visualise themselves as carried by other persons and, for better or worse, by their relations to others.

Complaining that human rights discourse renders people as little more than things is a customary Euro-American accusation (respect for individual persons is incompatible with treating them as things), and indeed the whole elevation of the victim's status to do with human rights violation could well have been premised on such accusations in the first place. The Melanesian construct, as I have synthesised it, of the reified person as a thing–image offers a different route, and one that dares us to begin specifying what it is as human beings we might own of one another.

### ACKNOWLEDGEMENTS

I thank Martha Mundy and Alain Pottage, organisers of the 1999 London School of Economics symposium, *Fabrications: the technique of ownership*, for forcing the pace on 'persons' and 'things'. I am especially grateful for provocation of John Muke's reflections. Cyndi Banks and Claudia Gross gave unstinting hospitality in Port Moresby in 1995 and 1997, including a visit that the British Academy supported, and supplied me with information about the Minj case. Parts of this account join with other issues in a chapter ('Global and local contexts') for a PTC volume, *Rationales of Ownership* (Kalinoe and Leach 2000). Lawrence Kalinoe provided the Papua New Guinea Law Report and many insights, as did James Leach. Eric Hirsch's study (1999) has been a stimulus for thinking about ones and multiples, as was the 1999 GDAT (Group for Debates in Anthropological Theory) debate at Manchester on human rights and Michael O'Hanlon's pertinent observations on the case. A final thanks to Lisette Josephides (2003) for her critique of some of the premises on which this argument is based; the piece comes as originally conceived, however, and I do no more than acknowledge her observations here.

# 6

⚭

# Divided Origins and the Arithmetic of Ownership

Borrowing information between groups characterises Papua New Guinea...The sharing of information only requires permission or the exchange of gifts. No actions should be taken that might stop the flow of information exchange through traditional channels.

Nick Araho, Seminar on Intellectual, Biological and Cultural Property, Port Moresby, 1997; Whimp and Busse 2000: 186–8

## I

*A*NTHROPOLOGISTS DO NOT GENERALLY GO ABOUT THEIR BUSINESS thinking that their subject matter is a contingency. Yet that invariably becomes the case when the ethnographic record – however vast – or models of social structure – however illuminating – are brought into relation with other bodies of material. They are hardly alone in this. Insofar as bodies of knowledge form systems, other efforts must lie outside, part of the environment not part of the system.

One body of knowledge that perpetually strives toward the systemic is law. Indeed this reflection on contingency is prompted by Barron's (1998) discussion of the influences that in 1991 were brought to bear on the Australian Federal Court that upheld (against his will in this case) the appropriateness of copyright as a property relation between an Aboriginal artist and his carving of a sacred emblem. In asking how this legal recognition had come about in the first place, she discusses a number of what she calls contingent issues, issues that in her view belonged to the environment not to the system. They included the newly discovered artistic value of Aboriginal art, not to speak of the thoroughly contingent place the genius of the Romantic individual holds in respect to copyright law in general. Copyright in this case was allowed to the artist as the originator of the work without invoking any stronger sense of creativity or merit. There are many cultural arenas of debate – and assumptions about the individuality of genius occur over and again in intellectual property discussions – that supply people rhetoric with which they may approach the law without being the basis of law. Of interest to the student of culture may well be the very fashioning of that rhetoric.

The boundaries are not always clear.[1] Two Australian legal theorists and feminists observe just that in considering whether persons can ever be property (Davies and Naffine 2001; see Chapter One). Property law, they argue, is surrounded by assumptions that act out the idea that one can have property in persons, or aspects of persons, even though the law is built on its denial. (They discuss mainly U.S., Australian and U.K. jurisdictions.) Indeed, they suggest that these days property in persons may be assumed in the very arena that legal thinkers once took as the radical divide that separated persons from things: self-ownership. Insofar as persons (as subjects) own themselves, no one else can own them (as objects).[2]

Now this state of affairs is at once interesting and unsettling for the anthropologist. It may be a contingency that one could ask similar questions of many of the kinds of societies anthropologists study, including those of Aboriginal Australia. But if the rhetoric then brings such societies into the orbit of debate they are likely to get pressed into other people's agendas. Thus, regardless of what national regimes of law do or do not allow, the international community may have its own interests in whether or not persons are treated as property. A contingency, in other words, of some effect.

To be blunt, the question of whether one can talk of persons possessing one another has dogged my own anthropological and feminist sensibilities for a long time. Ownership begins to look property-like in societies such as those of Melanesia where payments pass hands for all kinds of services and rights that people acquire in one another, where suitors expect to pay bridewealth and killers hope to escape revenge by handing out huge sums. In the coarse vocabulary of money, men and women may speak of buying and selling brides, of buying off the victim's kin.

Of course there are many ways in which people can negotiate interests without having property rights over one another, as there are diverse ways in which they might be said to own one another. What makes the question newly interesting are recent debates that have sprung up in relation to intellectual property. Along with them has come an arithmetic of sorts, that is, the 'discovery' that although there must be an identifiable originator of a work or product on whom the right is conferred (and this holds for works that meet the criteria of either copyright or patent), it is a contingency of some ethical moment that many others may also be involved in the working or supplying of raw material (e.g., Jaszi 1994; Woodmansee 1994; Biagioli and Galison 2003). The point was briefly raised in Chapter Three. If rights confer the opportunity of reward, the argument goes, these others should be rewarded too, whether or not they are recognised as owners. The others may be counted as many other individuals involved in making the thing in question or as a collectivity with prior interests in a commons.

Now this is the moment, as Davies and Naffine gesture at the end of their book, at which materials from beyond the Euro-American tradition may start to acquire comparative value. And where we may be reminded of the reason why the Aboriginal artist was trying to withdraw from a copyright agreement: it had led to the license holders to whom he had sold it to then sub-license the design, and others moved in to protest. The others included people he would count as kinsmen. It was clear that members of his clan both had claims to the design and claims over him; the design had originated in the clan, and the clan determined the conditions of its reproduction. I do not wish to step into the mire of what is collective or communal here;[3] the interests of a body of people may be conceived as either singular or plural depending on context and depending on whether one counts the claims or counts the people.[4] I focus instead on one type of multiplicity, in which more than one person means there is more than one (type of) claim being put forward. In respect of intellectual property rights, that in turn would imply more than one kind of originating activity. I believe that this focus could in the long run throw light on Euro-American assumptions about property in persons. However, the immediate enquiry springs out of Melanesian materials.

I wish to pursue a strong form of multiple claims in relation to certain Melanesian societies, all from lowland Papua New Guinea. Papua New Guinea is there in Davies and Naffine's book (2001: 172–3), where, following Pottage (1998), they discuss composite claims put forward in relation to a cell line developed from blood samples collected from that country; one of the 'inventors' named in the ensuing patent had been active as a facilitator not as a scientist. However, the materials I consider concern Papua New Guineans in their relations with one another. They offer some striking examples of multiplicity in the way they count persons, and it is persons vis-á-vis their origins of whom they are thinking. The origins are vested in parenthood and kinship relations; different types of claims yield different kinds of rights. This introduces a deliberate contingency into my narrative.

Melanesia aside, what has kinship to do with anything? English-speakers might use the language of ownership for kin, although explicitly without connotations of property rights (e.g., Edwards and Strathern 2000). Nonetheless, kinship is interestingly absent from the lawyers' questions about persons as property. In all the material they consider, Davies and Naffine may have

thought kin relations too far removed from their legal and quasi-legal concerns or that owning ('my' child) in such a context was merely a matter of
identification (as in my boss) or a reflex of belonging (as in my team). However, the cross-cultural point is that elsewhere many claims on both persons
*and things* that begin to look property-like, even taking one to court as in the
Aboriginal case, are premised on the rights kin have in one another.

The present narrative creates a question about multiple origins, then, from
a blatantly heterogeneous set of 'contingent intersections' or 'discontinuous
particularities'; the aim is to 'enable their intelligibility to be appreciated
differently' (Barron 1998: 42–3, after Foucault and Levinas). And severally.
Euro-American anxieties about property in persons, the role of the originator in intellectual property rights, along with the nature of Papua New
Guinean kinship transactions, and the way people envisage their origins in one
another: there are greater and lesser contingencies here. Clearly, the concerns
do not add up, but taken together perhaps the intelligibility of each is a little
increased.

## II

### *Counting People: Murik*

Imagine a party of NGO-driven Euro-American experts wanting to ascertain
precise genealogical relationships. This could be in the context of advice over
claims for natural resource extraction, possibly envisaged as royalties or as
recompense for indigenous knowledge (Posey 1996; Toft 1998). The experts
assume there will be no community leader – in any case, it is part of their
anthropologically informed critique of multinational corporations that these
extractors of resources do not pay attention to local divisions – and will be
sensitive to the fact that it is easy to overlook women's claims. In order to give
women space to speak, they decide to collect information from husbands and
wives separately.

If they were to go into a Murik village, as it existed in the Sepik River area
in the mid-1980s (Lipset and Stritecky 1994), they might have some surprises.
They would no doubt be attuned to the difference between biological and
social kinship, would not expect people to have any knowledge of genetics and
would be on the lookout for classificatory kin. Having done their homework,
they would be aware that these Papua New Guinean people allocate children
to bilateral kin groups on both the mother's and father's side. Indeed, knowing
that all four of the child's kin groups may make claims on it, they would also
be aware of the importance of nurture in the way claims were established. So

they would probably settle for the simplest kind of information, beginning with questions about the children people had. Here they might well be startled to find that husbands and wives can disagree. Each has his or her own version, and while often these tally this is not always true: not just the names and sex of children differ but so do the numbers. They do not count the children in the same way.

Oddly enough, the actual fieldworkers of twenty years ago who reported this were looking for *more* disagreement than they found. They had come with a theory of knowledge that posited that the sexes articulated cultural knowledge differently and that genealogical divergences would appear in their kinship discourses at large (Lipset and Stritecky 1994: 3, 18). Instead, they found considerable agreement, and the divergences in counting boiled down to two sets of differences. Murik men mentioned their adopted children more often than women, whereas women mentioned children who had died more often than men. I want to suggest that this piece of arithmetic needs a general mathematical solution. That is, it is not a question of people not able to add up properly or adding together incommensurables. Rather it is a question of the observer having to rewrite the sum as an equation: to rewrite the 'one' world that the observer sees, in which children are potentially countable, as 'two' worlds, perceived separately by men and women, in which children are divided from parents in different ways.

In this example, and those following, I have deliberately veered away from societies with what are known in an older literature as unilineal descent groups, that is, where people are clearly differentiated by the exclusive groups to which they are affiliated by ancestry through one parent alone.[5] Unilineal descent gives too quick an answer to the way people in Papua New Guinea can perceive origins. Ancestry appears as an origin in the idiom of an exclusive grouping that already presupposes belonging and the sense of ownership this brings,[6] and I want to arrive at some understanding of ownership rather than start with it.

What attracted me to the Murik account was Eduardo Viveiros de Castro's (1992; 1998) thesis of Amazonian perspectivism. By contrast with the commonly understood (Euro-American) sense of perspective in which a person's point of view creates an object (out there), Amazonian perspectivism creates the subject. For the original condition of humans and animals, he explains, is not animality ('nature') but humanity ('society'). Amazonian perspectivism implies that any being taking a point of view sees itself as human and as a person, and differences between points of view lie not in minds – they are all the same – but in bodies, and here all humans see some bodies as animal and others as human like themselves. To be a person is to register the point of view a subject takes. In the Melanesian analogue I earlier thought I had found (Strathern 1999a: 249–56), the pertinent divide would not be between humans and non-humans but between different kinds of humans, such as the persons of a son and a sister's son.[7] Their divergent affiliations axiomatically ensure that being a son is not the same as being a sister's son; the perspectivist point would be that these positions are not relative views on the (same) world but point to radically distinct states of being in non-similar worlds. Paternal kin claim their child in a very different way from maternal kin.

Now my example had explored gender, but it had also rested on the presence of group affiliation. For a division between father's side and mother's side on which the distinctiveness rests, that is, the division between parents, is iconic in descent group systems. The advantage of the Murik material is that it side-steps group assumptions about maternal and paternal connections yet locates an intriguing difference in how mothers and fathers view their children. We could even say, after Viveiros de Castro, that it is not that they count their children differently but what they count as children are different entities.

This probably seems a rather elaborate way in which to comment upon men's and women's diverse renderings of childbirth. Why not just accept them as holding different perspectives in the Euro-American sense of self-referential 'unique' points of view to put alongside numerous other self-referential and unique points of view (Strathern 1999a: 251)? The Euro-American stance implies diverse ways of 'knowing' the one world we all share but described from different viewpoints. However, knowing that knowledge matters when it comes to intellectual property, we might wish to dig a bit deeper.

## Analogous Worlds

What attracted me to Viveiros de Castro's Amazonian perspectivism is the clarity with which he locates it as a matter of ontology not epistemology. It is not about what one knows but about how one is, about the nature of the body with which one inhabits the world and apprehends it. The body is the organ of perception; perspectives are different according to the body one has. The reference to the body includes its affects, dispositions and capacities (Viveiros de Castro 1998a: 476, reiterated by Pedersen 2001: 420). In short, across species there is spiritual or intellectual unity, corporeal diversity. Now the Melanesian case does not present us with the viewpoints that humans and non-humans have on one another, and the parallel with Amazonian perspectivism must be tentative. But there is a kind of bodily perspective that does suggest differences of an ontological order.

Lipset and Stritecky (1994: 15–17) themselves dismiss some of the more obvious reasons why Murik men and women should count their children differently, arguing that the disparity is not just about women recalling stillbirths or men boasting about their social power. The reason Lipset and Stritecky put forward has to do with the bodily interior of each sex and the influences internal bodily powers have on others. It is simply that women are not bothered about mentioning dead babies, whereas men are very bothered indeed. Men are held responsible for the death of children at birth because this is a sign that they have failed to follow pregnancy protocols. Adultery, for instance, puts the husband's interior body into a state that is lethal for the young child. When it comes to adoption, women tend to mention children adopted-in but not children adopted-out. To men the traffic is all part of their larger nurturing roles (which they liken to mothering, specifically suckling),[8] including helping others by sending them children. It is women who see the children they have lost as truncating the kind of nurture they offer ('cutting the breast'). Like the observance of protocols at birth, the authors argue, women's nurture requires management of the interior body, for the nubile/parturient female body is otherwise dangerous to adults in general.

Very crudely, then, the signs switch: men mother (nurture) adults and are dangerous to children; women mother (nurture) children and are dangerous to adults. In this equation, the different *effects* that men and women have lie in their being, a matter not so much of managing knowledge as of managing the consequences of their bodily condition. The conditions are specific. Thus liability for danger comes from female bodies in the form of young women of childbearing age and from men's bodies when their wives are pregnant. Insofar as such internal dispositions shape the world that people perceive exists around them, then they (these dispositions) have ontological status.[9]

But in what sense are they different effects? Is this a case of what Pedersen (2001: 413, after Vivieros de Castro; cf. Wagner 1977) calls analogous identification? We may recall the perspectivist contrast, spiritual unity: corporeal diversity. In the Murik instance, male and female bodies seem alike in their inner capacities to influence others (inner unity); at the same time, bodies are differentiated along another axis altogether, in being responsive to other persons' bodies in particular states of childhood or adulthood (reproductive diversity.) For with some drama, Murik reveal a difference between male and female persons through this other difference between persons, that between adults and children.[10] Temporality, or stage of growth, introduces crucial distinctions, so that under certain (temporally bounded) conditions men's and women's bodies have differentiated effects on others.

It is clear that more than one kind of originating activity is going on. First as child and then as adult, the person owes health and vitality to the care that others take, and the care is of one of two kinds: observing rules or bestowing nurture. The inner powers of parents – both male and female – set different influences into motion depending on the reproductive stage of the child or adult. In turn, exterior form allows specific social origins to be claimed at certain moments.

Thus Murik men and women alike may claim the privilege of decorating children's bodies. Decorating takes place, for instance, at the climax of a series of rituals conferring entry into a ceremonial group, with its titles and insignia, and is the privilege of the title-holding senior of the group, male or female. Indeed, the capacity to bestow certain named ornaments is described by the ethnographers as a right and one exercised somewhat competitively. First born children in particular find themselves subject to the claims of more than one kin group that may be competing for the child (Lipset and Stritecky 1994: 5, 7). Note that these are not unilineal descent groups but ceremonial groups that may use ties through either sons (or brothers) or daughters (or sisters) to claim affiliates. Far from group affiliation being settled at birth, then, allegiance is established only once growth to adulthood is assured. The affiliation of the child is claimed by his or her seniors wishing to bestow their ornaments. We may conclude that the design of the ornaments tells you which group the child belongs to – and insofar as they declare the child's subject position then the child, so to speak, belongs to the ornaments.

### Counting Ancestors: Omie

How many bodies are made present when persons manifest their capacities as though they had both inner and outer versions and when they move through stages that may, as when maturation rites are performed, alter bodily states, temporally or permanently? Or when bodies also hold the imprint of their diverse kinship origins? The Murik child could be claimed by groups on either the mother's or the father's side, and it is his or her body that they in turn claim in decorating it. Where the bodies of children are held to take after the bodies of parents, procreation can introduce a further dynamic. If persons derive substance from both maternal and paternal kin, each generation has to take into account the fresh combination/division introduced by the new bringing together of the child's two parents.[11] But reproducing the *same* bodies in each generation means reproducing the same number of origins. This is an explicit aim of some Papua New Guinea kinship systems that consistently produce new generations out of old ones with the same number of antecedents. They achieve this by deliberately shedding earlier connections, as in the famous conception–deconception mathematics of the Bush Mekeo (Mosko 1983; 1985).[12] Far from the multiplier effect of Euro-American genealogies, each generation can point to an identical number of ancestral origins.

Some people bypass the mathematics altogether. They cut through the issues of multiplication and division by simply declaring that women belong to their mother's groups and men to their father's. Such systems are rare in the ethnographic record. Exclusive affiliation along gender lines seemingly flies in the face of the usual kinds of accommodations for combining group membership with reproduction based on parental pairing. However, in one famous case of 'sex-affiliation', the symmetry of same-sex identification leads to the extreme claim by the ethnographer that the sexes in themselves form 'distinct social groups'.[13]

Writing about the Omie of Papua New Guinea as things were some thirty years ago, Rohatynskyj[14] observed:

> It is clear that the sexes comprise two distinct groups. Men reside in collectivities on land with which they are identified through a set of *ma'i ma'i* [land specific totems] and the *anie* [plant emblems]. Interspersed among them are isolated women who, in consistently not bearing the *anie* of the groups within which they reside, stand as a whole in opposition to the groups formed by men.
>
> 1990: 449

She goes on to argue that men and women are equally persons and equally involved in group reproduction. This is through their *anie* affiliation, for women take their mother's and men their father's. And they have the same kinds of emblems because, it is reported, they also have the same kinds of bodies: Omie women have their mother's bodies and men their father's bodies.

Omie can think of themselves, then, as having *either* one (same sex) parent *or* as having two. In other words, they can count the number of parents they have in one of two ways. Rohatynskyj herself (1990: 434) opens her analysis by saying that it is the sex of the child that determines group affiliation. From the child's perspective, there is no alternative; each person has only one same-sex parent (male and female are analogous here). At the same time, the group affiliation that follows from this divides parents quite radically into two kinds. The opposite sex parent plays quite different and quite distinct roles; children may show this parent's imprint on their external features, for instance. But the overwhelming nature of the same-sex tie means not only that same sex parent and child belong to (are identified with) one another but also that it is the vital substance of that parent alone that causes the child to come into being and gives it an origin. This Rohatynskyj (1990: 439) refers to as *ownership*.

It is worth noting that the same-sex parent is duplicated, through marriage rules not necessary to spell out here, in that the girl is also, through this other route, identified with her mother's mother and the boy with his father's father. (Those who share the same plant emblem are spoken of as living together and here men take precedence; men's ties to the land introduce an important asymmetry between adjacent generations, which the marriage rules resolve in alternate generations.[15]) This shows in maturation rituals, some of which assume that male and female bodies are externally analogous, boys and girls having their septum pierced in the same way, and others of which diverge in order to ensure the appropriate development of internal capacities. Hence boys undergo re-birth at the hands of men, who refashion their insides through dietary and other rules, the fledglings emerging from the initiation nest to take the place of their grandfathers (father's fathers).[16] As they come out, senior men sing songs that the candidates' grandfathers composed personally, and from this moment the juniors are able to use their grandfather's totemic names. Girls are taken care of by senior women, taught appropriate bodily comportment, and we may, after Houseman 1988, read their own capacity to give birth as their inheritance of their own mother's and mother's mother's capacity. The generations are united by the vitality they show.

Perhaps there is a similarity here to identifications made elsewhere, and radically between dead and living. Pedersen's (2001) analysis of certain (southern) North Asian societies is germane. These people depart from the Amazonian-type of human/animal perspectivism also found in (northern) North Asia but instigate a perspectivism of sorts across interhuman relations and specifically relations between living persons and dead ancestor spirits. It takes shamans to move across the divide and see through ancestral eyes. In the Melanesia cases, there may be an equally dramatic denouement (a special performance), but it is one that takes phase as a stage in the reproductive process that reveals the unity of ancestors and descendants. An altered external body (the now mature child) points to the flow of internal powers across the generations. This is emphatically an embodied power; grandchildren appear as their grandparents.[17] Put otherwise, the grandchild makes the grandparent appear.

## Owners and Makers

Let me return to the issue of ownership. Rohatynskyj used the term when she described a parent being the cause of his or her child, by which she meant the cause of its being and condition in the world (battle for a child to be born as either its mother's offspring or its father's takes place, she observes, hidden away, within the womb). Yet there can be no 'original' in the infinite series

D–M–MM (daughter–mother–mother's mother), only the same state replicated. As Houseman (1988) demonstrates, reduplication is a sign of indeterminacy. Perhaps we can regard the opposite sex parent as a kind of negative presence, in which case its active elimination is the relational act that confers the same-sex parent's ownership.

Among its attributes, and like the songs sung at a boy's coming-out ceremony, the *anie* emblem presents an image of what it is of the person that can be replicated in the next generation.[18] The emblem belongs to more than one body, but is only produced through a particular body, that is, in being borne by a living person. So it is an image of his antecedents that a person owns, or equally we may say it is the image that owns the person (that is, through which these antecedents own the person). The *anie* endures; a succession of persons come to hold it, but the *anie* makes them all one (the son is both father and grandfather). If the same person (S – F – FF) is counted innumerable times, separate persons (S – F – FF) are equally counted as one. 'The one' may be singular; its power derives from its having passed through several bodies.

Now there is an issue of moment in similarities with Amazonian perspectivism and its emphasis on ontologically rather than epistemologically informed points of view. An epistemological viewpoint produces not diverse ways of being but diverse representations of the world. We may borrow the latter vocabulary to include persons' representations of themselves in the world. This is one sense in which Euro-Americans understand intellectual products. Yet the ornaments and songs and habits of comportment these Papua New Guinea people produce are not 'representations'. They are more like demonstrations or certificates, a point to which I shall return,[19] or like body products produced in the course of people's production of one another. Crook (1999: 237) recounts the dramatic gesture with which a senior man from Bolivip (Papua New Guinea), in wishing to convey what/how he was transmitting to the ethnographer, feigned an incision in his thigh; he had given over part of himself, meat, muscle. More generally, *knowing* the protocols is not sufficient for they cannot be represented in models for people to follow; in coaching the next generation, the seniors' job is not done until they have witnessed juniors acting out the protocols. The seniors are originators of the body transformations the juniors undergo.

What rescues this analysis from another Euro-American binarism (mind: body) is the perspectivist question about whether such bodies inhabit one or many worlds. Or rather, how many different *kinds* (Astuti 1995) of bodies there are. It would be absurd to argue that bodily distinctiveness alone means that people inhabit different worlds. But it is the case, across Papua New Guinea, that people deliberately attempt to make new bodies in order *to be* persons in a new world. Hirsch (2001) argues the point forcefully. Melanesians devise new ways to be persons, giving evidence of an ability to transform themselves in order to make themselves subjects in, have an existence in, a transformed world. He gives a telling example from the days of 'first contact' in Fuyuge, when people killed several pigs in order to convert a certain kind of headdress from a man-killing one to a pig-killing one. This transformation of the ornament meant that the headdress could continue to be worn but would give the body quite new connotations. No longer would its appearance point to prowess in killing people, but to the fact that its bearers were 'persons of a "new" kind, those who knew the 'law"' (2001: 245). More generally, people's understanding of transformations in their lives affects their interpretations of what it means to be the origin of something. Among recent transformations is a new language for the process of transformation itself that gives it an intellectual cast: focus is on the knowledge involved.

Rohatynskyj's (1997; 2001) description of present day Omie is apposite. Omie now work with the notion of themselves as a group with a unique culture (1997: 439), and this culture has become an 'origin' of their self-accounts. In this context, people talk about what happens to knowledge [in English] such as the knowledge their seniors have vested in the anthropologist.

To the anthropologist, her findings are inevitably representations; to the Omie, whether as a reliable guide to the working out of land claims or as a source of mischief used by the unauthorised, they are rather more than that. But 'knowledge' offers a new idiom in which to talk about new transformations, including people's perceptions of themselves as people with a 'culture', much of which in turn consists of cultural knowledge. Betrayal or loss of culture or knowledge is a language Papua New Guineans routinely adopt for their present condition (cf. Kirsch 2001). When talking of the disappearance of traditional songs, Omie thus lament, 'We have lost our customs' (Rohatynskyj 1997: 450). This is not the place to consider the nuances of Melanesian 'custom';[20] globally speaking, part of its power is the status the concept of cultural knowledge has in the international community. Knowledge pervades the language of UNESCO and WIPO.[21] In standing for what people transmitted to one another in the past, however, its usage may obscure an intergenerational dynamic in which, in the eyes of some (usually seniors), other people (usually juniors) appear to have lost interest in tradition (Sykes 2000; 2004).[22] It may also obscure an ongoing shift from an ontological to an epistemological sense of perspective.

New generation Omie no longer recognise the same-sex affiliations, *anie* and the totemic species through which people's claims on one another had once rested so firmly. In turn, the ethnographer (Rohatynskyj 2001) must ask questions about the nature of the transactions by which she came to acquire Omie cultural knowledge, what her ownership of it means and what then she must do with its form embodied in narrative on tape.[23]

## Propagating Images

Songs and narratives are forms of expression that Euro-Americans may class as intellectual. I have embedded some Papua New Guinean examples in what seems another description altogether, the way in which persons reproduce themselves over the generations. That is deliberate. In this part of the world, kinship relations offer a crucial clue to how such expressions are owned. Chapter Five suggested that kinsfolk own that part of the person that is an index of their relationship; here I stress a related point. When people are identified as members of kin groups, these groups are being defined by the interest they have in their members' *reproductive* capacity; they own persons through the perpetuation of the identity (e.g., name, insignia) that the person carries for them. More universally, we can talk of such persons as owning a reproductive interest in other persons. This is what axiomatically divides kin from non-kin, non-kin by definition having no such interest. I now wish to argue that what people can own in such persons is also what they can own in artefacts, namely, regenerative capacity.

A case can be made for considering a range of tangible as well as intangible artefacts here, including ornaments and decorations, although I particularly have in mind items that circulate in exchange relations. These may be generative in the weak sense of creating or sustaining relationship, but they may also be regarded as capable of magically multiplying themselves, as root crops in the ground multiply. The owner's own regenerative capacity is demonstrated to the extent that he or she exercises the power to reproduce the artefact. That in turn, the ownability of something, becomes one of its attributes. A case can also be made for claiming that these particular conditions have broad currency across Papua New Guinea. And although the data presented so far have been largely historical, they are not out of place in understanding much contemporary practice. Omie may have dropped *anie* and *ma'i ma'i* from the way they think about one another, but they are very much concerned about the form that various 'cultural expressions' take, including songs.

Items such as songs circulate readily between persons and groups.[24] And across Papua New Guinea they may do so precisely because of the mystical burden they carry in reference to fertility and potency. It is widely the case that although these forms of expression are in one sense detachable from persons, their reference to persons is emphatically part of their value. In other words, the origin of an artefact in the lives of others contributes to its distinctiveness and importance. Conversely, it demonstrates the reproductive power of those lives; the transferral of the right of possession is at once an example and a sign of such.

This description (Leach 2000: 66–7, paraphrased) comes from the Madang area of Papua New Guinea:

In 1998 people in a village called Goriong decided they wanted to purchase the tune, words and carvings of a particular Tamberan [ancestral] spirit from the neighbouring village of Seriang. Ten men who claimed to be the descendants of the originator of the spirit voice went to receive payment. The Goriong purchasers called each by name and placed money and other items in his hands, as well as handing over a live pig. The men took the pig back to Seriang, cooked it and distributed it among the villagers. Thus the transfer of the spirit voice was made public.

The transaction enabled the Goriong to sing and dance in the name of this spirit. Because they had made a payment, they became entitled to pass it on in turn and profit from the payments it would bring them. This contrasts with situations in which someone may ask permission to use a song or dance but acquires only use-rights, and not the right to be called an owner as the Goriong were now entitled to be. In the process, the Seriang lost nothing: they could still use the Tamberan (ancestral spirit) voice for their own celebrations.[25] What is important is that the songs are rendered in a way that keeps their integrity. They evoke memories of the dead and are highly charged for their original owners, and the new owners should do nothing to defame or mock the Tamberan spirit.[26]

The form eventually displayed may thus be an original and a derivative at the same time. The new owners acknowledge the source from which the Tamberan voice came, for it is a Tamberan originating at a particular place that they dance and sing. Transactions at the moment of transfer not only secure the release of the practices for use but multiply its origins; both those who had it and the those who obtained it may be considered sources of the new practices, even if not to the same degree. Beyond these originators, what is also brought into being are multiple destinations for the creation, in the people who will witness the display. The propagation of objects *means* attachment to new people (Demian 2001).

That such items can be transacted introduces a further possibility in the reproduction of persons: other people's generative power can be appropriated for oneself. So there is a form of generativity that can be transferred independent of the propagation of an 'originary' group. In addition to the logic of same-sex affiliation (if the same power is replicated over and over again, so too is reference to its origin) is the logic of dual parenthood. When origins are divided between persons, there need be no end to the process of division, to the number of borrowings and transfers that are recalled, although it is likely that distant antecedents will drop off. For interest is not just in the things acquired through transactions; explicit value is put on maintaining flow itself (Wagner 1977). Borrowing, sharing and exchanging are all effected through payments; keeping the flow going acquires generative connotations of its own. An ability to release generativity is bound up in the right to pass things on to others.

## III

### *Intellectual Products?*

The comparisons with intellectual property are becoming evident. I have been accumulating instances from this Melanesian material in which one might draw parallels with items that in Euro-American legal regimes can become subject to intellectual property protection. In addition to songs and names, we have encountered carvings, performance, moral rights (in the integrity of a piece of work), personal images or emblems and could even regard groups as having a proprietary identity to protect. Although they are made visible and manifest, many depend on performance to be so, so that they only appear for a while and in the interim exist as memories of designs, patterns and movements. Moreover, there are contexts in which control over reproduction is restricted. It is not surprising that copyright is often taken as a model for the protection of cultural property (Coombe 1998; Brown 2003).

The Papua New Guinean lawyer Kalinoe (2000) notes one bias that copyright would introduce. When contemporary artists draw on traditional art forms, such as Tamberan songs, copyright would appear to be the means to protect their artistic expressions. But although copyright declares their originality, as it is often said it does not deal with the other side of the equation – the simultaneously derivative nature of the work and its multiple origins.[27]

However, all this draws too quick a comparison between indigenous protocols governing the transmission and transaction of performances, artefacts and so forth, and regimes seeking to protect the products of intellectual work. We have already seen that loss of custom nowadays may be glossed as loss of (traditional/cultural) knowledge. It may be necessary to scrape off that gloss. Kalinoe (2000) has argued the case for considering the protection of various items of value, especially the class that he calls sacred (such as those with ancestral value, ancestral not because they are antique but because it is the living presence of ancestors in their descendants that guarantees continuity of inner power). Significantly, his proposal is that these should be treated, for legal purposes, simply as property – emphatically *not* as intellectual property.[28] This is worth pursuing.

The ethnographic record from Melanesia could have supplied many examples to convey the substance of the data presented here. Most notably, all the items just mentioned (songs, names, carvings, performance, moral rights, emblems, proprietary identity) could be bundled up in the single instance of Malanggan carvings in New Ireland and their accompanying displays, introduced in Chapter Four.[29] The instance would be doubly germane in respect to the designs worked on the carvings themselves, in that the way these figures are guarded from unauthorised imitation has compelled observers – as we saw – to use the vocabulary of intellectual property rights. Malanggan figures would also summarise some of the other features we have found. They recall the inner and outer bodies of the Murik in that the New Ireland carving is prototypically regarded as an external body for the departed presence of a deceased person whose potency is retained within. They echo the emergence of the Omie child/grandfather, for the sculpture gives an imagistic form to the name of an ancestor that, detached from the deceased's body, can then be passed on to an heir.[30] They point to the general difference between a history of exchanges and current ownership (the carved plane refers to the former and the painted patterns on it to the latter), and to a consistent orientation toward the future, in that the designs reflect anticipated claims for which the recipients make payments. Above all, the image is owned by, retained in the memory of, those who have the right to reproduce it.[31] But the one issue I wish to bring forward is Küchler's comment, 'Melanesia is a particularly clear example of a culture within which intellectual property is not an analogue of material property' (1999: 63). Given the mix of tangible and intangible items here, we might well ask what she means by that. The answer will open up the question of whether it is useful, in fact, to think of any of them as intellectual products.

The context of the remark is a discussion (begun by Harrison 1992; 1995) about the nature of mental resources in Euro-American societies of 'the modern industrial economy', which lay stress on 'material resources and productive capacity' (Küchler 1999: 62). The reproduction of mental products is here governed by a legal system in which intangible efforts have to be embodied in things for rights to be exercised over them. The contrast is with regimes, as in Melanesia, which have the kind of approach to the flow of information enunciated by Araho. Küchler describes intermittent Malanggan performances over a person's lifespan as part of 'a shared knowledge technology [that] assures the continuing generative and reproductive capacity of its intangible resources'

(1999: 63). She is referring the planned ephemerality of items produced for display, where (in her words) ownership centres less on the object as a material product than on the right to project or produce an image out of a repertoire of soon-to-be absent images. Particularly true of the Malanggan carvings, what is created to be passed on is not the thing itself (which is destroyed) but 'an inherently recallable image'. Her principal point is that the image is created as a *mental* resource precisely through the disappearance of the object.

Küchler arrives thus at a very specific definition of the mental, rather to one side of the Euro-American notion of intellectual creation that frequently informs the related concept of the intangible. My understanding is that the Malanggan image is indeed created as a *resource*, but is it a mental one in this second sense? Her phrase 'knowledge technology' is a pointer here.

As a resource it is an entity that can be reproduced again, often a generation hence, by the way it is recalled. So the knowledge in question is the memory that holds the image in people's mind. Another way of putting this would be to say that knowledge becomes a means to further reproduction (rather than an end in itself), the image being held in suspension, an outcome of what was seen in the original display when the rights were acquired or reconfirmed. Is the image in this sense inert? The mind (memory) of the holder–owner houses it as a kind of body part almost; while it may animate the person, the image as such is not affected by its location. It is perhaps not too extreme to suggest that being in the mind confers no further attributes or identity on the image; its mental or intellectual or intangible condition does not add anything. Although the image that is eventually reproduced will be negotiated from various anticipated claims on it, the holder–owner is not supposed to innovate on what he or she recalls. Indeed, that is heavily frowned upon. The end or aim, I infer, is the eventual reproduction of the memory as an image that is also a body, not as knowledge.

In other words, there is nothing particularly 'intellectual' about the fact that the image, like the words of a song or the design of an ornament, is a mental one,[32] and there is nothing to be gained in separating out a class of intellectual property. This also means we might be wary of those contexts in which knowledge is too easily brought forward as a gloss for intangible objects. It is at least worth hypothesising that such regimes treat knowledge practices as a means, literally as practices, not as an end or as objects with value to circulate.

## Ownership of Persons?

Harrison and Küchler's contrast between regimes holds, but we can add a proviso. Whether or not rights in these Melanesian forms of expression are treated as material property depends on what is material about property. Recall that the starting point of the discussion was the Euro-American presumption that intangible efforts must be embodied in material things for them to be apprehended as property in the first place (see Sherman and Bently 1999: 47; Bainbridge 1999: 45).

I return to the exegesis offered by Davies and Naffine and their interest in modern renditions of Hegel's forms of appropriation:

> Hegel argues that in becoming a person one must put oneself into the external world and then reappropriate the self through the appropriation of objects in the world. Taking the world unto ourselves is our method of completing our subjectivity and individuality, because it involves the purely subjective person externalising their personality and re-grasping it in the form of an external object.
>
> Davies and Naffine 2001 : 4; and see Miller 1995

Hence, '[p]roperty is seen as an extension of the person and as a means by which the person can relate freely and transparently with others. Property is seen to mediate our social relationships' (Davies & Naffine 2001: 6). Drawing in particular on the work of Radin (1993, 1996) for her advocacy of 'property for personhood', Davies and Naffine quote her observation that in order 'to achieve proper self-development – to be a person – an individual needs some control over resources in the external environment' (2001: 7). The property that a person uses in their self-construction, they go on to say, is in effect a relationship to an external thing that contributes to 'a person's feelings of well-being, freedom, and identity'.[33]

If property relations are part of the way in which people in modern industrial economies (Euro-American, that is) connect to the world, then they must both shape and take the shape of the way the world is perceived. To the extent that the world is thought of an assemblage of material things, it follows that property can only be claimed over material things. Property in this view *is* the condition of appropriating things from the world.

It also follows that an idea can only be claimed as an expression of a person's exertions and intellect when it is found in a 'thing'.[34] A more generalised version of this is that any human activity, including bodily exertion, can find expression in external things but by being embodied in something else is expressed in a condensed and abstracted (conceptual) form. For example, labour manifests an immediate bodily capacity, but what is incorporated in the products of labour is an abstraction, as when it is theorised (categorised) as 'labour power' in terms of social usefulness. However, there is a special inflection to mental activity, for the exercise of the intellect is closely associated with the exercise of the will, the distinguishing mark, in this Euro-American world view, of personhood (see Davies and Naffine 2001 : 104). The idea that must be incorporated in an artefact (thing) before it can be legally owned renders the mind's effects as separate from the body's, exactly as the individual's will is given expression and realised in a world separate from him or her. In short, in this view, inner energy is projected onto the world that returns evidence of it to its originator, as signs of the person (creative, productive outcomes of personal activity).

This line of thinking hardly needs further rehearsal. The point to draw from it is that we are not dealing with a simple contrast between owning things as material objects and the kind of situation (as described for Melanesia) in which there is no such restriction of materiality in the flow of assets. Rather, we might see in the Euro-American insistence on intangibles that can only be owned as embodied in concrete things something of a comparable reproductive moment. What is being reproduced? Minimally, what is reproduced is the self *and* its view on the world. This is true over and again. And it applies equally to that part of the external world that involves other persons; whatever encounters there are with social others, the reactions they elicit are absorbed back into the individual as its own feelings and sentiments. In other words, this (Euro-American) form of materiality is the condition under which perspective, a person's point of view, creates an object (out there). We could conclude that what is material about property relations is a function of an epistemological grasp of the world, that is, of knowing it as an object (of contemplation, say). The contrast is with the kind of perspectivism that creates the subject.

If anything like this (Amazonian) perspectivism holds in Melanesia, perhaps through it we can concomitantly imagine what is material about the processes of Melanesian reproduction. Perspective becomes an ontological way of being that alters the condition of the person ('creates the subject') so that everything in the perceived world (tangible or intangible) defines and contributes to that state of being.

Now if property, in the sense of the capacity to appropriate, is part of how Euro-Americans reproduce themselves, so too is knowledge. For what has to be returned to the self comes both as things for bodily consumption and as abstract qualities that enhance the equally abstract self, which is exactly where knowledge belongs. Knowledge of the world is a powerful means of connection to it (distinction from it). Yet, as we have already seen, for Euro-Americans it is much more than a means: knowledge about the world is returned to the person who already knows enough to seek it. Its end in fashioning subjectivity makes it something of an end in itself. For the mind reappropriates that connection to the world as intangibles appropriate to how it (the mind) is thought of itself (as so many thoughts, concepts, percepts, scapes, perspectives, and so forth). I am, obviously, speaking both culturally and synthetically.

As a consequence, Euro-Americans do value certain things as outcomes of the intellect. It does matter that there is a mental or intangible dimension to the products of that body location we think of as the mind. The translation from idea or effort into material object *and back again* marks the boundaries of the person. The corollary is that one cannot have property in those generative powers themselves, in the mental processes, because that would be tantamount to claiming property in persons. In liberal (industrial/Euro-American) societies, people cannot own other people's capacities as such (see Gray 1991: 299–300 for a different rendering). It is exactly the intangible nature of their mental processes that protects people from people. Property rights can only be exercised in relation to things in the world, and intellectual property can only apply to material objects that re-embody such intangible processes in things. In these views, creativity is not axiomatically embodied in the body, but is found either in the mind, on the one hand, or, on the other, in exactly those things in the world.[35]

The Melanesian data have pointed to people conceiving of owning what can also be transmitted and exchanged by virtue of being embodied. That embodiment is, however, in persons before it is in things (that stand for relations between persons). Persons are bestowed with human capacities and regenerative powers, such as the strength or life force that as a name, for example, becomes redistributable after death. Thus the Malanggan name is given form as an image that is itself considered to be generative (Küchler 1999: 66), in a quasi-procreative sense, and is passed on (transmitted and sold) in the form of rights to reproduce, to duplicate, the original. But one might wonder whether in the Melanesian case also it is the right not the potency that is owned and transmitted. This would be to ignore the lengths to which people go to turn potency into a visible and appropriatable phenomenon (Demian 2004).[36] It would also ignore a crucial difference.

The Melanesian 'right' to reproduce is sustained not by a legal apparatus but by the person being in the appropriate and necessary ontological state to exercise the right: sister's son, heir, purchaser, initiate or whatever (Kalinoe 2000). Moreover, the very exercise of the right is an instance of what it confers. Making duplicates *is* (to reproduce) the capacity for creation. Euro-Americans, on the other hand, value the right as having if not legal then moral or ethical sanction, and it is this value that allows its exercise to the benefit of the holder. *The source of creativity is not passed on*; that is left intact in the person of the original author or inventor.[37] We come back to the Euro-American significance of 'intellect'. Once embodied in a thing, mental processes can have further generative force only by being processed freshly (by the originator or by another) through someone's mind.

I have been deploying the term used by several writers, property, although we may ask what is propertied about the kinds of Euro-American ownership relations being considered here. One answer has to be that the holder of property rights and the subject of legal rights run together. The counterpart to the specific material thing in which efforts are embodied is the concrete person who can be a bearer of rights. (Rights are intangible before they are realised.) Personal concreteness is given form through individuality (see Sherman and Bently 1999 for a different rendering), so we arrive at the further well rehearsed point that exclusive interests define the individual's sphere of activities. What is enshrined in the law is emphasised by contingent values that lie outside it:

Property in things other than oneself has been said to enhance personhood, because it establishes an extended sphere of non-interference with one's person. . . . Property and personhood have also been linked in a more intimate manner by the assertion that persons may also be said to have property in themselves. [Contingently] [c]ommon to both approaches has been a desire to show how property interests express and secure the autonomy of the individual and hence their very personhood.

Davies and Naffine 2001: 6

The arithmetic here – the singular, recursive character of the origins of a person's actions in that very person – is evident.

## Single and Multiple Origins

Davies and Naffine (2001: 99) observe that the law – English, Australian, American, European law – 'fails to supply a sensible, credible understanding of our embodied selves'. The concept of the legal person cannot cope, for instance, with pregnant women or with the body at death. One of the problems, I would add, is that it cannot count. (It is not just the law; no one can.) The reason is evident: it is the body that normally bestows indivisibility on the person. So the law is baffled by a body within a body; it does not know how many persons a pregnant woman is, and resolution in terms of parts and wholes pleases no one.[38] In short, 'the possessive legal individual is rendered incoherent by the cultural and biological facts of reproduction' (2001: 92). Death creates a different problem, which is that the person's will lives on in disembodied form (in their testimonies and documents), and its wishes have to be given a finite life. The law has to kill off this disembodied personality, an uncanny echo of the way some Melanesians have to kill the (memory of) the dead through deliberate forgetting, by rendering the deceased absent

(Battaglia 1990). However, there seems a swifter resolution to the number of persons there now are because with the departure of the rational, sovereign will from the corpse, the authors argue, lawyers find little of the person there and tend to treat the corpse as a thing. But this brings its own anxieties about others, the deceased's relatives among them, laying claims to it.

I return to the numbers in a moment. First I note that the possessive in the 'possessive individual' (famously after McPherson 1962) refers to the simultaneous condition of being a proprietor and of being property as a result of having property in oneself, that is, a cultural contingency as far as the law is concerned. In some views, that property in oneself (self-ownership) is the guarantee of the freedom with which the will is exercised.[39] As noted at the outset, one philosophical justification is that insofar as persons own themselves, no one else can own them. The Melanesian material suggests that we parse the question about property through a more general question about embodiment. (Questions about persons and property thereby disappear from the account.)

Insofar as no one else can own what is self-owned, then, persons must be embodied *either* in themselves, that is, their own persons, *or* in artefacts, that is, external objects, but not in other persons. (The view that creativity regarded as a product of the intellect is embodied in the mind rather the body, rendering the body other to the mind, plays on an internal division of the person into self and other.) It is embodiment in things of the world that lays the conditions for property rights and for all the equivocations Davies and Naffine voice about the way people want to use the language of property rights for self-embodiment as well.

I have already noted a peculiarity about this Euro-American form of embodiment, that the incorporation of a person's efforts into things does not render those things person-like. On the contrary, they are detached from the generative or creative potential that remains within the person. The person has produced out of him- or herself an entity that now exists autonomously in the world as a 'thing'. If the claims through property are to keep those things within the person's orbit, they must rest on a reconceptualisation of the productive process consonant with the 'antinomy between objects and subjects of ownership ... [meaning that] subjectivity cannot reside in objects, as such, nor objectivity in subjects, as such' (Barron 1998: 55). The connection is simple. The producer is being imagined as the *origin* of the product. Conversely, there can be no property claim to a work (the reference is to copyright) 'without some author who can be said to originate it' (1998: 55).

Once imagined thus, there is no need to demonstrate anything more complex. This is the burden of Barron's explanation of how the Australian courts ever came to endorse copyright in an ancestral design. All that was necessary was to show that it was the artist and no one else who refashioned the design. She writes (1998: 56), 'in law, originality is simply the description of a causal relationship between a person and a thing'. It follows, in this view, that the law is less concerned with establishing the nature of creativity than with determining whether this or that person can demonstrate that he or she was the originator. Other claimants may of course be potential ones or exist as anticipated competitors, but they are the absent multitude against which any one person asserts originality.

There is no need to repeat the point that Euro-Americans equate sources of potency with an origin in the person as a singular entity, and the person is in this respect literally indivisible. It further follows that origins (in the sense pursued here) cannot be divided. What then do we make of the arithmetic in the observation that the Australian artist was 'an individual of several persons' (Barron 1998: 45, quoting Saunders and Hunter 1991). Anthropologically, I would put it that the Euro-American 'individual' is the person in its indivisible, embodied state, here taken for granted. The several persons correspond to the different social positions the artist holds. Barron lists them: author of the work (a legal status), a skilled artist (by reputation), an honoured citizen of Australia and local hero (acknowledged by the Northern Territory Government who had purchased his work), a successful entrepreneur (known through his dealings), as well as an Aboriginal person (whom some felt had desecrated a ritual object) and a member of a clan (whose ancestors were involved). To his legal status, then, were added many other possible statuses on which he could act. They are contingent to the law; nonetheless such positions affect the way the law's justice is perceived. This echoes the claims currently being made in relation to intellectual property rights elsewhere, which is how to acknowledge all those multiple others who participate in the productive process, except that here the multiple others are aspects of the one individual. Origins are singular, even when there are many of them.

### Applied Maths

Now the (Euro-American) view on the world that creates the world as object and the viewing self as subject generates a problem as far as other persons are concerned: what should be done with everyone else – how should they be counted? If that problem is among those still driving the extended Enlightenment project of 'making society', let me comment on a tiny movement within it. Property offers one obvious solution: keep others at bay. There are two related solutions. The first is rendering one person as several persons, as in the case of the artist. The second is sustaining a division between what is essential and what is contingent, for this allows several persons to be involved in producing things, and even to seek acknowledgement and reward, without being co-owners of the primary rights in the thing concerned.

Rendering one person as several persons abstracts or categorises the notion of person in terms of roles and statuses, and there may be as many of these as there are social niches. They can be added to over and again. But they do not add up. A glance at Barron's list shows that they are not commensurate entities, that the list is infinite (can be broken down into countless parts) and that the principal form of coherence is the individual's biography (an embodied life). A person moves between different domains as different persons; they overlap but that is all. This is equally true of the claims that are made to acknowledge co-workers who are not co-owners in a creative process. There may be a division of labour between all those involved in producing a book – the publisher, the binder, the printer and so forth – but each has competence in his or her own sphere or domain, which means that he or she can deploy the same skills for numerous other books as well. In every instance, they add their skills to the author's, but the contribution of each remains discrete and recognisable in the publication, the binding or whatever. A similar additive perception of multiple workers allows scientific investigators to build on one another's work so that they can distinguish the unique efforts of a team of inventors, who may publish as co-authors, from either the contingent technicians, funders and others necessary to the outcome or else the work of antecedent or competitive teams to which the inventors add the essential original input. This arithmetic enables multiple other persons to be recognised as inhabiting the same world without compromising anyone's unique perspective. Everyone has his or her own unique perspective, that is, is the originator of a singular view, and knowledge of this fact allows one to be added to another without expectation of closure or summation.

Another way of putting it is to say that however many others inhabit one's world in this Euro-American view, and however many specialised or exclusive domains there are in which one operates, every pointer of one's activity points to oneself. All that can be said is that the perspectives overlap; the signs do not change. It was one of the discoveries of twentieth century anthropology[40] that, by contrast, in many social regimes people imagine finite worlds in which there is a kind of division of labour between persons that stresses the dependency of each person's status on that of others. A shift of perspective does change the signs. An extreme example is exemplified in what we have learnt by applying the insights of Amazonian perspectivism to Papua New Guinean divisions between persons.

I return to the Melanesian formulation that being a son propels one into a different world from that one inhabits as a sister's son. In the world created between a son and his father, and I take a canonical example in a male voice, the mother's brother may be identified with his sister as a male mother. When someone instead acts as a sister's son (toward his mother's brothers) his own father is still in that world, he has not disappeared, but the signs have changed. The values put on the relationship are different. The father now appears (say) as an in-law to the mother's brother. The world alters not simply because the son comes to see his father through different eyes (his mother's brother's) but because the mother's brother has made a different subject out of him. He is now the son not of his father but of his mother's brother's sister's husband. This is hardly an alteration of perspective that the person can will into being. It is an ontological switch effected through the being and presence of the other relative.[41] One cannot in this situation 'add' other persons; new individuals become assimilated to positions already given. Another kind of mathematics is called for, one that describes the equations by which different sets of signs appear. The limitation of this perspectivism is that all one can do is change the signs; if one is not this, one is that.[42]

The Murik men and women who give different values to adopted and dead children or the Omie assimilating the boy to his grandfather are not confused about how many persons there are or to what generation people belong. To the extent that this kind of mathematics applies, the point is that there is no ultimate or single origin. Persons, subject positions, are created by the relations in which they must engage (Leach 2003). When, as they do, people emphasise specific origins or roots, this is to select particular relationships out of many, prioritising one over others. To use language appropriate to the Australian artist's copyright suit, for example, Barron (1998: 50, after Morphy 1991; cf. Kalinoe 2004) notes the different kinds of rights kin have in one another's ancestral designs. Thus someone may have the right to reproduce a painting from his mother's clan, or indeed from his mother's mother's clan, and will be consulted by them when they reproduce their own, even though his origins in that clan do not give him the rights that descendants of the father can claim. It is not a contingent or a subsidiary authority, but one that manifests a distinct order of relationships by which the person is *owned*.

Imagining how copyright ownership could be mapped onto Aboriginal concepts of clan ownership of images and designs, Barron (1998: 72) observes:

even if it could, the unification of copyright ownership in a single entity, albeit a collective one, would not mirror the distribution of rights among individual members of the clan [in their relations with members of other clans].

A judge, trying to convey how very 'other' Aboriginal concepts were from those found in the law of property, concluded a famous land claims case[43] with the remark he could have found in more than one anthropological text (and reduplicated in Murik ornaments and Omie emblems), namely, that the clan belongs to the land rather than the land belongs to the clan (quoted in Barron 1998: 54). The same could be said of sacred paintings. An artist belongs to the painting rather than the painting to the artist. For a painting executed in reference to ancestral images contains within itself its conditions of reproduction: like the Malanggan, it shows in its very designs who has the right to paint it. You have to be a person in an appropriate relationship to others who also have claims (not necessarily the same as yours) and who thus have claims over you. In this manner, the design authorises the painter.

## IV

It is exactly this kind of modulation of authority with which the Director of the Papua New Guinea National Cultural Commission has been concerned (Simet 2000; 2001 b) in relation to the Model Law on protection of cultural property in the Pacific.[44] This directive makes a case for setting up protection mechanisms outside intellectual property regimes, but it does so by insisting on the absolute claims of 'traditional owners'.[45] These are identified as groups. In implying they are singular in nature, and by implication homogeneous, it addresses the problem of collective ownership in terms that remain familiar counterfactuals to Euro-American private property thinking: 'community ownership', 'communal moral rights', 'cultural [as opposed to economic] or communal rights'.[46] The radical issue presented by the data from Papua New Guinea and Aboriginal Australia is how to accommodate multiple rights when they derive from incommensurable orders of relationship.

Simet observes of Tolai (PNG) (2000: 78):

One idea which might easily form part of the development of a mechanism for protection of indigenous knowledge is the assumption that all traditional knowledge is communally owned. [In fact] ... people were very particular about acquisition, ownership, transfer, protection and use of knowledge. Only some kinds of knowledge belonged to the public domain, while the rest belonged to individuals and social groups.

He goes on to explain (Simet 2001b) that Tolai individuals and groups are enmeshed in diverse relations with one another. A telling example is the way in which the signs of a clan's identity are distributed between its masks (*tubuan*) and the magic (*palawat*) that makes the masks effective vehicles of power. The *tubuan* is held by a clan member who acts as manager for the clan; the *palawat* is held by a non-member, who acts as a custodian on behalf of the clan and deploys the magic on its behalf. Clan members cannot use their own magic themselves.[47]

These groups and individuals are not the 'several persons' of Enlightenment arrangements of society. Persons exercise different kinds of authority depending on the relations that summon them, and they are made into different persons in the course of it. So contrasting types of multiplicity come into view. If we talk of multiple origins in relation to Euro-American works, then multiplicity comes from the way persons are added to one another's enterprises. If we talk of multiple origins in relation to their Melanesian counterparts, then multiplicity comes from the way people divide themselves from one another. Singularity (individuality) is an outcome not an origin.

This attempt at a comparison exposes an asymmetry. Some might find the substance of intellectual property issues in certain systems at odds with, as too contingent to, attention to kinship in others. I am not comparing like with like. Quite so. Precisely because the focus is on the things people produce in the one case, and on the persons they produce in the other, I am drawn to the parallel. Very differently construed as they are, one can nonetheless compare ideas of ownership imagined in intellectual property regimes with Melanesian notions of owning persons through kin ties. That is not where the asymmetry is. Asymmetry emerges if one takes what appears superficially similar. For if one looks closely, it is the kinship in the Euro-American case that appears fundamentally at odds with the Melanesian kinship material. What seems so similar, the concerns with ancestry, blood relations and the rest of it, not to speak of concerns with how children grow unblemished, is never quite in balance with comparable Melanesian notions. And that is because of the specific nature of the ambiguities at the heart of Euro-American kinship. (Other systems turn on other ambiguities.)

Davies and Naffine's observation about the way embodiment is treated in Western law sum up the ambiguities in question. The arena of family and kin relations is a prime place where the Euro-American arithmetic that creates distinct objects and singular originators is at once formed and confounded. Beside the creation of the individual person and of families as units, kin are also bound up with one another in dependencies that make counting difficult, where belonging is a kind of ownership but not quite, where persons both are and are not embodied in other persons, and where notions of property can only introduce complicating rather than simplifying factors.

ACKNOWLEDGEMENTS

I am grateful for the invitation from the Critical Theory Institute, University of California at Irvine, to lecture in the 2002 series, *Futures of Property and Personhood*, and for stimulating discussions. Conversations with Eduardo Viveiros de Castro started this topic off; without the interest of colleagues from Papua New Guinea, notably Lawrence Kalinoe, Andrew Moutu and Jacob Simet, there would have been less incentive to continue. Anne Barron, James Leach, Alain Pottage and Eduardo Viveiros de Castro all kindly read a draft, and I thank Marta Rohatynskyj for her generous comments.

# Notes

1. An explanation of the gloss of the more usual Western as Euro-American can be found in Edwards et al. 1999: 15–17. 'American' here derives from North America, 'European' from Northern Europe, but Euro-American influence is neither confined to these parts nor uniform within them (it has global spread, is locally patchy). I refer to a discourse not a people, although I personify the discourse in referring to its 'speakers' as Euro-Americans. The awkward term is meant to summon those whose cosmologies were formed by the religious and rationalist upheavals of the seventeenth and eighteenth centuries across Northern Europe, creating present-day America in their wake.

2. Miller says that he has often joked that much psychoanalytic theory about the formation of the early child sounds like the formation of the early parent, that the steps that the child follows mark the steps of the parent's delight, perplexities and sense of danger. 'The stages of development described by Klein [for instance] are not really about infants at all. Instead they describe the various stages which a parent goes through in order to develop as a mature parent' (1997: 67). It is the parent who sees the child as the good breast and bad breast, at once utterly wonderful and utterly appalling'.

3. I have made previous, rather similar, use of the notion of *a tool* in work arising from the PTC project mentioned in the Preface. The tool there (Strathern, 2004c) is the concept of 'transaction', a condensed definition of exchange relations of a kind useful largely for cutting, as in cutting through data; it belongs to and serves a rather narrow range of anthropological interests. In its generic form, here the tool I have in mind is as much like a function of the brain or like a body part as the artefact it also is. It is an implement for *separating*/holding *parts of itself*/things *from one another*/together (the sentence can be read in two ways, as indicated by the italics threading through one of them), a capacity for analysing (at once creating and handling) social complexity.

4. In lieu of the Old English *tool*, Rabinow's (2003) more sonorous and certainly more erudite sense of *equipment*, which I have since come across, searches for a continental toolkit of concepts for modern times.

5. Dovetailing science and kinship in this manner deploys anthropology's relation at various moments.

6. If this were a history one would no doubt be looking to numerous theological and ecclesiastical antecedents. If they are there, then perhaps this is a re-invention.

CHAPTER 1: RELATIVES ARE ALWAYS A SURPRISE: BIOTECHNOLOGY
IN AN AGE OF INDIVIDUALISM

1. 'Public opinion' is an elusive concept. For a European attempt to access public opinion, as initiated by anthropologists, see Lundin and Ideland 1997. Pálsson and Harðardóttir (2002) analysed newspaper reactions to the Icelandic biogenetic project, following the first bill on the Health Sector Database.

2. The reader may take 'we' and 'us' to refer to any one whose interests will have made them turn to the topic of this book. Yet if we are defined by shared concerns, that does not mean our perspectives are identical.

3. The case is from the United States. Non-parental visiting rights, including those of grandparents, have been the subject of legislation in most U.S. states so this is a bit of rhetoric on my part (Dolgin 2002: 371). It is always a hazard selecting particular cases from what is likely to be a whole gamut of potential circumstances and outcomes; one should also be aware of the special place that litigation carries in U.S. domestic life, and the special nature of arguments put forward in a court context. However, the two principal sources for this and other U.S. cases, Dolgin and Finkler, may be consulted for their own oversight of a wider scene. Their work enables the grandparents' suit to be put into the context of a range of similar and dissimilar cases being considered by the courts at about the same time.

4. Much of the case was to do with the constitutional argument about the extent to which the state could interfere in family life. Dolgin reports a confused and conflictual situation across the courts and among judges.

5. The individualism of members being separately autonomous to pursue their own choices; see Chapter Three for a brief reference to Dolgin's arguments about family types.

6. That is, the individualism of parental choice. Although choice is over the kind of relations one wishes with others (parents in respect of children), the source of choice is held to inhere in the parent's wishes and desires as an autonomous subject. One judge in the Washington grandparents' case invoked the 'fundamental right' of parents 'to make decisions concerning the care, custody, and control of their children' (quoted at Dolgin 2002: 390).

7. Not just in the general sense that everything one does contributes to what one is but because of the charged nature of techniques in relation to reproduction and the care of early life (see Alderson 2002).

8. Procedures in the United Kingdom for obtaining a woman's consent for use of fetal tissue (in research, after an abortion) explicitly prevent the woman from making any statement of preference about how she would like to see the tissue used (see Nuffield 2000: 9).

9. A central theme in the general discussions of assisted conception techniques that accompanied Australian arguments over stem cell research in 2001–2002. Monitoring disease and disability, for example, through pre-implantation (genetic) diagnosis, is another matter. The ethicist Savulescu interviewed by *The Age*, 19 June 2002, commented that many genes have nothing to do with the diseases by which advancement in gene research is often justified.

10. Public discussions about surrogacy in the 1990s are a case in point. The United Kingdom distinguished itself from the United States on the grounds of forbidding commercialisation, although the range of public opinion on that very issue (commercialism) was almost identical on both sides of the Atlantic. (As for commercialisation being 'un-British', the *Sunday Age* [9 June 2002] quoted an ethicist to the effect that paying IVF donors for their eggs would be un-Australian.)

11. This antinomy is part of an enduring Euro-American configuration (on diverse Euro-American inflections of altruism, Strathern 1992b: Chapter 6). I do not use the word altruism in its evolutionary psychology sense, for the way others are enrolled into the individual's projects for survival, but in terms of the capacity to put oneself into another's shoes and thus in the more general sense of social responsiveness.

12. But the case should not be overstated. Reponses to a U.K. consultation (HGAC 1998) on cloning issues had an emphatic 80% saying 'no' to the idea that the creation of a clone of a human being would be ethically acceptable. The same respondents were divided over the question, 'To what extent can a person be said to have a right to an individual genetic identity?' Forty-one percent thought they had this right while 50% queried the question on the grounds of the case of identical twins, objecting that identity is always more than genetic (context is obviously important). Savill (2002: 44) notes legal observations to the effect that the distinctive genotype of a fetus bestows individuality on it even while it is in the mother's womb.

13. As against the view, born of beliefs about genetic determinism, that there will be a decline in personal responsibility for behaviour and even 'the loss of individualism' voiced by the social philosopher Fukuyama (*The Australian* 27 May 2002). Biotechnology has us think more about these things, though one should not dismiss those who dismiss others (such as the researcher who, apropos debate over patenting human genetic material, referred slightingly to 'ethics and other irrelevant concerns' (quoted in Nelkin and Andrews 1998: 55)).

14. Not to play down the need here: Finkler tells of the distress caused by people not finding out early enough about what their close relatives ailed from (2000: 122–26).

15. However, the privacy of the individual with regard to his or her medical history or genetic information (central to Dolgin's interest in 'genetic families') is breached by the need that others in the family may have for it, as Chapter Three illustrates.

16. Something of a history of public reactions is given by Radick (2002); the U.K. Nuffield Council on Bioethics (2002: 22) includes a brief discussion under the rubric 'Genes as public property'. Justice Michael Kirby, of the High Court of Australia and member of the International Bioethics Committee, reported on an international symposium specifically called by UNESCO in 2001 to consider intellectual property and the human genome; this was in the context of concern that the results of genomic sequencing should be open to free access by the general scientific community.

17. And membership itself starts looking like an asset. Thus genetic heritage may be referred to with the ambiguous double entendre of the English term 'property' as 'the common property of humankind'. For an argument in favour of more explicit propertisation, for example, of genetic resources, see Laurie (2002: ch 6). Helmreich (2002) makes an interesting comment on the notion of the gene pool as an exploitable resource.

18. UNESCO's 2001 Universal Declaration on Cultural Diversity refers to 'the unity of humankind' and cultural diversity as 'common heritage of humanity'. When that place, as the heritage of humanity, is occupied by the human genome (1997

Universal Declaration on the Human Genome and Human Rights) it adds reference to the family ('the fundamental unity of all members of the human family').

19. The ruling from the Washington Superior Court, which had first tried the case, is worth giving in full (an oral not a written deliberation). 'The children would be benefitted from spending quality time with the Petitioners [the grandparents], provided that the time is balanced with time with the childrens' [sic] nuclear family. The court finds that the childrens' [sic] best interests are served by spending time with their mother and the stepfather's other six children' (as cited in Dolgin 2002: 375, including brackets). The U.S. Supreme Court, with its own reasons for putting a value on the nuclear family (to do with the mother's authority over her children), complained that the state trial court had favoured a family of extended kin.

20. Simpson's figures here come from *U.K. Marriage and Divorce Statistics 1990, 1994, 1997, 1998* and *Social Trends 1994*. Over the decade 1990–2000: one divorce for every two marriages; many people divorcing within three years of the wedding. The 2001 figures for Australia point to more than one third of all those remarrying as having children by a previous marriage, although as to the popularity of marriage it should be said that over the long term there has been a gradual decline in the crude rate of marriage (numbers per head of population) (Australian Bureau of Statistics, 2002). It is also reported that the number of de facto unions has been rising.

21. As given in the Sydney *Sun Herald* (23 January 2000), the statistics coming from *Australia now, a statistical profile* (Australian Bureau of Statistics), *Household and family projections* (ABS), *Births, Australia*, 1998 (ABS), the *Andrews Report*, House of Representatives Standing Committee on Legal and Constitutional Affairs, 1998.

22. Something of a corresponding figure is quoted by Dolgin (2002: 344); the proportion of children living with both 'biological parents' in the United States is 50%. This is not a proper statistical or demographic comparison, and I do not want to make too much of the figures. Quite wide variation in people's practices, both in range and rates, sits alongside some very similar evaluations and questionings about the nature of family life and future trends.

23. Her material documents the new prominence of the grandparent in France. Grandparenting has become part of networking, crucially backing up often fluid arrangements at the same time as grandparents are losing their place as obvious extensions of one or other parent. She asks, where do their obligations lie when grandchildren come visiting with their step siblings or half siblings? One in three French marriages end in divorce. When single fathers and mothers make new households, invariably it is the man who enters the household of a divorced or separated woman.

24. (And pose problem for other laws, such as property inheritance.) This kind of commentary has been made several times and notoriously in relation to motherhood; note from Segalen's account the emphasis put not on fragmentation but on recomposition.

25. See for example Dolgin (2000: 537). This was a divorce action over the parentage of twin girls conceived by egg donation; the 'biological father' asked for exclusive custody as the sole genetic parent (an argument rejected by the court, who regarded the recipient of the egg and intending mother as the 'natural mother' entitled to custody, with the husband eligible for visiting rights).

26. From this point of view one may look to the case involving a divorce between the intending parents of a child conceived in vitro outlined in Chapter Three. There

the trial court, faced with at least six potential parents only one of whom sought parentage or custody, concluded that the child was without parentage. Here, the combination of relationships that had produced the baby fell completely apart. However, the verdict was reversed on appeal, and some of the elements put back together again.

27. One would not have to go back very far in European history to find antecedents (including families made up of other families through death and widowhood), but the phenomenon described here is novel in originating in particular patterns of divorce and separation. Of course families could not recombine if they were not composed of elements with the potential for self-organisation. One of the readers of this book pointed out that genetic recombination depends on organic or molecular self-symmetry. In fact Pottage's (2004: 267–9) comments on what we now know of the self-producing properties of organisms, that is, organisms that cause themselves, indicate a revolution in the language of scientific description that extends the analogy.

28. And other close relatives, the basis of genetic screening programmes. The use of DNA-relationship testing is now carried out in the United Kingdom at a rate of nearly 10 000 cases annually (HGC 2002: 160).

29. Or an enlargement of 'the individual' as a reference point. The degree to which genetic determinism seized the public imagination in the 1980 and 1990s does not cease to amaze geneticists or ethicists. (Suvulescu, doctor and philosopher, is quoted as saying people have an 'irrational' approach to genes [*The Age*, 19 June 2002].) A description of the deterministic values of this period can be found, for example, in Nelkin (1996).

30. Indeed, the anthropologist's term *kinship* starts being useful. *Kinship* refers to relatives connected to one another without any supposition of what kind of social group or family they make up. So it can cover the connections and disconnections entailed in divorce, remarriage, adoption and visiting agreements, as well as in assisted conception arrangements.

31. As in Euro-American kinship practices that take 'after nature', this is a kind of kin reckoning that can be extended through any of the biotechnologies concerned with reproduction, including genetic transmission. Some general implications for the law for understanding 'the interconnectedness of bodies' is offered by Herring (2002: 44). He writes of organ donation 'as a reflection of the natural interdependence between our bodies'. Contrast MacIntyre's (1999) depiction of interdependence developed through relationships with specific others.

32. There is an integrity that rests not in defending boundaries, in keeping oneself inviolate or in asserting rights, but in entering into relationships with others – the relationship *creates* a differentiation that separates the parties. Indeed, every relationship is built on connection and disconnection; there would be no link if there were no differentiation (cf MacIntyre 1999). This is to argue on the grounds of social logic; the same ontology could be approached from other perspectives, notably psychology and psychoanalysis.

33. Whether or not *they* think of themselves as all members of 'a family' will depend on circumstances, or rather, we need to know how people apply the term. People draw the boundaries in different ways, as Simpson's data makes evident. In their brief as petitioners to the U.S. Supreme Court, the Washington grandparents

complained through their lawyer that the trial court had focused exclusively on the parent–child relationship, whereas in common parlance, the 'petitioners and their granddaughters would also be described as being part of the same "family", albeit in a somewhat broader sense. Grandparent visitation statutes are grounded on a recognition that grandparents are part of a child's family' (arguments as cited in Dolgin 2002: 389). The family, the grandparents argued further, should be seen as 'a collection of kin'.

34. He also compares different reactions between partners; in some cases there is a sense of a 'controlled expansion of relationships, possibilities and permutations', whereas in others there is instead unease with the messiness of overlapping relationships. People either emphasise the networks or else new, exclusive, nuclear families may emerge.

35. And more fundamentally, no relationship. However, I would give ontological status to the separation integral to relationships [see n. 32], whereas the versions described here are particular arrangements that draw on that universal condition of sociality but are not the only instantiations of it. In a merographic sense, there is endless fractal potential for the replication of combinatory phenomena across different scales, for persons are combined in relationships insofar as they are also separate from one another by being parts of other relationships.

36. Again, this is a merographic model for a Western culture, consistent with the model of reproduction I derive from English kinship (Strathern 1992a). The prior distinction of entities bound in relations ('with the environment', 'with the world') belongs to the model. (In the Melanesian case, on which I have also worked [1988], partibility takes different forms, and the composition of persons out of persons becomes the overt subject of public activity.)

37. The labour that goes into conceiving (confounding nature and nurture) is made visible: 'I hope she appreciates what we went through to have her', said the mother of an IVF baby now 21 years old (*The Age*, 24 July 2002) when, as the clinician noted, the procedure was more invasive than it is today.

38. As reported in the case of the first girl in Australia to be born to a surrogate mother from an IVF procedure. She is quoted as saying she has three mothers and three fathers, including the spouses of the surrogate mother and sperm donor, although 'I know I have only one mum and one dad' (the couple who bring her up) (*Sydney Morning Herald*, 11 May 1999). A commentator at this newspaper remarked that, in her experience, the business of keeping a family/household going as a functioning set of persons living together on an intimate, daily basis far outweighed thinking about origins.

39. Savill (2002: 65), quoting Karpin (1994: 41). See also her reference to an American observation on the creation of physicians' perceptions of the fetus as a separate patient (Savill 2002: 49).

40. She draws on Naffine, and her claim that 'law's conception of a person with discrete and unbroken bodily boundaries misrepresents the bodily reality of all human beings. But it particularly misrepresents the bodily realities of women whose deviance from this norm is most irrepressible when they are pregnant' (Naffine 2002: 46, notes omitted). As a so-called 'part' of the mother, the fetus cannot itself – in the received view – be a person (Davies and Naffine 2001: 91).

41. This I read into Savill's own gloss: she suggests Karpin intends that one should 'not draw boundaries within the maternal body in order to make it fit into a conceptual

framework that relies on individuation as a pre-requisite to selfhood, but rather, to accept the connections *and differentiations* of mother and foetus in their complexity, without undermining the selfhood and subject status of the pregnant woman' (Savill 2002: 66, my emphasis; see also Naffine 2002: 82). Karpin (1992: 326) earlier posited 'an empowering configuration' in which 'the woman's body is seen as neither container nor separate entity from the fetus. Until the baby is born the fetus *is* the female body' (original emphasis). A Melanesian perspective would make explicit the fact that a body can have relations internal to it.

42. There have been moments of exhaustion within biotechnology itself. Fox Keller (2000: 72) points to the very term gene as an impediment to exposition of genetics.

43. Without presupposing distinction. Savill objects (2002: 67) to 'a relational view' that would presuppose the fetus as an entity to which others could relate as a distinct person. But if one starts with the relationship rather than the entities, *nothing is presupposed* about dynamics of interaction, developmental trajectories or asymmetries. We might say that what is so important for Euro-Americans at birth is not just that a new person becomes visually apparent but (in that bodily separation) a new relation. In other cultural contexts, bodily separation itself can be delayed through various forms of postnatal identification between mother and child, and relations unfold in other ways.

44. The clinic (Sydney IVF) featured in both these stories. Of 1 000 IVF cycles now performed by this clinic annually, the newspaper noted that only about twenty are with donated sperm; almost all are with sperm from known donors.

45. Conversely, we might expect that donor anonymity comes into its own, not as an adjunct of concepts of the nuclear family whose integrity has to be preserved but by creating special kinds of connections (see Konrad 1988).

### CHAPTER 2: EMBEDDED SCIENCE

1. U.K. government initiatives have been fuelled by crises over food and technology and by apparently plummeting public respect accorded to science. The ICSU's (2003) preparatory document for its review was explicit: 'If ICSU is really to address some of the key "science and society" issues, then it may have to look beyond its current "academic" membership and seek partners representing other sectors of society. Building on commitments made during the World Conference of Science in 1999, this is something we have now committed ourselves to do in relation to the World Summit on Sustainable Development, where the international community has asked for "a new contract between science and society"'.

2. An engagement with society, environment turned actor ('the context speaks back'), replaces the old contract between relatively isolated experts who in return for being allowed (funded) to freely pursue research gave back public benefits from time to time. Much of this modelling of relations is spelled out by Gibbons 1999; Nowotny, Scott and Gibbons 2001. The Branco-Weiss international fellowship programme, *Society in Science*, which made its first appointments in 2003, was the inspiration of Helga Nowotny and colleagues (at the Swiss Federal Institute of Technology, Zurich). Strathern (2004a; 2004b) explores some of these arguments.

3. It will be appreciated that I present a highly focused (selected) version of anthropological history. For a fascinating account of kinship analysis reproducing capitalist economic utilities, see McKinnon 2001.

4. Among the four changes in knowledge about the natural world, with which Shapin (1996: 13) credits the seventeenth century, is the depersonalisation of natural knowledge and the growing separation of subjects and objects. The other three are mechanisation, that is, the use of mechanical metaphors to describe natural processes; mechanisation of knowledge-making, that is, the introduction of specific *methods*; and aspiration to deploy scientific knowledge in the service of moral or political judgement given that it itself was rendered disinterested, a point on which Haraway (1997) has famously written.

5. The legal versions take on attributes of their own, as we shall see in Part II. Many of these points are made in Alain Pottage's work, not separately referenced here.

6. *Theory*, from the same Greek root as *theatre*, a sight or spectacle, was in the seventeenth century expanded to encompass contemplation, a mental view, a conceptual or mental schema, and from there to a system of ideas or statements held as an explanation for phenomena or a systematic statement of general principles or laws.

7. *My very own medicine: What must I know?* (Melzer 2003) is the title of a review on information policy for pharmacogenetics completed for The Wellcome Trust by the Department of Public Health and Primary Care, University of Cambridge. Pharmacogenetics is the study of genetically determined variability in response to drugs and their application. (The clinical application of products involves the genetic testing of individual patients.) Prime ethical problems are envisaged in the disclosure of information to third parties (Corrigan 2004).

8. A qualification follows: 'with a shared interest in medical progress and the conquest of illness'. Molecular biology has grown up alongside the society-and-science debate.

9. For a discussion of material from U.S. law, see Dolgin (2000), discussed in Chapter One. The irony of *family* in this sense standing for society, however diminished by the epithet *micro,* will not be lost on feminist scholars.

10. 'Although considerations of genetic solidarity and altruism [acknowledging one's responsibilities without coercion] will generally take second place to the principle of respect for persons... [meaning, as human beings], there may be exceptional circumstances in which the contrary is true. In such cases the social interest – or the common good – may be weightier than the individual interest, and certain rights of the individual may take second place', an example being the storage of the genetic profiles of criminals (HGC 2002: 2.11). The concept of genetic solidarity is taken from the UNESCO Universal Declaration on the Human Genome and Human Rights adopted in 1997 (endorsed by the U.N. General Assembly in 1998).

11. He uses *relations* and *relationship* interchangeably. 'My view is that insofar as anthropology has a specific subject-matter at all, that subject-matter is social relationships – relationships between participants in social systems of various kinds' (Gell 1998: 4). 'Anthropological theories are distinctive in that they are typically about social relationships' (1998: 11). He goes on to say that this is not a matter of supplying contexts for interpreting art objects but of understanding the *relata* (here, art objects) as social agents.

12. Criticised by Dumont, whose argument was that social science was misled to think it should be seeking correlations or mechanisms and not intellectual coherence; it should not aim to be a causal science but the study of meaningful relations: 'For Dumont, studying a social system is studying a form of mind' (Descombes 2000: 40). Descombes focuses on the role of 'mind' in critiques of this position.

13. What religion had revealed was the relationship between man and God. Science hardly invented a self-referential universe (I am grateful to discussions with Alan Strathern on this point, but he is not responsible for my rendering of them). Fara (2003: 20–21) describes the pain felt by Linneaus's rivals 'who were trying to work out [discover] God's original blueprint for the universe, and … accused Linneaus of choosing [inventing] an arbitrary plan rather than one that was divinely ordained'. (Of course his system of classification subsequently became a blueprint against which further discoveries could be verified.)

14. And distinctions between elements that participate in one another's construction are propped up (Law 1994) by other distinctions. Barry (2001: 171–2) appropriately writes: '[T]he production of scientific information involves a double movement. On the one hand, the production of knowledge is a creative act. Reality is not merely reflected in the form of information or knowledge: it is creatively worked with and acted upon [movement within the movement] … Second, in order for the new object of information … to be produced it must be sustained and circulated. This necessarily depends not just on the use of scientific procedures and techniques, but also on political negotiations and bargains, government grants … a vast and increasingly transnational arrangement of technical, political and economic resources and agreements'.

15. Edmund Leach (1976) recapitulated some of the debate in his contrast between Radcliffe-Brown's suppositions and those of Lévi-Strauss.

16. Following the work of Gilbert (1989), he earlier used the example of a game of doubles tennis: one cannot confuse the individual agents who make up the adversaries from the social collective agent formed by two players who make up a team. Social actions always depend on partners. On second glance, the example is less than helpful; after all, there is a sense in which all the players, not just the doubles partners, are engaged in a common pursuit that defines them as parties to it.

17. *Monadologie et sociologie*, 1893. (Translated by Eduardo Viveiros de Castro, who relayed the passage to me on reading the text that became Chapter Six [this volume]; personal communications, 2002.)

18. Perpetual motion machine after Crook 2004. The Enlightenment made this explicit: 'natural philosophy had to be underpinned by ideas about it how it was possible to *know* "nature" at all' (my emphasis), and people were preoccupied with 'the relationship of man to nature, the very possibility of knowledge of the external world, and … the best way to organise such knowledge' (Outram 1995: 50, 48).

19. One example of a debate that seemingly followed these contours, of which I am obviously no judge at all, was reported by Israel (2001: 249–51). This concerns conflicting views over the laws of motion; Spinoza's views flew in the face of the majority: Descartes, Locke and others. They thought of motion as external to matter, introduced into the material world by God; Spinoza also held that God was the principal cause of motion but that by the same token it is inherent in things, and the only differences between individual bodies is in the proportion of motion and rest they evince. Everything is a balance of opposing pressures.

20. A merographic connection (also from Strathern 1992a). (I would imagine similar phenomena in other Euro-American contexts, but not necessarily in the form of class.) In this model, English ideas about kin relationships are *always* modified by other, non-kinship, elements. (For an arresting application of the merographic

connection to the field of pre-implantation diagnosis, see Franklin 2003; for an equally arresting elucidation with respect of ethnographic practice, see Schlecker and Hirsch 2001.)

21. In the Enlightenment, 'taxonomy' was 'the organising principle for *all* intellectual activity' (Outram 1995: 48, original emphasis, quoting Foucault's *The order of things*). According to Ziman 2000: 120 (notes omitted, my emphasis): 'something like the Linnaean system became necessary in the seventeenth century to cope with the world-wide diversity of local names for similar – often the same – biological species. Although designed around descriptive "family resemblances" rather than specific measurable properties, this system enabled naturalists to identify the subjects of their observations *to one another*, and thus brought order into biology'.

22. And indeed this characteristic also appeared in social anthropologists' approach to kin classification, as when structural functionalists were reproached for after all dealing with discrete units. In truth, it was simply that they had not gotten far enough; they could see the mother's brother as co-implicated in the definition of mother but did not totalise the insight, as Lévi-Strauss' atom of kinship did, to the relationship between affines and consanguines. Leach (1976) excoriated structural-functionalists' obsession with comparing societies as units.

23. Shapin (1996: 127, emphasis omitted) observes of the sixteenth and seventeenth centuries, '[M]ore and more gentlemen became avid consumers of a reformed body of knowledge. Practical ethical literature urged gentlemen to take up knowledge as an aid to virtue as well as civility'. Fara (2003: 57–58) reminds one of the intense sociability that crossed scientific, literary, diplomatic and artistic circles in eighteenth century London.

24. On observation as a collective enterprise, see the account of the tracking of the 1664 comet across the country (Shapin 1994: 268): '[T]he social stability of scientific knowledge is a reasonable indicator of its objectivity' (Ziman 2000: 6).

25. And the idea of *class* as an analytical unit, as in classification, can appear in this second guise. Leach complained (1976: 15) that in Radcliffe-Brown's treatment, '[T]he whole discussion focuses on the natural separateness of a class of real objects', an argument that led Radcliffe-Brown to define societies themselves as islands, 'conceptually isolated systems'. Leach commended those who appreciate 'that the way we cut up the empirical cake for the purposes of analysis is a matter of convenience rather than something that is given by nature' (1976: 19).

26. And house names were substituted by house numbers, as in streets (in England, however, surnames had been fixed for a long time). These concepts joined with that of 'the community of descent' or lineage that had its own history (Handler and Segal 1990: 32; Mitterauer and Sieder 1977: 10). Macfarlane (1986) opens with a fascinating account of the impediments that class or station were seen to put in way of marriage, which would upturn settled habits of association.

27. Although the notion of radical change was afoot then, Shapin (1996: 3) writes, 'the beginnings of an idea of revolution in science date from the eighteenth century writing of the French Enlightenment philosophers who liked to portray themselves ... as radical', while there were expert practitioners in the seventeenth century who 'identified *themselves* as "moderns" set against "ancient" modes of thought and practice' (1996: 5, original emphasis). See Outram (1995: 48–49).

28. She is drawing here on two ethnographic investigations by U.S. anthropologists, respectively Rapp (1999) and Finkler (2000), both of whose pioneering work I acknowledge.

29. Ultimately, society is thus made, created, in the positivist view. Hence society is different from all those systems that anthropologists constantly produce as counterfactuals in which people seemingly have no choice as to their associates. (The Euro-American 'father' may be acknowledged on diverse grounds, conventionally requiring social institutions such as the law to fix the determinants.)

30. Which give them their so-called nature. Hence nature is different from all those systems that anthropologists constantly produce as counterfactuals in which 'biological' kin are seemingly invented. (The Euro-American mother conventionally derives definition from nature, axiomatically created in the very process of giving birth to the child.)

### CHAPTER 3: EMERGENT PROPERTIES

1. Litigation offers an arena that may be frustrating for social analysis but fascinating for cultural understanding. Lawyers are paid to stretch the imagination – the question is whether their arguments will stick. (On the stretching capacities of contest, see for example the NRT debates preceding British embryology and fertilisation legislation [Edwards et al. 1999; Mulkay 1997].) However, as with the appearance of new items of vocabulary or of interpretation, it may matter little if a phrase begins life as some outrageous conceit; what is revealing about the culture is how the phrase does or does not pass into general use. My appropriation of legal opinion for 'cultural understanding' conceals the extent to which judges' written opinions (the bulk of the material referred to here) are produced in the very awareness 'that what they write gets picked up as the stuff of cultural criticism' (Annelise Riles, personal communication).

2. Dolgin uses *traditional family* as shorthand for what emerged during the early years of the industrial revolution, a family 'constructed as the cultural antithesis of the domains of commerce produced by industrialization' (2000: 524).

3. In this case, the court refused to order blood testing or to take DNA evidence into account; it relied on the facts about the relationships. A father suing for paternal rights may be confronted with the argument that a proper familial relationship needs to include the ability to set up home with the child's mother (Dolgin 2000: 533).

4. *In re the Marriage of John A. and Luanne H. Buzzanca*; I am very grateful to Janet Dolgin for sending me the record from the California Court of Appeal, March 10, 1998.

5. It could find no biological tie between any of the potential parents and the then three-year-old girl. The gestational surrogate (who had given birth) was not her 'biological' mother, and ipso facto her husband did not count; Luanne could not be the mother because she had neither contributed her egg nor given birth; John could not be the father because he had contributed no biological material; the donors did not come into the picture.

6. This was argued on a parity of reasoning with the existing ruling that a husband's consent to his wife's artificial insemination makes him the lawful father: by consenting to the medical procedure, the couple had put themselves into a position similar to an IVF husband. Note the reference also to their 'initiating' the procedure:

'Even though neither Luanne nor John are biologically related to [the child], they are still her lawful parents given their initiating role as the intended parents in her conception and birth'. (California Court of Appeal 1998: 72 Cal. Rptr. 2d at 291). In the final verdict, both the Buzzancas were declared the lawful parents, and the birth certificate altered accordingly.

7. Biagioli (2003) refers to the long chain of names that accompanies authorial claims in scientific writing. In reproductive medicine, the possibilities continue to grow. Thus tetraparenthood refers to the technologically feasible creation of an embryo from the genetic materials of four partners (Brazier et al. 2000, Chapter VII).

8. Without choices having to be asserted or claims being made, perhaps the concept of technology would not have the same purchase on the imagination as it does: I take as cultural fact the widespread perception of 'technology', especially when it carries the epithet 'new', as a force in everyday contemporary life. Thus Justice Panelli, in the surrogacy case noted below (*Johnson v. Calvert*), opened with the general observation (my emphasis), 'In this case we address several of the legal questions *raised by* recent advances in reproductive technology' (851 P. 2d. 776).

9. Values of individuality and choice would seem to lie behind *both* the guidelines *and* this form of protest against it. Dolgin (cf. 1997) has more than once commented on legal situations in which the same values are pressed into service for different ends.

10. The particle physics laboratory, Fermilab; approved in 1998, the proposals are said to be extended to the European physics laboratory complex, CERN.

11. Those who made the work possible; thus Biagioli points to discussions about the authorial input of peer reviewers or journal editors. (The term 'corporate' carries here resonances with commercial corporations and the market rather than ideas about a commnuity of scholars.) Haraway (1997: 7) makes a similar point: 'Only some of the necessary "writers" have the semiotic staus of "authors" for any "text". . . . Similarly, only some actors and actants that are necessarily allied in a patented innovation have the status of owner and inventor, authorized to brand a contingent but eminently real entity with their trademark'.

12. In Biagioli's view, the basic problem of how to divide attributable claims from acknowledging the support that made them possible is not solved by the corporate model. This problem is embedded in an epistemological issue about the relationship between specificity (of a particular piece of work) and the general conditions of (its) possibility. It probably goes without saying that there are also likely to be perennial political issues, leading to variation in practice between different laboratories (Susan Drucker-Brown, personal communication).

13. In 1999, the U.K. Association of Learned and Professional Society Publishers proposed that the 'license to publish' would entail publishers relinquishing copyright to authors. Authors could publicly self-archive their work, online for example, and would be free to give it away, whereas all rights to sell (on paper or online) would be held by the publisher. (Since widely adopted.)

14. A 1997 Draft Declaration produced by the first National Consultation of Academic Authors, a preliminary feeder document initiated by the Authors' Licensing and Collecting Society, simply saw claiming moral rights as a warranty of authorship to the publisher.

15. 'Moral rights' point clearly to the originator but, unlike property rights, cannot be sold or otherwise assigned (they may be waived). Long established in much of the

rest of Europe (nineteenth century French judges allowed relief for moral rights, Rose 1993: 18), although foreign to U.S. copyright law, moral rights were introduced into English law through the U.K. 1988 Copyright, Design and Patent Act.

16. Intellectual property law offers a legal avenue to claims of a potentially economic nature. What is meant by *intellectual?* An intellectual property rights system 'creates incentives for the accumulation of useful knowledge' (Swanson 1995: 11); exclusive property rights depend in turn on the demonstration that the knowledge offers 'novel information'. Swanson, writing in the context of biodiversity issues, readily talks of the creation of 'knowledge' (also prominent in debates over indigenous knowledge) where others may stress the protection of ideas. To paraphrase a 1990s managers' guide (Irish 1991): IP is a general term for different types of ideas protected by legal rights; the law recognises that the time spent originating new concepts is an investment that needs protection. Or: 'Intellectual property is a generic term which refers to the rights attached to the products of human creativity, including scientific discoveries, industrial designs, literary and artistic works' (Tassy and Dambrine 1997: 193). The emphasis on *products* (particular physical objects as the outcome of effort) has traditionally dominated the British view. ('It is often said of modern British intellectual property law, with its pragmatic and positive heritage, that it is not and never has been concerned with creativity... and that it is more concerned with the sweat of the brow than the brain' [Sherman and Bently 1999: 43], a view [as they suggest] that overlooks early modern concerns with creativity as a process.) (Thanks to Alain Pottage for drawing this to my attention.)

17. Lone literary authors can, of course, take a collective view, although they may have in mind a community that comprises audience as well as fellow writers. The first paragraph of the U.K. Draft Declaration (n. 18) opens: 'Academic authors communicate and share ideas, information, knowledge and results of study and research by all available means of expression and in all forms. They recognise that participants in this scholarly communication process include academic editors, publishers and presentation experts'. A more radical although well-worked theorisation of multiple authorship is argued through the postmodern text, always a tissue of other texts, as we are reminded, for example, by Coombe (1998: 284). Rose (1994: viii) notes that one stimulus for his historical enquiry into the notion of the individual creator, on which copyright is based, was his experience of the entertainment industry, where almost all work is both formulaic and corporate.

18. The Draft Declaration states: [3.1.] 'The legal framework of publishing in an electronic age must be reevaluated in order to establish a fair balance between the needs of creators, other rightholders and users'; [1.3.] 'in particular the needs of the user community must be taken into account'.

19. I have drawn from before (see Strathern 1999a: 165), and it is one of the starting points of Strathern (1995). Derek Morgan (see Morgan 1994) originally sent me a typed report of *Anna Johnson v. Mark Calvert et al.* (California Supreme Court 1993: 851 P. 2d at 776) and I have since received the printed version from Janet Dolgin. My thanks to them both.

20. 'We conclude that although the Act [Uniform Parentage Act, California, 1975] recognizes both genetic consanguinity and giving birth as means of establishing a mother child relationship, when the two means do not coincide in one woman, she who intended to procreate the child – that is, she who intended to bring about the birth of

a child that she intended to raise as her own – is the natural mother under California Law' (California Supreme Court 1993: 851 P.2d at 776).

21. The commentator continued: 'The mental concept must be recognized as independently valuable; it creates expectations in the initiating parents of the child, and it creates expectations in society for adequate performance on the part of the initiators as parents of the child' (851 P.2d at 782). Another had argued that reproductive technology extends 'affirmative intentionality' and that intentions voluntarily chosen should be determining of legal parenthood. Dolgin (2000) points out that the doctrine of intent can thus support either a *traditional* view of the family (it points to the likelihood of enduring relationships) or a *modern* view (it suggests choice and negotiation).

22. Of course the majority had not argued that children were property either; they had simply talked of the conceivers and prime movers who produced the child and of the intention implied in the original contract with the surrogate mother (Roberston 1994; Ragoné 1994). 'Intending parents' were covered in model legislation drawn up in 1988, but California had not adopted it, and the case had to be argued afresh (Morgan 1994).

23. When it is impossible to separate idea from expression because of the limited ways in which, for example, ideas in a computer programme can be expressed (Bainbridge 1992: 63).

24. And in the case of patents it would also have to be a commercially exploitable outcome. Apropos the point to follow about copyright, new performers' rights (after the 1988 U.K. Act) deal with protecting something that is unique but still copiable (Arnold 1990).

25. It seems that after relatively stable arrangements in the sixteenth and seventeenth centuries, agitation first by booksellers and then by writers, in response to a growing reading public and the possibility of generating income from writing, saw a new regime developing over the course of the eighteenth century; this was when copyright in England took its present form. Evidence comes from debates published in journals and broadsides and from attempts to pass bills through Parliament, which did not stop with the famous Statute of Ann in 1710, and from legal suits.

26. Other figures 'employed to represent the author's relation to his writing' included 'the author as singing shepherd, tiller of the soil, vessel of divine inspiration, magician, and monarch' (Rose 1993: 38). The following account draws heavily, and gratefully, on this secondary source.

27. Although there was an enduring identity (propriety) between the author and his work insofar as the author might be punished for libel or sedition. There was in any case a general understanding that it was improper to publish an author's work without permission; however, this controlling interest in its publication was closer to a moral right than to a property right (Rose 1993: 18).

28. An idiom authors borrowed from stationers (printers and booksellers). The latter had long argued that their copies (property that was at once the manuscript and the right to multiply copies of a particular title) were the equivalent of other people's estates. Rose (1993: 40) cites the Company of Stationers' petition of 1643 which pleaded that 'there is no reason apparent why the production of the Brain should not be as assignable [sellable] . . . as the right of any Goods or Chattells'.

29. Opposers of this view argued that there could be no property without the *thing*, the corpus (Rose 1993: 70; also Woodmansee 1994: 49–50). The debate rumbles on. Whether or not copyright can be property is still sometimes questioned; this is partly because of its unusual legal status (it exists not in fact but only in law, it can be infringed but not stolen and rather than being a thing that is protected for as long as it exists it suddenly ceases to exist at the end of a set term), but partly because 'a sizeable body of otherwise intelligent persons . . . argue from the mistaken premise that something cannot be truly "property" unless it is solid and has the attributes of a physical presence' (Phillips and Firth 1990: 107). But a caveat must be registered: what constitutes a thing will shift not just across historical periods but across disciplines; for a commentary on Rose's treatment see Sherman and Bently (1999: Chapter 2). They also make clear the extent to which the concept of 'creativity' has its own complex history.

30. Said in the context of an analysis of continuity between the generations. 'For patriarchalists inheritance mattered because the right to rule was transmitted from father to son. For liberals it was the mechanism through which property was transferred, and property was the basis of political rights' (Jordanova 1995: 375).

31. It is Rose himself who extrapolates here, and says that the analogy could never have got very far when the issue of authors' rights turned to the pursuit of profit in the marketplace. However, another historian notes (Jordanova 1995: 378): 'Many eighteenth century commentators did indeed see production as a form of reproduction; they could therefore conceptualise children as commodities', although she qualifies this by also likening them to capital, that is, something in which parents invest. (*Conceptualise* is not the same as *realise*; the issue is the kind of space that ideas create for one another. Children were thought about through many other idioms too. As Jordanova comments, 'reproductive processes and products were imaginative spaces that could be filled up in a variety of ways' [1995: 379].)

32. Though there are some striking current day and not dissimilar instances of combined positions held with no difficulty at all. Within the compass of one sentence, in reference to indigenous rights: 'Indigenous people have shared this knowledge freely in the past [they circulate it without recompense] and have rarely received proper compensation or recognition for it [they ought to receive recompense]' (1997 *Guidelines for environmental assessments and traditional knowledge*, Report to World Council of Indigenous Peoples, Centre for Traditional Knowledge, Toronto, Canada).

33. If I were to write that it was the way in which the text is distinctively moulded and shaped (so the text not the volume becomes the 'body') that was being seized upon, it would be with an uncanny sense of déjà vu in so far as similar phrasing has been used in a locus classicus of anthropological debate on so-called conception theories, the Trobriand father's role in procreation as moulder of the child's external features. Note that I use *text* here in a non-technical way; it receives quite different value, for instance, in Barthes' hands (1977; 1986, discussed by Coombe 1998: 284).

34. But perhaps not too wildly. Dorinda Outram (personal communication) has since pointed out the evolution of salon circles in eighteenth France where aspiring scholars found a kind of 'second family'. This often seems to have involved removal from the first and in particular from the biological father. For the fledgling savant, 'the freedom to pursue innocent knowledge . . . could only occur as a result of . . . rejection of parental authority' (1987: 21).

35. Possessiveness lay generally in identity or likeness, a sense of 'ownness' between parent and child and, in the ideas of the time, parental authority and power over the child. However, there were specialised arenas of debate that argued about the consequences of identity. Some of the seventeenth century philosophers discussed by James (1997) distinguished the spiritual unification of oneself with one's object of knowledge, likened to the benevolent love of the father, from physical union, as in the mother's effects on the unborn child, which exposes the mind to 'inescapable afflictions of sense' and the person to too much influence from others to be able to form a clear knowledge of a world (1997: 248–52). An alleged change took place over the eighteenth century in the so-called natural association of the child with the parent: from the father to the mother (Jordanova 1995: 373, 379).

36. Value was put on innovation. Woodmansee (1994: 38) quotes Wordsworth from 1815 regarding the great author who, through his originality, has the task of creating the taste by which he is appreciated. (Here as elsewhere I retain the masculine pronoun.) Wordsworth: 'Genius is the introduction of a new element in the intellectual universe' (Woodmansee 1994: 39).

37. It is to be understood that these are cultural categories not psychological ones. Now if it (the work) is less obviously a child and he (the author) is less obviously the father, then is it (the work) more like (the author) himself? Woodmansee's own argument ends with a comment on the concomitant emergence of the notion that work could be read in order to uncover the author's personality. Coombe (1998: 219) can thus generalise – like the commentator cited by Justice Kennard – that copyright laws came to protect works 'understood to embody the unique personality of their individual authors'. The Romantic view has to allow the observer's direct sensibility, correspondence, to what is being observed. Creativity becomes assigned on the evidence of the resultant work.

38. Focus is not on his or her vision but on the quality of information which that vision produces, verifiable by comparison with other pieces of information. The procedure is not, of course, restricted to science; in discussing the nature of evidence, Hume (1748) succinctly remarked that a reason for a fact will be another fact. Haraway's (1997) critique of the modest witness lies precisely in observing that the juncture at which facts become visible is the juncture at which the witness becomes invisible. 'This [modesty] is one of the founding virtues of the modern world. This is the virtue that guarantees that the modest witness is the legitimate and authorized ventriloquist for the object world, adding nothing from his mere opinion . . . ' (1997: 24).

39. If we take Biagioli's point about the present-day importance of accountability in science, then the handling of information in the humanities and social sciences follows a similar model. Paul Connerton has observed (personal communication) that conventions in citation have hardly stayed still themselves, and this complicates whatever it is one might mean by multiple authorship. (Pre-modern compositions might consist of whole strings of citations; it was the job of authors to assemble [previously deceased] authors. The knowledge practices of which Shapin writes newly implicated relationships with living people.)

40. The people were men (cf. Haraway 1997: 27). Shapin examines the different kinds of testimony that men allowed, and thus the evaluation of that testimony (see Shapin 1994: 212). Shapin's overall thesis concerns the conventions of decorum and integrity by which the trustworthy made themselves evident – necessarily drawing on existing

credentials (e.g., gentlemanly behaviour) – that in effect defined as a class those able to vouch for one another and that had to discount other contributors to knowledge-making.

41. My term: a rhetoric of equality had displaced old canons of authorisation. 'The Royal Society's "modern" rejection of authority in scientific matters quite specifically mobilized codes of presumed equality operative in early modern gentle society. Just as each knowledge-claim was to make its way in the world without help or favoritism, so all participants played on a level field' (Shapin 1994: 123). (This did not mean that everyone had to be personally acquainted, only that they held the status to be counted as trustworthy.) From another time and place, the young savants mentioned by Outram (see n. 34) were specifically fledgling scientists, and in escaping their birth origins were escaping 'the tainted world of career-making, patronage, and advantage' (Outram 1987: 21).

42. Shapin (1994: 258) gets close to this when he says that having 'knowledge about the nature of people allowed experience to be brought back from distant times and places and transformed into public knowledge'.

43. 'It is evident that there is a principle of connection between the different thoughts and ideas of the mind, and that ... they introduce each other with a certain degree of method and regularity' (Hume, 1748: 320). All objects of human enquiry may, he averred, be divided into two kinds, relations of ideas and matters of fact. As far as 'connections among ideas' are concerned, we find three principles: resemblance, contiguity and cause or effect. And when it comes to reasoning over matters of fact, this is largely founded on the last, the relation of cause and effect: 'by means of that relation alone we can go beyond the evidence of our memory and senses (1748: 322)'. '[A]ny idea ... may be the occasion why the mind thus brings two things together, and as it were, takes a view of them at once, though still considered as distinct; therefore any of our ideas might be the foundation of relation' (Locke 1690: 234).

44. In the last chapter of *The order of things*, Foucault addresses the delimiting effects of knowledge that knows itself as finite. We may see the relation (in the sense used here) as an effect of just such a limitation, in that scientific knowledge conceives of things as 'seeking the principle of their intelligibility only in their own development (1970: xxiii) or as 'contain[ing] the principles of their existence within themselves' (1970: 317). Although medieval doctrines of resemblance were ostensibly thrown out to be replaced by comparison through measurement and order, what he writes of analogy continues to apply to cultural practices of persuasion. It is, he observes, one among many devices by which 'the world must fold in on itself, duplicate itself, or form a chain with itself' (1970: 25–6). For a critique of twentieth century examples from biology, see Fox Keller (1992).

45. Technical authority had to be demonstrated through the replicability of experiments. Both connections and facts required allies (Latour 1986).

46. Outram (1995: 53) quotes de Condillac from the *Treatise on sensations*, Paris, 1754: 'Ideas in no way allow us to know beings as they actually are; they merely depict them in terms of their relationship with us'.

47. At once social and intellectual. The same applies to property practices. Consider Macfarlane's (1998) challenging account of developments stemming from feudal law in England, which utilised the concept of relations in a particularly flexible manner. By contrast with Roman law, where property lay in a thing to be divided among

claimants, feudal lawyers 'saw the thing as indivisible, but the rights in it, that is the relationships between people, the bundle of social ties between people and resources, were almost infinitely expandable' (1998: 113, emphasis removed; 1986: 339–40). He goes on to quote from Stein and Shand's *Legal Values in Western Society* and say that the idea of multiple relations in respect of a thing assisted the common law acceptance of abstract rights such as copyright, patents, shares and options as forms of property (1998: 111–12).

48. Connections *within* may be seen as another example of connections *between*; see Ollman's discussion of 'The philosophy of internal relations' (1971). He quotes Leibniz: '[T]here is no term so absolute or so detached that it doesn't enclose relations and the perfect analysis of which doesn't lead to other things and even to everything else, so that one could say that relative terms mark expressly the configuration which they contain' (1971: 31).

49. The phrasing is from Ollman and his chapter on the philosophy of internal relations (1971: 27) concerning Marx's attempt to distinguish two types of relations (cf. Marfarlane 1998: 104–5). But the notion that seemingly absolute terms contained relations within them was already familiar from philosophy (see Locke 1690: 235).

50. A homely parallel is the way English-speakers commonly talk of a *relation* between individual and society: the relation is bringing together phenomena of quite different scale. An apparent counter-example makes the point. Bouquet (1993: 172), reflecting on Portuguese perpelexities over British anthropological theorising on kinship, notes that there is, in Portuguese, 'no separation, such as the English might make, between the [private] person and [public] ... conventions'. One cannot, in Portuguese, it would seem, contrast persons and system, and therefore one cannot, in this sense, relate them or derive each from the other. Yet even this relation of identity acknowledges the terms (public, private) separately from their fusion.

51. Technology holds within itself ideas, concepts, information. Technology has no other form than a working form; a failed technology is no technology. We may say it is like a device that works to make other things work. This is the strong sense in which I call 'the relation' a tool (see Introduction: Part I), by contrast with the weak sense in which all concepts have an effect as vehicles of communication.

52. From the perspective of certain seventeenth century philosophers, for instance, it has been argued that it would be a mistake to treat knowledge as an intellectual matter divorced from emotion or the urge to act. Rather, '[t]he view that emotions are intimately connected to volitions enabled the philosophers ... to make space for a conception of knowledge as feeling' (James 1997: 240). It was not, in this sense, independent from the knowing subject.

53. At least if we can go by the citations in the *Oxford English Dictionary* [1971 edition]. These do not work simply as figures of speech (metaphors or similes in respect of one another), although through explicit analogy (when their different domains are compared) they may become so. Note that *kinship* is a thoroughly modern term (*kin* and *kinsfolk* are ancient, but *kinship* as at once a relationship by descent or consanguinity and a relationship in respect of quality or character was coined in the nineteenth century). I use *knowledge* rather than (say) *logic* for the second set from the hindsight of certain contemporary usages.

54. In the dual senses of receiving seed (becoming pregnant) and taking something into the mind (grasping an idea); however we may note that only later, and it is

recorded thus from the seventeenth century, is *conceive* used more loosely to cover both conception (by a woman) and begetting (by a man).

55. A usage that seems to have become prevalent, in certain circles at least, in Jane Austen's time. Handler and Segal (1990: 33) suggest that *connection* stressed the socially constructed and mutable (their phrasing) dimension of the kinship tie as opposed to its natural basis in blood. *Family* seems to have referred to the household and to those related through common descent before it became, in the seventeenth century, a term for an assemblage of items.

56. When they are made explicit, the effect is indeed often that of 'a dreadful pun' because English-speakers will hold that the connections are not really intrinsic or else that the similarities may seem altogether too obvious or altogether too obscure. Yet the parallels have kept going for three hundred years, and the doubles entendres are as persistant. English-speakers thus persist in using the same words to talk about intellectual propagation as they do procreative acts, and then they do it all over again in connecting concepts together in order to instruct themselves about the nature of the world and connecting persons together whom they wish to acknowledge as members of a common kin universe. Sometimes the connections have been explored in fiction. Beer hints that George Eliot's novel *Middlemarch*, published in 1872, may be read as a narrative of double relationships: what happens when relations of love and marriage are eclipsed by the obsessive pursuit of relations and connections between infinitely compilable facts.

57. Although Haraway would prefer to dispense with the idea of kinship altogether, this offers a parallel to her supposition about gender relations. She asks 'if gender, with all its tangled knots with other systems of stratified relationships, was at stake in key reconfigurations of knowledge and practice that constituted modern science' (1997: 27).

58. The original reads: 'having the notion that one laid the egg out of which the other was hatched, I have a clear idea of the relation of dam and chick between the cassowaries in St James's Park; though, perhaps, I have but a very obscure and imperfect idea of those birds themselves' (Locke 1690: 237). The cassowaries would have been one in a long line of unusual creatures kept on public display, many of which set puzzles for the 'classifying imagination' (Ritvo 1997).

59. Whether through a comparison of similarities or, as in metaphor, through describing one thing via what is sustained (domained off) for the very purpose of comparison as an entirely different thing. 'Making sense' is of course too passive a rendering when one considers the transformative effect of mimesis and the 'epistemic awareness' it generates (Gell 1998: 100, after Taussig 1993).

60. If so, it is almost as though he were also insisting that the language of kinship is no analogy either. Scientists who were dealing with living, and thus reproducing, organisms had the particular advantage of being able to close whatever gap 'between metaphor and actuality' that existed. Beer (1983: 170) cites Darwin in this connection. In *The origin of species* the idea of family is given a genetic actuality when descent becomes 'the hidden bond of connexion which naturalists have sought under the term of the Natural System' (1983: 170). Kinship was no figure of speech but conveyed 'true affinities' between living things. He had been arguing that 'all living and extinct forms can be grouped together in one great system ... [such that] several members of each class are connected together by the most complex and radiating lines of affinities'

(quoted from *The origin of species*, Beer 1983: 167). Beer notes that family, and what we might call a network of connections, were one among several idioms to which Darwin had recourse, others including tree and web. Thus the notion of generation yielded 'the tree, the great family, the lost parent, the "changing dialect" of life' (1983: 55). We might see a similar situation (on the borders of biological connection) among present day artificial life workers: 'kinship terms from the Euro-American lexicon have been read onto biogenetic connections and *then used to structure knowledge about biogenetic categories themselves*. One genetic algorithmist ... did not stop with "parents" and "children" in describing relationships between bit strings but added terms like "grandparent," "aunt, "cousin"' (Helmreich 1998: 152, my emphasis).

61. In the sense, for instance, in which Arnold (1990: 1) uses it: 'Copyright is a member of *the family* intellectual property' (emphasis displaced).

62. Alone in the span of kin relations, those between parent and child are duplex (mutually implicated, pulling two ways, offering views on the world that are alternatives to, and thus presuppose, each other). Most kin relations are mediated (e.g., siblings are related through mutual parents). To hear an English-speaker call someone a *relation* tells you there is some other reason for the connection than simply acknowledging it; he is known to be a relative by marriage or she a relative through an aunt. English-speakers can think of parent–child relations this way too: the bond appears mediated by other things (by the facts of life, by knowledge of those facts, and so forth); but they may also posit an (unmediated) identity between parent and child.

63. Godelier (1986), intending a universal observation, puts it powerfully, 'Kinship is not just recognition of father, mother. . . . But it is equally and just as much knowledge of father's father ... mother's mother ... and so on. This then entails recognition of a network of transitive relationships which in turn presupposes the ability to perceive relations between these relationships'.

64. That is, the analogy between the way things or persons are known. My question ('was new impetus given to the legal axiom that between mother and father only the mother is known with certainty?') and the observations following are my extrapolations; it may not even be a sensible question to ask. Out of interest, to add to the demise of idioms of paternal begetting in the context of copyright, idioms of carnal knowledge (*knowing* for sexual intercourse) were also fading at the time.

65. Regardless of whether the knowledge is absolute or contingent, a difference highlighted in the traditional difference between mother and father. In a way not true of mothers, fathers are vulnerable to 'discovering' they are not fathers after all, as in the case briefly mentioned at the beginning of this chapter.

66. On choice in English kinship also see Strathern (1992a); for North American see Hayden (1995); Robertson (1994); Weston (1991 ).

67. And, as Dolgin puts it, in complete disregard for traditional understandings about the parent–child relationship. However, we might note the momentum from reproductive technology involving gamete donation where the so-called right of the child to know about its genetic origins is increasingly taken as normal and justifiable.

68. She has already pointed out the possibility that hereditary traits that appear to apply to overall ethnic or racial groups could be taken as evidence applying to individual members of them. See Rabinow (1996a: Chapter 6).

69. She is not overlooking the fact that a parent affects a child's genetic disposition, not the other way around, and that genealogical distance also affects genetic probablities.

Rather, Dolgin's focus is on the way in which neither families nor family members can protect their secrets from outside professionals newly obliged to reveal rather than withhold genetic information and, in this circumstance, family members are all alike.

70. Contexts merge: the genetic family is indifferent to distinctions between social domains – it belongs neither to home nor to work but to both at once (Dolgin 2000: 564) – for genetic traits are carried into the workplace, may be vetted for insurance purposes, and so forth. This is not new or otherwise inconceivable. One can think of past ways in which, in certain circles at least, family reputation travelled likewise, or situations in which kinspersons have been reduced to otherwise interchangeable replicas through the monetary value their inheritance might hold for others (Paul Connerton, personal communication).

71. Only to note that this resonates with what is happening in the way people have been setting up new procreative units. One can have reproductive relatedness (quasi-kin, friends as family) without relatives; the new 'kin' detach relationships from kinship. Weston's (1991) work is the classic here; I would also refer to Bonaccorso's study (2000) of Italian family ideology in the context of gamete donation.

72. Sometimes to embrace all those connected as kin, at other times to detach relatedness from kinship, as in the case of a woman who was urged by her genetic counsellor to contact various people she did not count as her relatives (although she referred to them as cousin', 'uncle', 'aunt'; Finkler 2000: 67).

73. Finkler's argument is that otherwise loosely connected kin are re-connected through the emphasis given to genetic ties and thus linked through a sense of shared body and 'blood bonds'. This may overlay existing ties: 'People are compelled to recognize consanguinity even when in the lived world . . . [the] family . . . may be grounded in friendship or sharing of affect and interest' (2000: 206). Logically, however, the reasons for the genetic relations have an independent existence. Dolgin (2000) similarly observes that the (abstract) idea of sharing genetic connection develops a reality of its own; it becomes a (concrete) social reality under the requirements of genetic testing and diagnosis. The connotations Haraway (e.g., 1997: 141 f.) gives to corporealization in this context, a new reification of familial relations, are discussed by Battaglia (1999: 135).

74. The breast cancer patients whom Finkler interviewed uniformly absolved their ancestors of responsibility for transmitting genetic disease: how could they, as individuals, help it? At the same time, as she says (2000: 208), DNA encourages neither the reinvention of the self nor the embellishment of past ancestry. Truth will out! (cf Edwards 1999). It may, however, allow one to claim as an ancestor someone with whom one has no traceable connection but through the DNA, that is, through a history of disease (Finkler 2000: 196). It should be added that these data refer to negotiation in family relations. In other circumstances, for example, in the study of human genetic diversity, the revelation of genetic connection may lead to expressions of solidarity. even injunctions of the order that the demonstration of common kinship should lead us to all assuming responsibility for one another. I am grateful to Adam Reed (personal communication) for this observation.

75. Confidentiality of information may or may not fall under intellectual property rubrics. The need to protect industrial secrets, at least in the early stages of development, while encouraging the dissemination of information, is one of the backbones

of IPR regimes. Dolgin notes that the impetus toward refining informed consent comes largely from insurance and health care provisions, but clearly works in the interests of the biotechnology industry as well.

76. Their interchangeability is recognized in the kind of agency that donation brings: 'donors not only (symbolically) contain inside their anonymized bodies the imaginary persons of many (unknown) women – they *are* these many persons' (Konrad 1998: 655, original emphasis).

77. I cannot develop the point here but several hints in Konrad's paper point to the worlds of donors and recipients as (regarded as) simultaneously separate, conjoined and parallel with or *analogous* to one another. (Were donors and recipients to become involved in one another's lives, the analogy would collapse into a different kind of relationship.)

78. By interesting contrast with the emphatic kinship perspective recorded by Edwards (2000). As one egg donor put it, 'I've just provided the means for the pregnancy, and as far as I am concerned once my eggs have gone, that's fine by me' (Konrad 1998: 652). Konrad (1998: 659) proffers the epithet *transilient* for persons formed through extensional relatedness via multiple other persons.

### PART II: INTRODUCTION: THE ARITHMETIC OF OWNERSHIP

1. I am thinking of anthropology's relation here, but of course the question can also be put to science's relation. (There are potentially innumerable duplex possibilities; the interest is in the hold of a salient few.)

2. Though colloquially, and I have done so myself, one may speak of multiple perspectives creating multiple worlds. The colloquialism refers to an effect of infinity – to the myriad positions made possible by the myriad individuals in the world – that is held to cast in different lights the physical and environmental world that can be known in diverse ways but exists in one.

3. Knowledge of the world and, recursively, knowledge of the practices and methods that build knowledge of the world, and thus the grounds on which it is held.

4. But for a very different anthropological rendering, on another trajectory, consult Rabinow (2003).

5. A famous boy character (aged thirteen and a three-quarters) in contemporary English fiction whose 'diaries' are intended for child as well as adult audiences. 'It's my mother's fault for not knowing about vitamins', Adrian Mole: Jan 2nd, on the spot on his chin (Townsend 1989).

### CHAPTER 4: THE PATENT AND THE MALANGGAN

1. The basic Malanggan concepts drawn on here are shared across the region (Küchler 1987: 239 and n. 4); Küchler points particularly to Lewis (1969). Matrilineal clans are dispersed across the whole area, being locally concentrated as village-based kin groups and conceptually brought together under a region-wide name. The significance of Küchler's (1987: 249) remark that the 'relationship between localised units of a matrilineal clan is apprehended in terms of places and movements of people between places' will become apparent later.

2. There are several illustrations in Lincoln (1987) and, after this piece was first written, Küchler (2002).

3. There is only one term here (*skin*, *tak*, Küchler [1992: 100]); the Malanggan momentarily replaces the rotting body of the deceased, which is, in one way or another, then left to rot itself.

4. Casey (1996: 39) notes Heidegger's insistence that it is 'in dwellings that we are most acutely sensitive to the effects of places on our lives' (place here refers to embodiment).

5. See the Acknowledgement for the source of these analogies. I am not sure about borrowing terms, notably 'dwelling', from general philosophical arguments about conceptual and bodily orientations that prefigure the perceived world (Heidegger, Merleau Ponty) and then applying them to culturally conceived contexts or environments. The borrowing has some purchase perhaps in the form of a question: how do people fabricate the idea of a world *containing* things or persons within it?

6. Anthropologists have drawn on dwelling to develop a dialectic not with technology but with travelling (Battaglia 1999: 129, citing Feld and Basso 1996) or, explicitly after Heidegger, building (Ingold 1995). For a full length ethnography that marvellously explores some of these ideas, see Weiner (1991).

7. Technical virtuosity points to the sheer control necessary to produce these effects out of these materials: light, airy flowing structures from solid wood (though no more amazing, than the cathedral made of matches [Gell 1999b: 167; n. 10]). In pre-steel days, much of the work was done by burning.

8. Partly because this is not a concept reified in their thinking, partly because they do not have an environmentalist view of what Euro-Americans call the natural world in which they seem to be situated.

9. It is the cultural role that technology has come to play in Euro-American perceptions of their place in the world that has in turn given an impetus to the concept of intellectual property; intellectual property rights (IPR) hold up a mirror to the dazzle of creativity. For 'intellectual property' points simultaneously to an item or technique made available to knowledge, authorising its use and circulation, and to the knowledge, on which claims are made, that has made it into an item or technique. Inventions are impotent if there is too great a technology gap between the idea and its application (Phillips and Firth 1990: 42).

10. An important part in the production of their effects is the dazzle of technical virtuosity (the enchantment of technology). His terms are deliberately recursive. Apropos art and magic, '[I]t seems to me that the efficacy of art objects as components of the technology of enchantment . . . is itself the result of the enchantment of technology, the fact that the technical process, such as carving canoe boards [which have magical properties], are [known to be] construed magically so that, by enchanting us, they make the products of these technical processes seem enchanted vessels of magical power' (Gell 1999b: 166). Apropos the matchstick model of Salisbury Cathedral that awed him as a boy, '[T]he matchstick model, functioning essentially as an advertisement, is part of the technology of enchantment, but it achieves its effect by the enchantment cast by its technical means, the manner of its coming into being, or, rather, the idea which one forms of its coming into being' (1999b: 167).

11. As a concept, technology 'essentially refers to the rational principles [*logos*] governing the construction of artifacts and indicates a move away from artisan or craft

production [*techne*] to the possibilities of embedding skills in machines which can then be "operated" by relatively non-skilled workers' (Harvey 1997: 6, after Ingold 1988, 1997). As Ingold (1997: 131) observes, the creative part of manufacture ceases to be found in the application of the craftsman's skills and becomes instead found 'in the element of design or planning' by which the machine itself was conceived.

12. On the empowerment of anonymity, see Konrad (1998). Creativity might be thought individual and idiosyncratic, thereby deserving of personal reward (cf Khalil 1995: 243), but Euro-Americans also imagine their civilisation to be characterised by technical innovation at large.

13. In the arena of the once-called new reproductive technologies, arguments are frequently heard that technology supplies a means, and it is for society to sort out the ends to which it will be put (see Edwards et al. 1999).

14. For example, by dividing technology off from other things, we create the materials on which technology gets to work. A language that divides off technology as a marked form of human industry from everything else is consonant with one that divides the scientific observer from the observed, culture from nature, and modernity from tradition, not to mention the mechanical from the organic, human intervention from self-reproduction, and so forth. There is no end to the number of conceptual supports by which each division is held up through related but distinct divisions (cf. Pottage 1998: 745). Bits of this ancient enchantment of the Euro-American world are endlessly destroyed (by critics) only to spring up again (in new contexts).

15. See Miller (2000) on Trinidadian websites. These can be understood as creating 'aesthetic traps that express the social efficacy of their creators and attempt to draw others into social or commercial exchange with those who have objectified themselves through the internet. [As in Melanesian exchange] . . . these websites attempt to expand their creators through casting themselves out into a larger world of exchange with distant places' (2000: 6).

16. Whalers, labour recruiters and traders followed Cartaret's 1767 determination that New Ireland was an island, and encounters with New Ireland people were frequent. After 1885, colonisation by Germany added intensive commercial and missionary activity (Bodrogi 1987: 17; Lincoln 1987: 35). But the area had been known since Tasman's voyage of 1643, and carvings (not Malanggan in this case) were recorded from that earliest moment in the seventeenth century (Gunn 1987: 74).

17. Küchler (1987) explains that vertical and horizontal Malanggan may act as *tree* and *branch* in relation to one another, whereas in some areas (e.g., Tabar island) *houses* take over from *trees*. These structures are at the basis of mnemonic techniques required for the recall of designs.

18. For Tabar, Gunn (1987: 75) gives a list of diverse occasions that provide the immediate reason for display, but the logic of the display is based on the same premise that a person honours the dead of their spouse's kin group (from the opposite moiety) when they deploy Malanggan in an appropriate context. Across the Malanggan-making region, occasions include intitiation, ceremonies to renconcile parties after quarrelling, validation of land transactions, removal of social prohibitions, as well as a host of new events (Sykes personal communication). I am abbreviating and eliding information and analysis from several distinct social traditions; my principal published source is Küchler (1987, 1992) and Gell's (1998) rendering of her data, along with the examples described in Lincoln (1987).

19. Malanggan may be made for deceased men or women, but they are sponsored and made by men; the owner in question will be someone who shared rights in the Malanggan with the deceased person (Küchler 1987: 240).

20. Rather like the Hagen headdress (Strathern 1999a: Chapter 2), every such figure, every construction of identity, is an amalgamation of figures, of social identities derived from others. On places as events rather than things, or as location rather than geography, and on the general significance of emplacement as the gathering together of perceptions, see Casey (1996).

21. Weiner (1990: 71) comments on an early anthropological observer of Melanesian languages who said that habits of speaking (through locatives and so on) implied that everybody or everything was either coming or going, now in one place now in another.

22. As a virtual body, the clan contains all the persons and actions, past and future, that constitute it, and clanship means for any one individual both the possibility of living through all these others and the possibility of benefiting from its numerous connections; not the clan as a discrete unit but the clan and its relationships with others is what envelops persons (Wagner 1991). Note that, for simplicity's sake, I argue through the concept of *clanship* in order to summon the collective dimension in rights to produce Malanggan. The reality is complicated by the identities of and interrelations between localised subclans or clan segments. (Küchler [1987: 251] suggests that the transactions over and sharing in Malanaggan across the northern New Ireland region offer their own sources of sociality connected to but separate from the organisational role played by the dispersed matrilineal clans.)

23. The phrase is from Gell (1998: 225): 'On death the agency of a [deceased] person is in a dispersed state', and through the Malanggan the dispersed social effectiveness of the person becomes 'something to which a single material index may be attached'. Compare Hirsch (1995).

24. 'Absorbed into the artistic system, this life-force is rechannelled to the living in the form of power. This power constitutes political authority and is derived from the control over the re-embodiment of the memorised imagery into new sculptures' (Küchler 1987: 240). This is highly pertinent to relations between land-holding units, whose claims relative to one another are mapped out through their rights to reproduce particular Malanggan.

25. There are both inter-place and inter-clan relations here, not distinguished in this account. The right to reproduce Malanggan may be transferred between parts of the same matrilineal clan living in different localites or between affinal clans linked in a history of inter-marriage and co-residence (Küchler 1987: 240).

26. Thereby, for example, ratifying new claims to landholdings after the person's death. In the area where she worked, recently settled by immigrants from elsewhere in the region and where land was very short, Küchler notes particular emphasis on the readjustment of land claims. It is the anticipated claims that the Malaggan records.

27. On gathering and dispersal as a recurrent template to social arrangements in PNG, see Hirsch (1995). From the perspective of Actor Network Theory (Law and Hassard 1999), the Malanggan is a temporary passage point (see Callon 1986).

28. Tassy and Dambrine (1997: 193) are explicit: 'Intellectual property is a generic term which refers to the rights attached to the products of human creativity'. Patent law is 'inherently designed to cope with new technology' (Phillips and Firth 1990: 273).

29. Specifications of the invention must be of a detail to be intelligible to anyone in the position to exploit it. Disclosure must be total, with nothing of substance withheld; otherwise, no one could make use of the invention when the patent expires (Bainbridge 1999: 317). (I refer to inventor, but the eventual patent-holder and owner of economic rights in the invention may be other social entities as well, for example, an industrial sponsor.)

30. Recent impetus is given to this perspective by what is perceived as the galloping rate of technologisation, the size of commercial investment, the emergence of biotechnology as a major player, and the accelerated pace at which scientific research is becoming subject to proprietary interests (cf Nelkin 1984).

31. Bainbridge (1999: 349) quotes two commentators, the first to the effect that inventions are either new ways of producing something old or old ways of producing something new; the second to the effect that every invention is a 'new combination of pre-existing knowledge'. In itself, a single invention may also consist of several subinventions that are allowed together under the one patent as a substantive package.

32. 'The fact that [certain] material previously occurred in nature does not prevent it from being patented if it is isolated from its natural environment or produced by means of a technical process' (Bainbridge 1999: 378), interpreting Article 2 of the 1998 European Parliament and Council Directive on the legal protection of biotechnological inventions. There are differences here between European and American patent rights. Thus, in the United States, it is possible to obtain a patent for a new breed of animal (Bainbridge 1999: 377).

33. Among those with whom Küchler worked, the carver will have inherited his skill of carving along with knowledge of the magic to induce a vision of the image to be carved. He has already had the image described to him by the person in the clan responsible for producing the sculpture and what he is told will include not only this memory but also all of the modifications that current transactions require (1992: 103). Gunn (1987: 74) says it might be thirty years between acquiring rights and passing them on to be reproduced again by the next generation.

34. To follow the non-productionist locations of technology in Weiner's (2004) and Leach's (2004) debates with Gell.

35. This can be read as referring to an owner and carver; to a procreative couple who bear a child or to a localised kin grouping in which spouses will always have a distinct identity from one another so that no set of siblings replicates any other.

36. This contributes to Harrison's (1992: 235) argument about what is owned as intellectual property, not things but classes of things ('their images or typifications'). See Chapter Six.

37. Lincoln (1987: 34) puts this altogether more positively. A clan depleting its wealth when it pays for Malanggan is in effect converting money and labour into enduring prestige. Moreover, she adds, the ownership rights it has acquired, which 'will likely be resold, constitute a sort of semiliquid asset'.

38. However, Gunn (1987: 79–80) distinguishes two modus operandi on the Tabar Islands. Once a major series of Malanggan have been shown and transferred, the original owner cannot display that Malaggan again. This applies to Malanggan transferred across generations within the same clan or subclan. However, when rights to a single sculpture or motifs from a sculpture are transferred across group (e.g., from father to son in this matrilineal system), it is possible to allocate usage and

reproductive rights alone, with the owner retaining rights to his own ceremonies. Here we can say that the Malanggan is copied.

39. Unlike copyright (and design right), which comes into effect automatically on publication, patents have to be registered (designs may be), and there is no equivalent to such a process in this case. If one pursues these analogies, however, then more appropriate forms of intellectual property protection might be found in performers' rights or in the relatively new concept of design rights.

40. A point that is held to perplex some legal commentators: the law has brought a thing into existence and then at the end of a set term the thing winks out of existence (Phillips and Firth 1990: 24). Euro-Americans are also alleged to be mystified by the way in which so much effort goes into producing Malanggan when they are then so quickly destroyed or otherwise discarded.

41. The Patent Office holds specifications and abstracts for every British patent dating from 1617, more than two million inventions, and twenty-three million patent publications from overseas (Bainbridge 1999: 335). Population for population, it is conceivable that there have been almost as many northern New Ireland Malanggan as there have been British patents.

42. The figure of 5000 comes from Küchler (1992: 97) with reference to the period approximately 1870–1990; it not the whole output of course because many more will have been burnt or buried away from sight with the dead in caves (Gunn 1987: 74). Lincoln (1987: 40) gives the figure of 15 000 for all kinds of material culture objects from New Ireland (principally masks and sculptures) finding their way into European and American museums from the 1885–1914 German period alone. Some of this prodigious production, she speculates, must have been in response to outside demand. There have no doubt been cycles of productivity. Lincoln (1987: 39) suggests that the use of metal introduced into carving in the 1850s, and the experience of colonisation in general, stimulated the production of Malanggan.

43. And today, alongside other rights such as cultural property rights (Sykes 2004). The term *Malanggan* always included ceremonial and other events surrounding the revelation of the carving and, these days, New Irelanders may extend the term across a range of customary practices.

44. As Harrison (2000) reminds us, the dialectical relationship between invention and convention in Melanesian life, and how we attribute these values, is complicated (Wagner 1975). In the end, however, the Malanggan is an invention without innovation. Although each re-combination is freshly inspired, each individual element is also recalled from some other, the creation of entirely new images (through dreaming) being regarded as hazardous; there has been immense stability in the repertoire of forms over the years (Küchler 1987: 239).


CHAPTER 5: LOSING (OUT ON) INTELLECTUAL RESOURCES

1. Sources include Gewertz and Errington's (1999) commentary on both the preliminary hearing (June 1996) and the court's determination (February 1997); newspaper reports (Palme 1996; Dorney 1997), and notes from a seminar paper given to the Cambridge Social Anthropology Department in October 1996 by John Muke, who was to provide an affidavit to the court. Banks (2001) became available while this

was being revised. Miriam is quoted as saying that she found it embarrassing to be referred to as the *compo girl* (*Post Courier* 20 February 1997).

2. Either women for women, for example, through sister exchange, or women for wealth, as when marriages are arranged with bridewealth payments from the groom's to bride's kin; the transactions could be easily (mis)understood as implying a kind of commodity exchange. Anthropologists predicating their analysis on women exchanged as objects, one argument went, ran the risk of rendering them less than subjects in their own accounts (see Hirschon 1984).

3. As Gewertz and Errington also argue, with rather different intent. They discuss the case for the light it sheds on their thesis about new social differences (incipient class differences) springing up in Papua New Guinea. (These are based on middle class estimations of people's worth and life chances that drive a wedge between those with and without realistic monetary prospects.) Here, they argue, testimony came from a small handful of educated persons who spoke on behalf of others and who became arbiters and exemplars of 'reasonable' and 'ordinary' behaviour. As to the concept of person, I deploy this in the Papua New Guinea context in a manner somewhat analogous to the legal understanding of person: an entity elicited by relationships and thus by procedures that enact them (e.g., exchange transactions).

4. At that time, the Papua New Guinea *kina* was worth approximately £0.5 sterling, so that the amount here is some £10 000. For simplicity I use the tribal names for these patrilineal groupings, although the relevant units of action were clans or subclans from within the tribes (Tangilka Kumu Kanem and Konombuka Tau Kanem).

5. The PNG Constitution provides for the recognition of customary law (it can be argued in court as relevant fact) to the extent that it does not conflict with constitutional law, which includes the promulgation of several rights, or is not repugnant to the general principles of humanity. When the story was first exposed by the *Post Courier* (9 May 1996), and before ICRAF had laid their complaint, Justice Injia had initiated enquiries on the grounds that the National Court has the jurisdiction to itself bring action for the enforcement of constitutional/human rights.

6. That no specific partner had been identified was used on both sides, one to say that her freedom of choice was intact, the other that this could expose her to abuse. Note two contrasting incidents reported earlier by O'Hanlon and Frankland (1986: 189–90). In the first, a woman's personal choice of lover was retrospectively judged as satisfying a debt between two groups; in the second, a girl was marked in compensation, although no particular partner was designated for her, and she was dragged off against her wishes. O'Hanlon (personal communication) subsequently writes that Wahgi people sharply distinguish between love matches and forced marriages, *regardless* of the rubric under which the unions are classified.

7. This was the provocation of Clifford's (1988) argument apropos the Mashpee Indian land case. People laying claims were required to demonstrate pure cultural continuity.

8. To one ethnic society, Justice Injia said, the custom of head pay involving women may sound offensive although it may not be to the ethnic group practising it; the legislators of the constitution were thinking about a modern Papua New Guinea and about the 'promotion of good traditional customs and the discouragement and elimination of bad customs as seen from the eyes of an ordinary modern Papua New Guinean' (Gewertz and Errington 1999: 132).

9. With any argument that brings in slavery, we should remember that Euro-American moderns all know what slavery means (an assault on human dignity) and (following that knowledge) what their attitudes ought to be (it was a 'bad' custom); after all, historically speaking, its abolition was bound up with the very development of the notion of human rights. Invoked, it presents the strongest possible image of the inalienability of the person-body seen as an entire entity.

10. Unless we take the references to human beings as a background argument here, for example, as in the statement that a prime ethical consideration is to show respect 'for human beings and their bodies' (1995: 124, or 'human lives' and 'the human body', Chapter 6). By contrast, debates concerning the embryo invariably touch on concepts of personhood.

11. Except in marginal cases, such as surgeons' specimens. The traditional English view derives from, among other things, practices to do with disposal of corpses; the dead body lacking animation but potentially being able to be reunited with its soul was a kind of limiting case (intellectual resource) for thinking about living bodies. Human corpses as whole bodies cannot be property, although there is a duty to effect a decent burial and a corresponding right to possession for that purpose.

12. The report cites a case from Maryland in the United States, in which abandonment is taken as an alternative to a person's intent to assert 'his right of ownership, possession, or control over [bodily] material', as an example of 'a property approach'. It suggests that some English statutory language implies a property approach – it is the language 'of things, of property, of the reification of blood and body parts' (Nuffield Council 1995: 70). It also mentions the notorious *John Moore vs Regents of University of California* (1990, 13p 2d) case, in which Moore failed to lay claim to the profits of a cell line developed from his spleen because his claims to a property right failed. The equivocations are as notorious; the following comes from Rabinow (1996a: Chapter 7). The first (Superior Court) held that Moore's informed consent to medical procedures had released his detached spleen for the doctors to work on. The second (Court of Appeals) reversed the decision. The majority verdict was that surgically removed tissue was held to be the patient's 'tangible, private property'; without Moore's explicit permission, there had been a conversion – his property (cells and blood products) had been converted for someone else's profit. (A minority dissent argued against the application of private property principles without legislative guidance.) Finally, the Supreme Court argued that although U.S. law recognises a variety of interests in one's own body, it never created a property right in surgically removed parts. Because therapeutic tissue no longer supports the person's life, the law regarding its disposition must be that of community health; there was no interference with Moore's right of ownership or possession because he had no title in the first place. California statutes in relation to organs, blood, fetuses and so forth, deal with human biological materials as *res nullius* (as things but belonging to no one).

13. My comment. An example of a non-property gift would be 'the gift of life'.

14. A Canadian working paper on human tissue and organs (cited in Nuffield Council, 1995: 70–71) presented the traditional view that there is no property in the body against the view that those from whom tissue is removed have some claim to it, and resorts to consent for disposal as a way around the impasse. It thus cites a French ruling that frozen sperm was not property on grounds that human reproductive material was neither inheritable (!) nor an object of commerce. But it did recognise

a claim arising from the terms under which the sperm had been deposited in a sperm bank. 'In the name of dignity of the person, French law basically refuses the individual the right to dispose of his or her body and its parts; American law has allowed a greater latitude for proprietary and commercial relations concerning the body and person, privileging autonomy and value over an inherent and inalienable dignity' (Rabinow 1999: 93). Dignity rather than informed consent is at the basis of French law according to Pottage (1998: 745).

15. I feel comfortable about using the term 'thing' only because of the analytical support I can give it; in an abbreviated version, I take a different tack (Strathern 2000). Harrison (1992) deploys the concept of property in analysing Melanesian material while respecting the peculiarity of a gift as opposed to commodity economy. Interestingly, he avoids the person–thing distinction until right at the end of his article. Like black boxes, one suspects that such (partial) eliminations are basic to any exposition of complex data.

16. Politico-ritual, hereafter ritual, is an encompassing phrase for the public techniques through which a person is made (created, brought forth) to appear in a transformed state, including bridewealth and mortuary ceremonies or, in the past, initiation. In the Papua New Guinea context, it offers an analogue to legal intervention.

17. However many images it is also composed of. I am using Wagner's (1986) wonderful insight here; you can have an image of half a something but, logically and phenomenologically speaking, you cannot have half an image. A Melanesian take on Amazonian perspectivism (Viveiros de Castro 1998) might be to say that you can only own your own (not another's) relationship to another person.

18. For a summary of reificiation and personification, see Strathern (1999a: Chapter 1; 1988: 176–182). The term entification (Ernst 1999) has been introduced to draw attention to contemporary engagements with the political and legal processes of development that lead to people presenting themselves and their land as entities or units (see Hirsch 2000). I keep to reification as including indigenous modes of (aesthetic, formal) presentation.

19. A ritual exists as a shared thought–object, 'a piece of frozen, objectified social action, with all contingency and indeterminacy reduced to a minimum . . . to perform it is to try to express that pre-existing intellectual object in social action' (Harrison 1992: 235). He argues more generally, and beyond Melanesia, for seeing insignia, ceremonial and religious practices in this way.

20. Although my generic formulation is meant to be applicable across a range of Melanesian situations where people envisage what Euro-Americans might call the concept of a person as a person's image, I am particularly stimulated by de Coppet's (1994) account from the Solomon Islands. 'Are'are distinguish the body both from its animation and from its name or image.

21. Or the MB (mother's brother) as a root to the Zch (sister's child) as a 'cutting' (O'Hanlon and Frankland 1986: 185).

22. When relationships are made visible through things appearing in a specific form, we can refer to a person's relationships with others being embodied in an artefact, wealth item or whatever (hence the wealth accompanying Miriam as the 'bones' of the deceased man). Because the entire relationship between the two clans is summed up in those bones, the bones exist not as a part but as an entirety: *how the person now looks from the perspective of that relationship*. (The flesh and blood they helped

make come back to them in the form of bones; the classic reference here is Wagner 1977; see also Viveiros de Castro 1998a, b). Abstract as these formulations seem, they come from the analyses of ethographic data by many Melanesianists.

23. Or a surrogate, a classificatory granddaughter who could stand for such a person. The significant tie of descent here was from the ancestress to the man or men who bestowed the woman in marriage. O'Hanlon and Frankland (1986: 189) observe that at stake was less ensuring a marriage between partners already in a pre-existing relationship (as anthropologists have often analysed prescriptive marriage rules between cross-cousins) than meeting a debt created by a previous marriage. The debt might or might not be tied into death compensation payments; it could be settled by a man dispatching any girl whose marriage choice he controlled. However, such arrangements had to preserve the concept that the woman was acting as a third generational return ('granddaughter') for a woman previously given. Whoever occupied this role, genealogical surrogate or no, occupied a specific role (granddaughter) because of the specifity *of the grandmother* to whom the transaction referred. The return was not for any woman in the previous generation but for a particular female ancestress whose identifiable progeny bore concrete testimony to the fertility of her natal clan. (We do not know, says O'Hanlon [personal communication] whether Miriam had already been designated in this way, but the evidence suggests not.)

24. Recalling the question, prompted by the Nuffield Report, about why body parts continue to be called *parts* (in their detachability they are things without necessarily being commodities), we may say that it is the Melanesian person, as described here, who is in a state of perpetual detachability. The partible person is constituted in the process of detaching relations from relations. (On singular and plural, see Strathern 1988: Chapter 1. As to the conceptual distinction between person and agent: 'The person is construed from the vantage point of the relations that constitute him or her: she or he objectifies and is thus revealed in those relations. The agent is construed as the one who acts because of those relationships and is revealed in his or her actions' [1988: 273].)

25. My observation: her agency, manifest in her orientation toward these diverse kin, is not to be denigrated. Recall O'Hanlon's observation about free and forced marriages (n. 6). In itself, the 'skull in a netbag' arrangement is often a matter of retrospective classification if a match can be found to fit the bill; these are not 'remorseless customary practices which demand to be over-ridden by respect for individual autonomy' (personel communication). Jolly's (1996: 183) comments from Vanuatu add a qualification to the notion of tradition relevant to Miriam: 'human rights are not necessarily inconsistent with *kastom* (Bislama, 'tradition')...[and] tradition is not a static burden of the past but something created for the present'.

26. Although he criticises anthropologists who avoid universalisms and retreat into cultural relativities, Wilson acknowledges the out-of-date concept of culture that the critics of cultural relativism in turn often use. Yet, he argues, to insist on the relativism of cultural diversity, as he claims anthropologists often do, is to neglect both the forces of hybridisation and globalisation *and* a principal contemporary arena in which ideas about common humanity are voiced: human rights discourse. Where, he asks, have the anthropologists been in developing notions of common humanity?

27. For an exploration of this dilemma in a Melanesian context, see Jolly (1996); Banks' (2000) criminological perspective on cultural specificity is germane.

28. Many of the contributions (to Wilson 1997) address context – historical, social/ cultural, politico-economic – without exploring the issue of concrete relations. In respect of a murdered Guatamalan anthropologist, Wilson points out that none of the human rights reports deal with her (interpersonal) situation as a professional social researcher, nor was there any mention that her child was in the field. 'By disengaging an agent from their socio-historical circumstances, what we are left with is a universal decontextualised individual which is the basic unit of liberal political, economic and legal theory' (1997: 148). He contrasts this with the regular anthropological view: 'As opposed to a universal maximising individual with a natural set of rights, there are [in the anthropological view] social persons who are engaged in the making and remaking of complex interconnected social processes, and whose rights in those contexts are not natural, but are the results of historical struggles for power between persons and corporate groups' (1997: 148).

CHAPTER 6: DIVIDED ORIGINS AND THE ARITHMETIC OF OWNERSHIP

1. Understood as signs of 'overlap and intersection' (Barron 1998: 44). Note that Barron intervenes in a debate that asserts *either* that the author defined by copyright is a Romantic individual *or* that there is no connection at all. She argues that the connection is one of resemblance between different systems of practice, that is, a contingency. Sherman and Bently (1999, Chapter 2) draw out the role that ideas about creativity played in earlier developments of IPR, and argue that in pre-twentieth century IPR thinking the intangible was thought of not so much as a thing as an action or performance – the productive effort – embodied in material form (1999: 47–48). Insofar as it is arguable that this is still an element in contemporary thinking, the position of Davies and Naffine that I take up for its reading of an Euro-American approach is controversial. Finally, I would note the eloquent discussion of Aboriginal authenticity in 'art' and 'ownership' proffered by Myers (2004).

2. Or God owns them (but not another human being). This is a truncated, and democratised, version of a devolution of ideas that began with the patriarchal formula that there was only one self-owner, God's steward Adam, who owned all progeny. From what should have been evident in Chapter Five, I talk about ownership of 'persons' not 'bodies'; ideas about bodies are usefully analysed as contributing to different modes of being a person in the world. (It should be acknowledged that there is a strong sociological tradition that takes bodies as the primary entity [so that persons are whole bodies and body parts part bodies], summarised, for example, by Richardson and Turner [2002].)

3. This has been one of the running concerns of the PTC project (see Preface). The discussions by Blakeney (1995; 2000) and Weatherall (2001) deal with aspects of the Australian situation with reference to communal ownership.

4. The basis of the claims *and* the nature of the rights may differ; per contra, one can imagine different reasons for making a claim but similar rights of possession and disposal being conferred. The 'joint ownership' provisions in Euro-American property law are not helpful to the present case.

5. Given the role that such societies played in diverse earlier accounts of mine, this set of apparently contingent materials is a challenge (what counts as a group is a separate problem); Crook (in press) and Leach (2003) have been influential here. The present discussion does not observe the usual anthropological distinctions between kinship and clanship.

6. That does not mean that people's claims on one another are uniform. In talking about clan interests in the Australian case, Barron does an excellent job of pointing out how the exact rehearsal of someone's claims depends on diverse factors in their own life history, the reproductive stage they are at and allegiances they have elsewhere.

7. The sense in which persons inhabit different life-worlds is not a matter of where you are on a genealogical grid (Leach 2003); Pedersen (2001: 413) uses 'grid' to distinguish totemic difference from animist/perspectival relations.

8. Suckling can be a form of fathering too (Strathern 1988); the recursiveness of closed or finite perspectives is endless ([one set of] relations become metaphors for [another set of] relations).

9. Andrew Moutu (National Museum of Papua New Guinea) writes on ontology and on the limits of Euro-American epistemology in conceiving relations. However, as his own work was in progress when this was being written, I have avoided drawing on it directly and hope I do not trespass inadvertently. See Moutu 2003.

10. The stages are subject to transformation through ritual. Conversely, gender can be used to discriminate between stages of growth, as in rites that pass boys from one gendered state to another as their bodies grow. Astuti (2000: 93–4) comments on changing perspectives in Vezu, a cognatic/kindred based Madagascan society (where a person's reproductive stage is crucial to the world of kin groups and descendants he or she perceives).

11. Which in turn involves the suppression of some of what the parent passes on. In unilineal descent group systems, each of the parents, themselves made up of differentiated elements, passes on one of a pair of differences.

12. In sustaining a quadripartite structure to their kin universe so that a person always has four originary clans, the Mekeo have to de-conceive earlier unions in order to create fresh possibilities for new unions. Only then will a person's child also have four originary clans.

13. And to a criticism of the partible model of person that rests on the child recreating the relationship between parents (Strathern 1988), insofar as here the interest of one parent in the procreative outcome is actively eliminated (Rohatynskyj 1990: 437).

14. In addition to published work (1990, 1997), I draw on her contribution to the 2001 PTC conference (2001); permission to cite and quote from the written version is much appreciated.

15. Patrilateral cross-cousin marriage overcomes the asymmetry of residence; when it is followed, grandchildren replace the original grandparental sibling pair residing together in a locality (Rohatynskyj 1990: 439). *Anie* can also refer to local group (1997: 441).

16. The assumption is that by this point their grandfather will be deceased, or if not then nearly so (and in any case ancestral). Boys acquire the adult male power that at this point can damage women and children, even as contact with women's power would stunt the boys' growth, and their manifestations of fertility are generally dangerous for the opposite sex (Rohatynskyj 1990: 445; 1997: 443).

17. And vice versa. In Amazonian perspectivism, the departure of the body causes problems for living/dead identification; the dead, without body to see with, are no longer human (but for an important qualification, which introduces a difference of perspectives between human beings related to the deceased, see Vilaça [2000: 94]).

18. de Coppet (1981) describes how 'Are'are specifically detach the deceased's image from the body at its mortuary ceremony. Note that just as an Omie person acquires names, the land also has names, and a man learns about his land rights through learning the names of the totemic species *(ma'i ma'i)* that reside there. They advertise who has the right to work.

19. Note Hirsch (2000) on Fuyuge origin stories: the knowledge is not a representation but an instruction to the knowledge-holder to look after (caretake, nurture) the things, places and persons referred to in the myths.

20. Bolton (2003) offers a synthesis based on Vanuatu materials. Blakeney (2000: 251–2) observes that replacing *folklore* with *traditional knowledge* in the IPR deliberations 'significantly changes the discourse', from copyright-related concerns to patent law and biodiversity concerned with, for example, knowledge about the medicinal qualities of plants.

21. See Hirsch and Strathern (2004). In the draft Model Law for the Pacific, *traditional knowledge* covers all tradition-based innovations and creations, including literary, artistic and scientific works, along with names, symbols, information and such.

22. In the same way as the discourse of property, Brown (1998) argues, obscures or displaces what should be moral discussion on the implications of exposing Native people's sacred knowledge to unwarranted scrutiny.

23. People's interest in their futures goes alongside new ethnographic sensibilities about ownership of knowledge nurtured from two distinct sources: postcolonial critique and an IPR-sensitive world. For a robust criticism along these lines of my own research (and that of others) in Mt. Hagen, see Muke (2000).

24. A timeless statement to convey neither the imputation that it is only 'today', with commodification, that such things circulate nor the imputation that 'traditional' reasons for such circulation have lost all significance.

25. At the same time, the spirit is now lodged in another network of people and, hidden from view, people may dream of new designs or forms. 'Tamberan [spirit] songs are being innovated all the time' (Leach 2000: 69) and this includes the dreaming of new Tamberan, made public with the distribution of pork everyone can eat, that is, among the villagers who become its co-owners. Although an innovation may have a single creator, it is owned by the residential group, who would together be paid if it were transferred to another.

26. Growth or creativity, the time when people hatch innovations for the designs they own, come from experiences that occur out of public view. Leach contrasts this with the world of local business and marketing enterprises in this area where no one owns the innovations people try out, and everyone rushes to imitate other people's little inventions.

27. An analogue in Euro-American contexts might be conflicting demands on copyright as applying to something both individual and replicable (Sherman and Bently 1999: 55).

28. He writes that finding a suitable regulatory regime for 'indigenous cultural and intellectual property and traditional knowledge' can be enhanced if we separate the

issues relevant to a regime for the preservation of culture from those relevant to IPR protection. One reason Kalinoe offers for avoiding the IPR route in the protection of cultural property is because IPR brings things into the public eye. The limited restriction guaranteed by IPR protection is nothing compared to the long-term publication entailed when copyright (say) expires. He is discussing items identified with particular groups – perhaps secret property, not unlike the Tamberan songs described earlier – that should only be revealed under controlled conditions, for example when the moment for their reproduction is ripe. The public domain aspect of IPR causes problems for this kind of resource (Brown 1998; Brush 1999).

29. I draw on Küchler (1987, 1992, 1999); Lincoln (1987); Sykes (2004). Much of the phrasing in what follows comes directly from Küchler's various writings; Malanggan is also spelled Malangan. For a critical comment on emphasising display, see Küchler (2002: 170).

30. Küchler observes: 'names, as the carriers of a transcending body politic, are considered the property of the ancestral domain, are "found" and recollected through dreaming [prior to being reproduced] to be validated and transferred as images' (1999: 66). The named image that is the subject of such rights and that can be exchanged is what kin own of one another.

31. Figures or effigies ('skins') appear as material objects in a particular form, and once they have disappeared, what is retained is the memory of this form as an abstract image. Unless otherwise indicated from its context, *image* refers primarily to the latter. What is owned includes the capacity to turn such a memory into a realisation and make a new effigy (Küchler 1992: 105, 107).

32. To say it is held in the head (and mind) would already be a Euro-American perspective; to say body would already be a Melanesian view, in the most appropriate but still inadequate vocabulary the English language can offer.

33. They note that Radin's emphasis on property for personhood compels her to produce an alternative category ('fungible property') to cover property that is interchangeable with other things and exists largely for wealth creation. We can see this as a Romantic version of the legal assumption that the law makes possible rights of ownership and thereby the exchange of commodites by creating the individual as a bearer of rights, the starting point of Barron's (2002) re-examination of the legal properties of art.

34. In law, a necessary condition for dealing with the intangible, which must be turned into an object that 'can be incorporated in a commodity and subjected to the process of [commercial] exchange' of the kind with which the law deals (Barron 1998: 56). I have since read Barron (2002), which puts it all much more succinctly (e.g., her comment that copyright's requirement of embodiment or fixation means fixation in a thing; materialisation of work cannot be a human being as such).

35. This is why performers who make their bodies creative – in dance, song, athletics, acrobatics, sport – are, exactly, out of routine, are performers. I should add that throughout the discussion I have assumed that property is a relation (between persons, with respect to things). It is the concept of the 'thing' which is of interest here.

36. In the Malanggan case, Küchler (1999: 67) remarks that the names and imaged forms of Malanggan are produced out of a source (*wune*) that refers to an originary womb or water source, the template for the construction of an image (1992: 97); this source is transmitted at the same time as the image.

37. This is quite explicit. Elsewhere in the book I have noted that the current distinction in U.K. and European copyright between economic rights acquired through intellectual property protection and moral rights identifying the author as the originator of the work. Rights acquired through patenting may belong to any one of a number of owners of the scientific work that went into the invention, separate from the reputation that the inventors can acquire through scientific publishing.

38. Treating a fetus as part of the person (the mother) resolves the dilemma as to whether 'the woman or the foetus is the person' (2001: 91). A Melanesian response would point to the obvious, that she manifests the multiple embodiment that characterises all persons; persons are made up of persons.

39. Davies and Naffine (2001: 9) quote the observation that Western property is based on self-possession as a primordial property right, which grounds all others. This axiom holds whether or not the self-owning individual is given in the world (being ultimately owned by God, Locke) or has to fashion that condition out of it (through its own struggling, Hegel).

40. Most explicitly in structuralism, but with antecedents in comparative endeavours to classify kinship terminologies or group structures that stumbled on relations between relations.

41. Leach (e.g. 2003: 24, 195) observes of the Nekgini speakers of Madang Province that when they use kinship names, these usages are not classificatory or taxonomic but part of the process by which persons are made to appear, in the perception of others, as standing in a particular relationship to them and to one another.

42. This is not to rule out creativity. People may elaborate on sign switching, and indeed such switching runs throughout revelatory practices in Melanesia; a notable example is the Barok (Wagner 1987) demonstration that by changing positions one can make male appear female and old appear young. Reed (2003) offers a provocative present-day commentary on revelation and concealment.

43. Compare de Coppet 1985, and I may add Bamford (2004: 294) on Kamea. Australian precedents lie in Aboriginal land claims (Barron 1998: 52–3) such as this. The courts had to confront the fact that people may relate to land *either* as members of a territorial band *or* as members of a clan that has its sacred imprint on the landscape. Neither together nor apart do the claims add up to property in the legal sense. They are two ways of being, a position the court came close to endorsing in interpreting them as two entities with different spheres of activity ('economic' and 'spiritual'). The judge could also have been drawing inspiration from the Torrens system of land registration in Australia, by which title relates not to an owner's various holdings but to a holding's various owners (Riles 2003).

44. Under the auspices of UNESCO and WIPO: a Model Law for the Protection of Traditional Knowledge and Expressions of Culture in the Pacific Islands. At the time of Simet's observations, it was being discussed at various fora, including the South Pacific Commission (e.g., Kalinoe 2001); it has since been partially adopted.

45. Indigenous systems, the principal architect of the Model Law (Puri 2002) opines, 'are driven by characteristics of trans-generational, non-materialistic, and non-exclusive or communal ownership of rights', which make IPR inappropriate. (For a critique, Hirsch and Strathern 2004.) Nonetheless, the Model Law deliberately uses the term *property* in accord with international usage, thus conferring a 'property right' on

those who own traditional knowledge and expressions of culture and seeks to have 'true owners' identifiable in each case.

46. The Model Law is based on an explicit objection to Western forms of private property, and regards the Pacific counterpart as communal property. Notes (from a draft) appropriately observe that rights over a work of art are generally distributed over several individuals or groups of individuals but then interprets the relevant subject of traditional ownership as a group or community. Hence under 'collective ownership' it is noted that 'property rights in traditional knowledge and expressions of culture can vest only in a group, clan or community of Pacific Islanders' or 'ownership and control over the reproduction of works is vested in the group, clan or community'. Simet (2000) wishes to make a strong distinction between a community as a kind of public domain in which certain types of knowledge circulate on a non-exclusive basis and clans or groups that assert exclusive claims, as may individuals. But, in Simet's view, exclusive access does not mean that the clan or group has control over all its property: aspects of *its* property may be under the control of *others* (non-members) who act as custodians or guardians of it.

47. In this matrilineal system the relevant non-members are children born to male members of a clan. The reproductive model is evident here (and is mirrored in rules of exogamy; a clan is not auto-fertile but depends on other clans for its spouses). Tolai land usage repeats the division, between the 'owners' of land and the 'custodians' of the history associated with it that is in the safe keeping of non-owner children.

# References

Alderson, Priscilla. 2002. The new genetics: Promise or threat to children? *Bulletin of Medical Ethics* 176: 13–18.

Arnold, Richard. 1990. *Performers' rights and recording rights: UK law under the Performers' Protection Act 1958–72 and the Copyright, Designs and Patents Act 1988*. Oxford: ESC Publishing Ltd.

Astuti, Rita. 1995. *People of the sea: Identity and descent among the Vezo of Madagascar*. Cambridge: Cambridge University Press.

Astuti, Rita. 2000. Kindreds and descent groups: New perspectives from Madagascar, in *Cultures of relatedness: New approaches to the study of kinship*, edited by Janet Carsten. Cambridge: Cambridge University Press.

Augé, Marc. 1995. *Non-places: Introduction to an anthropology of supermodernity*. London: Verso.

Bainbridge, David. 1992. *Software copyright law*. London: Pitman.

Bainbridge, David. 1999. *Intellectual property*. 4th ed. London: Financial Times Management and Pitman Publishing.

Bamford, Sandra. 2004. Conceiving relatedness: non-substantial relations among the Kamea of Papua New Guinea. *JRAI (Journal of Royal Anthropological Institute)* (NS) 10: 287–306.

Banks, Cyndi. 2000. *Developing cultural criminology: Theory and practice in Papua New Guinea*. Sydney, Australia: Sydney Institute of Criminology.

Banks, Cyndi. 2001. Women, justice and custom: The discourse of 'good custom' and 'bad custom' in Papua New Guinea and Canada. *International Journal of Comparative Sociology* 42: 101–22.

Barron, Anne. 1998. No other law? Author-ity, property and Aboriginal art, in *Intellectual property and ethics*, edited by Lionel Bently and Spyros Maniatis. London: Sweet and Maxwell.

Barron, Anne. 2002. The (legal) properties of art. UCL/Birkbeck conference, *Marxism and the Visual Arts now*. London.

Barry, Andrew. 2001. *Political machines: Governing a technological society*. London: Athlone Press.

Barthes, Roland. 1977. *Image-music-text*, translated by S. Heath. New York: Hill & Wang.

Barthes, Roland. 1986. *The rustle of language*. Translated by R. Howard. New York: Hill and Wang.

Battaglia, Debbora. 1990. *On the bones of the serpent: Person, memory and mortality among the Sabarl Islanders of Papua New Guinea.* Chicago: University of Chicago Press.

Battaglia, Debbora. 1995. On practical nostalgia: Self-prospecting among urban Trobrianders, in *Rhetorics of self-making,* edited by Debbora Battaglia. Los Angeles: University of California Press.

Battaglia, Debbora. 1999. Towards an ethics of the open subject: Writing culture in good conscience, in *Anthropological theory today,* edited by Henrietta Moore. Cambridge: Polity Press.

Beer, Gillian. 1983. *Darwin's plots: Evolutionary narrative in Darwin, George Eliot and nineteenth century fiction,* London: Routledge and Kegan Paul.

Beer, Gillian. 1996. *Open fields: Science in cultural encounter.* Oxford: Clarendon Press.

Bell, Vikki. 2001. The phone, the father and other becomings: On households (and theories) that no longer hold. *Cultural Values* 5: 383–402.

Berg, Paul, David Baltimore, Sydney Brenner, Richard O. Roblin III, and Maxine Singer. 2002. Summary statement of the Asilomar conference on recombinant DNA molecules (1975), in *The ethical dimensions of the biological and health sciences.* 2nd ed., edited by Ruth Bulger, Elizabeth Heitman, and Stanley Reiser. Cambridge: Cambridge University Press.

Biagioli, Mario. 1998. The instability of authorship: credit and responsibility in contemporary biomedicine. Life Sciences Forum. The Federation of American Societies for Experimental Biology: *The FASEB, Journal* 12: 3–16.

Biagioli, Mario. 2003. Rights or rewards? Changing frameworks of scientific authorship, in *Scientific authorship: Credit and intellectual property in science,* edited by Mario Biagioli and Peter Galison. New York: Routledge.

Biagioli, Mario. In prep. Scientists' names as documents, in *Documents: Artefacts of modern knowledge,* edited by Annelise Riles.

Biagioli, Mario, and Peter Galison, eds. 2003. *Scientific authorship: Credit and intellectual property in science.* New York: Routledge.

Blakeney, Michael. 1995. Protecting expressions of Australian Aboriginal folklore under copyright law. *European Intellectual Property Review* 9: 442–45.

Blakeney, Michael. 2000. The protection of traditional knowledge under intellectual property law. *European Intellectual Property Review* 6: 251–261.

Bodrogi, Tibor. 1987. New Ireland art in cultural context, in *Assemblage of spirits: Idea and image in New Ireland,* edited by Louise Lincoln. New York: George Braziller, in association with the Minneapolis Institute of Arts.

Bolton, Lissant. 2003. *Unfolding the moon: Enacting women's custom in Vanuatu.* Honolulu: University of Hawai'i Press.

Bonaccorso, Monica. 2000. The traffic in kinship: Assisted conception for heterosexual infertile couples and lesbian-gay couples in Italy, PhD dissertation, Cambridge University.

Bouquet, Mary. 1993. *Reclaiming English kinship: Portuguese refractions of English kinship.* Manchester: Manchester University Press.

Brazier, Margaret, Sara Fovargue, and Marie Fox, eds. 2000. Reproductive choice and control of fertility. *Report for Commission of European Communities, Biomedical and Health Research Programme (Biomed 2),* Manchester: Centre for Social Ethics and Policy.

Brown, Michael. 1998. Can culture be copyrighted? *Current Anthropology* 39: 193–222.

Brown, Michael. 2003. *Who owns Native culture?* Cambridge, Mass.: Harvard University Press.

Brush, Stephen. 1999. Bioprospecting in the public domain. *Cultural Anthropology* 14: 535–55.

Butler, Judith. 2000. *Antigone's claim: Kinship between life and death.* New York: Columbia University Press.

California Supreme Court. 1993. *Anna Johnson v. Mark Calvert et al.* (851 P.2d 776–800).

California Court of Appeal. 1998. *In re the marriage of John A. Buzzanca and Luanne H. Buzzanca* (72 Cal. Rptr. 2d 280).

Callon, Michel. 1986. Some elements of a sociology of translation: domestication of the scallops and the fishermen of St Brieuc Bay, in *Power, action and belief: A new sociology of knowledge*, edited by John Law. London: Routledge.

Carsten, Janet. 2004. *After kinship.* Cambridge: Cambridge University Press.

Casey, Edward. 1996. How to get from space to place a fairly short stretch of time: Phenomenological prolegomena, in *Sense of place*, edited by Stephen Feld and Keith Basso. Santa Fe: School of American Research Press.

Chambers, Robert. 1969 [1844]. *Vestiges of the natural history of creation*, London.

Clifford, James. 1988. *The predicament of culture: Twentieth century ethnography, literature and art.* Cambridge, Mass: Harvard University Press.

Coombe, Rosemary. 1998. *The cultural life of intellectual properties: Authorship, appropriation and the law.* Durham, NC: Duke University Press.

Corrigan, Oonagh. 2004. Informed consent: The contradictory ethical safeguards in pharmacogenetics, in *Donating and exploiting DNA: Social and ethical aspects of public participation in genetic databases*, edited by Richard Tutton and Oonagh Corrigan. New York: Routledge.

Corsín Jiménez, Alberto. 2004. The form of the relation, or anthropology's enchantment with the algebraic imagination. Manchester: University of Manchester. Manuscript.

Crook, Tony. 1999. Growing knowledge in Bolivip, Papua New Guinea. *Oceania* 69: 225–42.

Crook, Tony. 2003. After the relation. Presentation at AAA panel, *Towards an anthropology of uncertain moments*, convened by Iris Jean-Klein and Annelise Riles, Chicago.

Crook, Tony. 2004. Transactions in perpetual motion, in *Transactions and creations: Property debates and the stimulus of Melanesia*, edited by Eric Hirsch and Marilyn Strathern. Oxford: Berghahn.

Crook, Tony. In press. *Kim kurukuru: An anthropological exchange with Bolivip, Papua New Guinea.* London: British Academy Publications.

Cummins, Jim. 2002. Unresolved and basic problems in assisted reproductive technology, in *Assisted reproductive technology: Accomplishments and new horizons*, edited by Christopher De Jonge and Christopher Barratt. Cambridge: Cambridge University Press.

Davies, Margaret, and Ngaire Naffine. 2001. *Are persons property? Legal debates about property and personality.* Aldershot: Ashgate/Dartmouth.

de Coppet, Daniel. 1981. The life-giving death, in *Mortality and immortality: The anthropology and archaeology of death*, edited by Sally Humphrey and Helen King. London: Academic Press.

de Coppet, Daniel. 1985. Land owns people, in *Contexts and levels: Anthropological essays on hierarchy*, edited by Robert Barnes, Daniel de Coppet, and Robert Parkin. Oxford: JASO.

de Coppet, Daniel. 1994. 'Are'are, in *Of relations and the dead: Four societies viewed from the angle of their exchange*, edited by Cecile Barraud, André Iteanu, and Raymond Jamous, translated by S. Suffern. Oxford: Berg.

Demian, Melissa. 2001. Claims without rights: Stable objects and transient owners in Suau, presented to panel, Intellectual and Cultural Property Rights, at *Rights, Claims and Entitlements*, ASA conference, Sussex.

Demian, Melissa. 2004. Seeing, knowing, owning: Property claims as revelatory acts, in *Transactions and creations: Property debates and the stimulus of Melanesia*, edited by Eric Hirsch and Marilyn Strathern. Oxford: Berghahn.

Descombes, Vincent. 2000. The philosophy of collective representations. *History of the Human Sciences* 13: 37–49 (translated by A. C. Pugh).

Dolgin, Janet. 1990. Just a gene: Judicial assumptions about parenthood. *UCLA Law Review* 40: 637–94.

Dolgin, Janet. 1997. *Defining the family: Law, technology and reproduction in an uneasy age*. New York: New York University Press.

Dolgin, Janet. 2000. Choice, tradition, and the new genetics: The fragmentation of the ideology of family. *Connecticut Law Review* 32: 523–66.

Dolgin, Janet. 2002. The constitution as family arbiter: A moral in a mess? *Columbia Law Review* 102: 337–407.

Dorney, Sean. 14 February 1997. The constitution, change and custom – Miriam wins. Port Moresby: *The Independent*.

Eco, Umberto. 1995. *The island of the day before*, trans. W. Weaver. London: Secker and Warburg.

Edwards, Jeanette. 1999. Explicit connections: Ethnographic enquiry in north-west England, in *Technologies of procreation: Kinship in the age of assisted conception*, by Jeanette Edwards, Sarah Franklin, Eric Hirsch, Frances Price, and Marilyn Strathern. 2d ed. London: Routledge.

Edwards, Jeanette. 2000. *Born and bred: Idioms of kinship and new reproductive technologies in England*. Oxford: Oxford University Press.

Edwards, Jeanette, Sarah Franklin, Eric Hirsch, Frances Price, and Marilyn Strathern. 1999. *Technologies of procreation: Kinship in the age of assisted conception*, 2d ed. London: Routledge.

Edwards, Jeanette, and Marilyn Strathern. 2000. Including our own, in *Cultures of relatedness: New approaches to the study of kinship*, edited by Janet Carsten. Cambridge: Cambridge University Press.

Ernst, Thomas. 1999. Land, stories, and resources: Discourse and entification in Onabasalu modernity. *American Anthropologist*, 101: 88–97.

Fara, Patricia. 2003. *Sex, botany and empire: The story of Carl Linnaeus and Joseph Banks*. Cambridge: Icon Books Ltd.

Feld, Steven, and Keith Basso, eds. 1996. *Sense of place*. Santa Fe: School of American Research Press.

Finkler, Kaja. 2000. *Experiencing the new genetics: Family and kinship on the medical frontier*. Philadelphia: University of Pennsylvania Press.

Foucault, Michel. 1970. *The order of things: An archaeology of the human sciences*, translated. London: Routledge.

Foucault, Michel. 1972. *The archaeology of knowledge*, translated by A. M. Sheridan Smith. London: Routledge.

Fox Keller, Evelyn. 1992. *Secrets of life, secrets of death: Essays on language, gender, and science*. New York: Routledge.

Fox Keller, Evelyn. 2000. *The century of the gene*. Cambridge, Mass.: Harvard University Press.

Fox, Robin. 1993. *Reproduction and succession: Studies in anthropology, law and society*. New Brunswick: Transaction Publishers.

Franklin, Sarah. 2001a. Biologization revisited: Kinship theory in the context of the new biologies, in *Relative values: Reconfiguring kinship studies*, edited by Sarah Franklin and Susan McKinnon. Durham, NC: Duke University Press.

Franklin, Sarah. 2001b. Culturing biology: Cell lines for the second millennium. *Health* 5: 335–54.

Franklin, Sarah. 2003. Re-thinking nature – culture: Anthropology and the new genetics. *Anthropological Theory* 3: 65–85.

Franklin, Sarah, and Susan McKinnon, eds. 2001. *Relative values: Reconfiguring kinship studies*. London: Duke University Press.

Gatens, Moira. 2002. The politics of 'presence' and 'difference': Working through Spinoza and Eliot, in *Visible women: Essays on feminist legal theory and political philosphy*, edited by Susan James and Stephanie Palmer. Oxford: Hart Publishing.

Gell, Alfred. 1998. *Art and agency: An anthropological theory*. Oxford: Clarendon Press.

Gell, Alfred. 1999a. Strathernograms, in *The art of anthropology: Essays and diagrams*, edited by Eric Hirsch. London: Athlone.

Gell, Alfred. 1999b. The technology of enchantment and the enchantment of technology, in *The art of anthropology: Essays and diagrams*, edited by Eric Hirsch. London: Athlone.

Gewertz, Deborah, and Frederick Errington. 1999. *Emerging class in Papua New Guinea: The telling of a difference*. Cambridge: Cambridge University Press.

Gibbons, Michael. 1999. Science's new social contract with society. *Nature* 402 (Supplement): C81–4.

Gilbert, Margaret. 1989. *On social facts*. London: Routledge and Kegan Paul.

Gilbert, Sandra M., and Susan Gubar. 1979. *The madwoman in the attic: The woman writer and the nineteenth-century literary imagination*. New Haven: Yale University Press.

Godelier, Maurice. 1986. Generation and comprehension of human relationships and the evolution of society. Herbert Spencer Lecture. Oxford: Oxford University. Mimeograph.

Gray, Kevin. 1991. Property in thin air. *Cambridge Law Journal* 50: 252–307.

Gunn, Michael. 1987. The transfer of Malagan ownership on Tabar, in *Assemblage of spirits: Idea and image in New Ireland*, edited by Louise Lincoln. New York: George Braziller, in association with the Minneapolis Institute of Arts.

Haimes, Erica. 1990. Recreating the family? Policy considerations relating to the 'new' reproductive technologies, in *The new reproductive technologies*, edited by Maureen McNeil, Ian Varvoe and Steven Yearley. London: Macmillan.

Haimes, Erica. 1992. Gamete donation and the social management of genetic origins, in *Changing human reproduction: Social science perspectives*, edited by Margaret Stacey. London: Sage.

Handler, Richard, and Daniel Segal. 1990. *Jane Austen and the fiction of culture*. Tucson: University of Arizona Press.

Haraway, Donna. 1997. *Modest_witness@second_millennium.femaleman(c)_meets oncomouse [tm]: Feminism and technoscience*. New York: Routledge.

Harrison, Simon. 1992. Ritual as intellectual property. *Man* (NS) 27: 225–44.

Harrison, Simon. 1995. Anthropological perspectives on the management of knowledge. *Anthropology Today* 11 : 10–14.

Harrison, Simon. 2000. From prestige goods to legacies: Property and the objectification of culture in Melanesia. *Comparative Studies in Society and History* 42: 662–79.

Harvey, Penelope. 1997. Introduction: Technology as skilled practice, *Social Analysis* (*Technology as skilled practice*), special issue edited by Penelope Harvey. 41: 3–14.

Hayden, Corinne. 1995. Gender, genetics and generation: Reformulating biology in lesbian kinship. *Cultural Anthropology* 10: 41–63.

Hayden, Corinne. 2003. Presumptions of interest, in *When nature goes public: The making and unmaking of bioprospecting in Mexico*, Princeton: Princeton University Press.

Helmreich, Stefan. 1998. *Silicon second nature: Culturing artifical life in a digital world*. Los Angeles: University of California Press.

Helmreich, Stefan. 2002. Comment on Gísli Pálsson and Kristín Harðardóttir, For whom the cell tolls: Debates about biomedicine. *Current Anthropology* 43: 289–90.

Heintze, Dieter. 1987. On trying to understand some Malangans, in *Assemblage of spirits: Idea and image in New Ireland*, edited by Louise Lincoln. New York: George Braziller, in association with the Minneapolis Institute of Arts.

Herring, Jonathan. 2002. Giving, selling and sharing bodies, in *Body lore and laws*, edited by Andrew Bainham, Shelly Day Sclater, and Martin Richards. Oxford: Hart Publishing.

HGAC (Human Genetics Advisory Commission) and HFEA (Human Fertilisation and Embryology Authority). 1998. *Cloning issues in reproduction, science and medicine: A report*. London: HGAC and HFEA.

HGC (Human Genetics Commission, UK). 2000. *Whose hands on your genes? A discussion document on the storage, protection and use of personal genetic information*. London: Department of Health.

HGC (Human Genetics Commission, UK). 2002. *Inside information: Balancing interests in the use of personal genetic data, A Report*. London: Department of Health.

Hirsch, Eric. 1995. The 'holding together' of ritual: Ancestrality and achievement in the Papua Highlands, in *Society and cosmos: Their interrelation or their coalescence in Melanesia*, edited by Daniel de Coppet and André Iteanu. Oxford: Berg.

Hirsch, Eric. 1999. Colonial units and ritual units: Historical transformations of persons and horizons in Highland Papua. *Comparative Studies in Society and History* 41 : 805–28.

Hirsch, Eric. 2000. Mining boundaries and local land narratives in Central Province, in *Rationales of ownership*, edited by Lawrence Kalinoe and James Leach. New Delhi: UBS Publishers' Distributors Ltd.

Hirsch, Eric. 2001. Making up people in Papua. *Journal of the Royal Anthropological Institute*. (N.S.) 7: 241–56.

Hirsch, Eric. 2004. Boundaries of creation: The work of credibility in science and ceremony, in *Transactions and creations: Property debates and the stimulus of Melanesia*. edited by Eric Hirsch and Marilyn Strathern. Oxford: Berghahn.

Hirsch, Eric, and Marilyn Strathern, eds. 2004. *Transactions and creations: Property debates and the stimulus of Melanesia*. Oxford: Berghahn.

Hirschon, Renée, ed. 1984. *Women and property, women as property*. London: Croom Helm.

Houseman, Michael. 1988. Towards a complex model of parenthood: Two African tales. *American Ethnologist* 15: 658–77.

Hume, David. 1748. An inquiry concerning human understanding, reprinted in collection, *Essays, literary, moral, and political* 3rd ed. World Library Edition, London: Ward, Locke and Co.

ICSU (International Council for Science). 2003. The rights and responsibilities of science and society: Defining the future role for ICSU. Paris: Background document for discussion. (Manuscript).

Ingold, Tim. 1988. Tools, minds and machines: An excursion into the philosophy of technology. *Techniques et Culture* 12: 151–76.

Ingold, Tim. 1995. Building, dwelling, living: How animals and people make themselves at home in the world, in *Shifting contexts: Transformations in anthropological knowledge*, ASA Decennial Conference series, edited by Marilyn Stathern. London: Routledge.

Ingold, Tim. 1997. Eight themes in the anthropology of technology, *Social Analysis (Technology as skilled practice)*, special issue edited by Panelope Harvey, no. 41.

Irish, Vivien, ed. 1991. *Intellectual property: A manager's guide*. London: McGraw Hill.

Israel, Jonathan. 2001. *Radical enlightenment: Philosophy and the making of modernity, 1650–1750*. Oxford: Oxford University Press.

James, Susan. 1997. *Passion and action: The emotions in seventeenth century philosophy*. Oxford: Clarendon Press.

James, Susan, and Stephanie Palmer, eds. 2002. *Visible women: Essays on feminist legal theory and political philosphy*. Oxford: Hart Publishing.

Jaszi, Peter. 1994. On the author effect: Contemporary copyright and collective creativity, in *The construction of authorship: Textual appropriation in law and literature*, edited by Martha Woodmansee and Peter Jaszi. Durham, NC: Duke University Press.

Jolly, Margaret. 1996. Woman ikat raet long human raet o no? Women's rights, human right and domestic violence in Vanuatu. *Feminist Review* 52: 169–90.

Jordanova, Ludmilla. 1995. Interrogating the concept of reproduction in the eighteenth century, in *Conceiving the new world order: The global politics of reproduction*, edited by Faye Ginsburg and Rayna Rapp. Los Angeles: California University Press.

Jorgensen, Joseph. 1979. Cross-cultural comparison. *Annual Review of Anthropology* 8: 309–31.

Josephides, Lisette. 2003. The rights of being human, in *Human rights in global perspective: Anthropological studies in rights, claims and entitlements*, edited by Richard Wilson and John Mitchell. London: Routledge.

Kalinoe, Lawrence. 2000. Ascertaining the nature of indigenous intellectual and cultural property and traditional knowedge and the search for legal options in regulating access in Papua New Guinea. Presented to PTC Colloquium, *Intergenerational and intergender transactions.* Cambridge.

Kalinoe, Lawrence. 2001. Expressions of culture: A cultural perspective from Papua New Guinea, presented to *Intellectual Property, Genetic Resources and Traditional Knowledge*, WIPO Sub-Regional Workshop, Brisbane.

Kalinoe, Lawrence. 2004. Traditional knowledge and legal options for the regulation of intellectual and cultural property in Papua New Guinea, in *Transactions and creations: Property debates and the stimulus of Melanesia*, edited by Eric Hirsch and Marilyn Strathern. Oxford: Berghahn.

Kalinoe, Lawrence, and James Leach, eds. 2000. *Rationales of ownership: Ethnographic studies of transactions and claims to ownership in contemporary Papua New Guinea.* New Delhi: UBS Publishers' Distributors Ltd.

Karpin, Isabel. 1992. Legislating the female body: Reproductive technology and the re-constructed woman. *Columbia Journal of Gender and Law* 3: 325–49.

Karpin, Isabel. 1994. Reimagining maternal selfhood: Transgressing body boundaries and the law. *The Australian Feminist Law Journal*, 36.

Khalil, Mohamed. 1995. Biodiversity and the conservation of medicinal plants: Issues from the perspective of the developing world, in *Intellectual property rights and bio-diversity conservation: An interdisciplinary analysis of the values of medicinal plants*, edited by Timothy Swanson. Cambridge: Cambridge University Press.

Kirsch, Stuart. 2001. Lost worlds: Environmental disaster, 'culture loss', and the law. *Current Anthropology* 42: 167–98 [with commentary].

Konrad, Monica. 1998. Ova donation and symbols of substance: some variations in the theme of sex, gender and the partible person. *Journal of the Royal Anthropological Institute* (NS) 4: 643–67.

Konrad, Monica. 2005. *Nameless Relations: Anonymity, Melanesia and Reproductive Gift Exchange between British ova donors and recipients.* Oxford: Berghahn.

Küchler, Susanne. 1987. Malangan: Art and memory in a Melanesian society. *Man* (NS) 22: 238–55.

Küchler, Susanne. 1988. Malangan: Objects, sacrifice and the production of memory. *American Ethnologist* 15: 625–37.

Küchler, Susanne. 1992. Making skins: Malangan and the idiom of kinship in New Ireland, in *Anthropology, art and aesthetics*, edited by Jeremy Coote and Anthony Shelton. Oxford: Clarendon Press.

Küchler, Susanne. 1999. The place of memory, in *The art of forgetting*, edited by Adrian Forty and Susanne Küchler. Oxford: Berg.

Küchler, Susanne. 2002. *Malanggan: Art, memory and sacrifice.* Oxford: Berg.

Latour, Bruno. 1986. Visualization and cognition: Thinking with eyes and hands. *Knowl-edge and society: Studies in the sociology of culture past and present* 6: 1–40.

Latour, Bruno. 1993. *We have never been modern*, translated by C. Porter. London: Harvester Wheatsheaf.

Laurie, Graeme. 2002. *Genetic privacy: A challenge to medico-legal norms.* Cambridge: Cambridge University Press.

Law, John. 1994. *Organizing modernity.* Oxford: Blackwell.

Law, John, and John Hassard. 1999. *Actor network theory and after.* London: Routledge.

Leach, Edmund. 1976. Social anthropology: A natural science of society? The Radcliffe-Brown Lecture, London: The British Academy.

Leach, James. 2000. Multiple expectations of ownership. *Melanesian Law Journal* 27: 63–76.

Leach, James. 2002. Drum and voice: Aesthetics, technology, and social process on the Rai coast of Papua New Guinea. *Journal of the Royal Anthropological Institute* (NS) 8: 713–34.

Leach, James. 2003. *Creative land: Place and procreation on the North Coast of Papua New Guinea.* Oxford: Berghahn Books.

Leach, James. 2004. Modes of creativity, in *Transactions and creations: Property debates and the stimulus of Melanesia,* edited by Eric Hirsch and Marilyn Strathern. Oxford: Berghahn.

Lewis, Philip. 1969. The social context of art in Northern New Ireland. *Fieldiana: Anthropology* 58, Chicago: Field Museum of Natural History.

Lincoln, Louise. 1987. Art and money in New Ireland, in *Assemblage of spirits: Idea and image in New Ireland,* edited by Louise Lincoln. New York: George Braziller, in association with the Minneapolis Institute of Arts.

Lipset, David, and Jolene Stritecky. 1994. The problem of mute metaphor: Gender and kinship in seaboard Melanesia. *Ethnology* 33: 1–20.

Locke, John. 1690. *An essay concerning human understanding.* World Library Edition, London: Ward, Lock and Co.

Lundin, Susanne, and Malin Ideland. 1997. *Gene technology and the public: An interdisciplinary perspective.* Lund: Nordic Academic Press.

Macfarlane, Alan. 1986. *Marriage and love in England, 1300–1840.* Oxford: Basil Blackwell.

Macfarlane, Alan. 1998. The mystery of property: Inheritance and industrialization in England and Japan, in *Property relations: Renewing the anthropological tradition,* edited by Christopher Hann. Cambridge: Cambridge University Press.

MacIntyre, Alasdair. 1999. *Dependent rational animals: Why human beings need the virtues.* London: Duckworth.

Melzer, David, Ann Raven, Don Detmer, Tom Ling, and Ron Zimmern. 2003. *My very own medicine: What must I know?* Cambridge: Department of Health and Primary Care, Cambridge University.

McKinnon, Susan. 2001. The economies in kinship and the paternity of culture: Origin stories in kinship theory, in *Relative values: Reconfiguring kinship studies,* edited by Sarah Franklin and Susan McKinnon. Durham, N.C.: Duke University Press.

McPherson, Crawford Brough. 1962. *The political theory of possessive individualism: Hobbes to Locke.* Oxford: Clarendon Press.

Miller, Daniel. 1995. Introduction: Anthropology, modernity and consumption, in *Worlds apart: Modernity through the prism of the local,* edited by Daniel Miller. ASA Decennial Conference series. London: Routledge.

Miller, Daniel. 1997. How infants grow mothers in North London. *Theory, Culture and Society* 14: 67–88.

Miller, Daniel. 2000. The fame of Trinis: Websites as traps *Journal of Material Culture* 5: 5–24.

Minnegal, M., and P. Dwyer. 1997. Women, pigs, god and evolution: Social and economic change among Kubo people of Papua New Guinea. *Oceania* 68: 47–60.

Mitterauer, Michael, and Reinhard Sieder. 1977. *The European family: Patriarchy to partnership from the middle ages to the present*, translated by K. Oosterveen and M. Hörzinger. Oxford: Basil Blackwell.

Moore, Henrietta. 1996. The changing nature of anthropological knowledge: an introduction, in *The future of anthropological knowledge*, edited by H. Moore. London: Routledge.

Morgan, Derek. 1994. A surrogacy issue: Who is the other mother? *International Journal of Law and the Family* 8: 386–412.

Morphy, Howard. 1991. *Ancestral connections*. Chicago: University of Chicago Press.

Mosko, Mark. 1983. Conception, de-conception and social structure in Bush Mekeo culture. *Mankind* 14: 24–32.

Mosko, Mark. 1985. *Quadripartite structures: Categories, relations and homologies in Bush Mekeo Culture*. Cambridge: Cambridge University Press.

Mosko, Mark, and Fred Damon, eds. In press. *On the order of 'chaos': Social anthropology and the science of chaos*. Oxford: Berghahn.

Moutu, Andrew. 2003. *Names are thicker than blood: Concepts of ownership and person among the Iatmul*. Doctoral dissertation, Cambridge University.

Muke, John. 1996. The case of the Compo Girl: Kinship on trial. Paper presented to the Department of Social Anthropology, Cambridge University.

Muke, John. 2000. Ownership of ideas and things: A case study of the politics of the Kuk prehistoric site, in *Protection of intellectual, biological and cultural property in Papua New Guinea*, edited by Kathy Whimp and Mark Busse. Canberra (Australia): Asia Pacific Press.

Mulkay, Michael. 1997. *The embryo research debate: Science and the politics of reproduction*. Cambridge: Cambridge University Press.

Myers, Fred. 2004. Ontologies of the image and economies of exchange. *American Ethnologist* 31: 5–20.

Naffine, Ngaire. 2002. Can women be legal persons?, in *Visible women: Essays on feminist legal theory and political philosphy*, edited by Susan James and Stephanie Palmer. Oxford: Hart Publishing.

Nelkin, Dorothy. 1984. *Science as intellectual property*. New York: Macmillan.

Nelkin, Dorothy. 1996. The social dynamics of genetic testing: The case of fragile X. *Medical Anthropology Quarterly* 10: 537–50.

Nelkin, Dorothy, and Lois Andrews. 1998. Whose body is it anyway? Disputes over body tissue in a biotechnology age. *Lancet* 351: 53–57.

Nowotny, Helga, Peter Scott, and Michael Gibbons. 2001. *Re-thinking science: Knowledge in an age of uncertainty*. Oxford: Polity.

Nuffield Council on Bioethics. 1995. *Human tissue: Ethical and legal issues*. London: Nuffield Council on Bioethics.

Nuffield Council on Bioethics. 2000. *Stem cell therapy: The ethical issues. A discussion paper*. London: Nuffield Council on Bioethics.

O'Hanlon, Michael, and Linda Frankland. 1986. With a skull in the netbag: Prescriptive marriage and matrilateral relations in the New Guinea Highlands. *Oceania* 56: 181–98.

Ollman, Bertell. 1971. *Alienation: Marx's conception of man in capitalist society*. Cambridge: Cambridge University Press.

Osborne, Thomas. 1998. *Aspects of enlightenment. Social theory and the ethics of truth*. London: UCL Press.

Outram, Dorinda. 1987. Before objectivity: Wives, patronage and cultural reproduction in early nineteenth century French science, in *Uneasy careers and intimate lives: Women in science 1789–1979*, edited by Pnina Abir-Am and Dorinda Outram. New Brunswick, N.J.: Rutgers University Press.

Outram, Dorinda. 1995. *The enlightenment*. Cambridge: Cambridge University Press.

Palme, Robert. 9 May 1996. Miriam: Torn between her tribe and herself. Port Moresby: *Post Courier*.

Pálsson, Gísli, and Kristín Harðardóttir. 2002. For whom the cell tolls: Debates about biomedicine. *Current Anthropology* 43: 271–301.

Parkin, Robert, and Linda Stone. 2004. *Kinship and family: An anthropological reader*. Oxford: Blackwell.

Pedersen, Morten. 2001. Totemism, animism and North Asian indigenous ontologies. *Journal of the Royal Anthropological Institute* (NS) 7: 411–27.

Phillips, Jeremy, and Alison Firth. 1990. *Introduction to intellectual property law*, 2d ed. London: Butterworths.

Pinney, Christopher, and Nicholas Thomas, eds. 2000. *Beyond aesthetics: Art and the technologiest of enchantment: Essays for Alfred Gell*. Oxford: Berg.

PNGLR. 1997. In the matter of an application under Section 57 of the Constitution: Application by Individual and Community Rights Forum Inc. (ICRAF) in re: Miriam Willingal, National Court of Justice, *Papua New Guinea Law Reports*, Port Moresby.

Posey, Daryll. 1996. *Traditional resource rights: International instruments for protection and compensation for indigenous peoples and local communities*. Cambridge: International Union for Conservation of Nature.

Pottage, Alain. 1998. The inscription of life in law: Genes, parents, and bio-politics. *Modern Law Review* 61: 740–65.

Pottage, Alain. 2004. Our original inheritance, in *Law, anthropology, and the constitution of the social: Making persons and things*, edited by Alain Pottage and Martha Mundy. Cambridge: Cambridge University Press.

Puri, Kamal. 2002. Traditional knowledge and folklore. *Sustainable Developments* 70: 3 [report from Conference of the U.K. Commission on International Property Rights: *How intellectual property rights could work better for developing countries and poor people*, London].

Rabinow, Paul. 1996a. *Essays on the anthropology of reason*. Princeton, N.J.: Princeton University Press.

Rabinow, Paul. 1996b. *Making PCR. A story of biotechnology*. Chicago: University of Chicago Press.

Rabinow, Paul. 1999. *French DNA: Trouble in purgatory*. Chicago: University of Chicago Press.

Rabinow, Paul. 2003. *Anthropos today: Reflections on modern equipment*. Princeton, N.J.: Princeton University Press.

Radcliffe-Brown, Alfred Reginald. 1952. *Structure and function in primitive society*. London: Cohen and West.

Radick, Gregory. 2002. Discovering and patenting human genes, in *Body lore and laws*, edited by Andrew Bainham, Shelley Day Sclater, and Martin Richards. Oxford: Hart.

Radin, Margaret. 1993. *Reinterpreting property*. Chicago: University of Chicago Press.

Radin, Margaret. 1996. *Contested commodities: The trouble with trade in sex, children, body parts, and other things*. Cambridge, Mass: Harvard University Press.

Ragoné, Helena. 1994. *Surrogate motherhood: Conception in the heart.* Boulder, Colo.: Westview Press.

Rapp, Rayna. 1999. *Testing women, testing the fetus: The social impact of amniocentesis in America.* New York: Routledge.

Rapport, Nigel. 1998. The potential of human rights in a post-cultural world. *Social Anthropology* 6: 381–88.

Reed, Adam. 2003. *Papua New Guinea's last place.* Oxford: Berghahn.

Reiser, Stanley. 2002. The ethics movement in the biological and health sciences: A new voyage of discovery, in *The ethical dimensions of the biological and health sciences.* 2d ed., edited by Ruth Bulger, Elizabeth Heitman, and Stanley Reiser. Cambridge: Cambridge University Press.

Richardson, Eileen, and Bryan Turner. 2002. Bodies as property: From slavery to DNA analysis, in *Body lore and laws*, edited by Andrew Bainham, Shelley Day Sclater, and Martin Richards. Oxford: Hart Publishing.

Riles, Annelise. 2000. *The network inside out.* Ann Arbor: University of Michigan Press.

Riles, Annelise. 2003. Law as object, in *Law and empire in the Pacific: Fiji and Hawai'i*, edited by Sally Engle Merry and Donald Brenneis. Santa Fe: School of American Research Press.

Ritvo, Harriet. 1997. *The platypus and the mermaid, and other figments of the classifying imagination.* Cambridge, Mass: Harvard University Press.

Roberston, John. 1994. *Children of choice: Freedom and the new reproductive technologies.* New Jersey: Princeton University Press.

Rohatynskyj, Marta. 1990. The larger context of Omie sex affiliation. *Man* (NS) 25: 434–53.

Rohatynskyj, Marta. 1997. Culture, secrets, and Omie history: A consideration of the politics of cultural identity. *American Ethnologist* 24: 438–56.

Rohatynskyj, Marta. 2001. Omie myths and narratives as national cultural property, presented to Becoming Heirs workshop at *Innovation, creation and new economic forms: Approaches to intellectual and cultural property*, PTC Conference, Cambridge.

Rose, Mark. 1993. *Authors and owners: The invention of copyright.* Cambridge, Mass: Harvard University Press.

Rose, Mark. 1996. Mothers and authors: Johnson versus Calvert and the new children of our imagination. *Critical Enquiry* 22: 613–33.

Sahlins, Marshall. 1993. Goodbye to tristes tropes: ethnography in the context of modern world history, *Journal of Modern History* 65: 1–25.

Saunders, D., and I. Hunter. 1991. Lessons from the 'Literatory': How to historicise authorship. *Critical Inquiry* 17: 479.

Savill, Kristin. 2002. The mother of the legal person, in *Visible women: Essays on feminist legal theory and political philosphy*, edited by Susan James and Stephanie Palmer. Oxford: Hart Publishing.

Schlecker, Marcus, and Eric Hirsch. 2001. Incomplete knowledge: Ethnography and the crisis of context in studies of the media, science and technology. *History of the Human Sciences* 14: 69–87.

Segalen, Martine. 2001. The shift in kinship studies in France: The case of grandparenting, in *Relative values: Reconfiguring kinship studies*, edited by Sarah Franklin and Susan McKinnon. Durham, N.C.: Duke University Press.

Shapin, Stephen. 1994. *A social history of truth. Civility and science in seventeenth century England*. Chicago: University of Chicago Press.

Shapin, Steven. 1996. *The scientific revolution*. Chicago: University of Chicago Press.

Sherman, Brad, and Lionel Bently. 1999. *The making of modern intellectual property law: The British experience, 1760–1911*. Cambridge: Cambridge University Press.

Simet, Jacob. 2000. Copyrighting traditional Tolai knowledge? in *Protection of intellectual, biological and cultural property in Papua New Guinea*, edited by Kathy Whimp and Mark Busse. Canberra (Australia): Asia Pacific Press.

Simet, Jacob. 2001a. Conclusions: Reflections on cultural property research, in *Culture and cultural property in the New Guinea Islands region: Seven case studies*, edited by Karen Sykes. New Delhi: UBS Publishers' Distributors Ltd.

Simet, Jacob. 2001b. Custodians by obligation, presented to Becoming Heirs workshop, at *Innovation, creation and new economic forms: Approaches to intellectual and cultural property*, PTC Conference, Cambridge.

Simpson, Bob. 1994. Bringing the 'unclear' family into focus: Divorce and remarriage in contemporary Britain. *Man* (NS) 29: 831–51.

Simpson, Bob. 1998. *Changing families: An ethnographic approach to divorce and separation*. Oxford: Berg.

Strathern, Marilyn. 1988. *The gender of the gift: Problems with women and problems with society in Melanesia*. Los Angeles: University of California Press.

Strathern, Marilyn. 1991. *Partial connections*. ASAO Special Publication 3. Savage, Md.: Rowman and Littlefield.

Strathern, Marilyn. 1992a. *After nature: English kinship in the late twentieth century*. Cambridge: Cambridge University Press.

Strathern, Marilyn. 1992b. *Reproducing the future: Anthropology, kinship and the new reproductive technologies*. Manchester: Manchester University Press.

Strathern, Marilyn. 1995. The relation. Issues in complexity and scale. Cambridge: Prickly Pear Pamphlets no. 6.

Strathern, Marilyn. 1996. Cutting the network. *Journal of the Royal Anthropological Institute* (NS) 2: 517–35.

Strathern, Marilyn. 1998. Surrogates and substitutes: New practices for old?, in *The politics of postmodernity*, edited by James Good and Irving Velody. Cambridge: Cambridge University Press.

Strathern, Marilyn. 1999a. *Property, substance and effect: Anthropological essays on persons and things*. London: Athlone Press.

Strathern, Marilyn. 1999b. Refusing information, in *Property, substance and effect: Anthropological essays on persons and things*. London: Athlone Press.

Strathern, Marilyn. 2000. Global and local contexts, in *Rationales of ownership*, edited by Lawrence Kalinoe and James Leach. New Delhi: UBS Publishers' Distributors Ltd.

Strathern, Marilyn. 2004a. *Commons and borderlands: Working papers on interdisciplinarity, accountability and the flow of knowledge*. Wantage, Oxford: Sean Kingston Publishing.

Strathern, Marilyn. 2004b. Robust knowledge and fragile futures, in *Global assemblages: Technology, politics and ethics as anthropological problems*, edited by Aihwa Ong and Stephen Collier. Oxford: Blackwell.

Strathern, Marilyn. 2004c. Transactions: An analytical foray, in *Transactions and creations: Property debates and the stimulus of Melaresia,* edited by Eric Hirsch and Marilyn Strathern, Oxford: Berghahn.

Swanson, Ted. 1995. *Intellectual property rights and biodiversity conservation: An interdisciplinary analysis of the values of medicinal plants.* Cambridge: Cambridge University Press.

Sykes, Karen. 2000. Losing interest: The devaluation of Malanggan in New Ireland. Presented to PTC Colloquium, *Intergenerational and intergender transactions,* Cambridge.

Sykes, Karen. 2004. Negotiating interests in culture, in *Transactions and creations: Property debates and the stimulus of Melanesia,* edited by Eric Hirsch and Marilyn Strathern. Oxford: Berghahn.

Tassy, J., and C. Dambrine. 1997. Intellectual property rights in support of scientific research. *European Review* 5: 193–204.

Taussig, Michael. 1993. *Mimesis and alterity.* London: Routledge.

Thompson, Charis. 2001. Strategic naturalising: Kinship in an infertility clinic, in *Relative values: Reconfiguring kinship studies,* edited by Sarah Franklin and Susan McKinnon. Durham, N.C.: Duke University Press.

Townsend, Sue. 1989. *The secret diary of Adrian Mole aged 13³/₄.* London: Teens Mandarin.

Toft, Susan, ed. 1998. *Compensation and resource development in Papua New Guinea.* Canberra: Australian National University, and Port Moresby: Law Reform Commission.

Toren, Christina. 2002. Comparison and ontogeny, in *Anthropology, by comparison,* edited by André Gingrich and Richard Fox. London: Routledge.

Trench, Richard. 1882. *On the study of words.* London: Macmillan and Co.

Vilaça, Aparecida. 2000. Relations between funerary cannibalism and warfare cannibalism: The question of predation. *Ethnos* 65: 83–106.

Vilaça, Aparecida. 2002. Making kin out of others. *Journal of the Royal Anthropological Institute* (NS) 8: 347–65.

Viveiros de Castro, Eduardo. 1992. *From the enemy's point of view: Humanity and divinity in an Amazonian society,* translated by C. V. Howard. Chicago: University of Chicago Press.

Viveiros de Castro, Eduardo. 1998a. Cosmological deixis and Amerindian perspectivism. *Journal of the Royal Anthropological Institute* (NS) 4: 469–88.

Viveiros de Castro, Eduardo. 1998b. Simon Bolivar Lectures, University of Cambridge.

Viveiros de Castro, Eduardo. 1999. Animism revisited: Personhood, environment and relational epistemology. *Current Anthropology.* 40 (suppl): S67–91.

Viveiros de Castro, Eduardo. In prep. The gift and the given: Three nano-essays on kinship and magic, in *Genealogy: Beyond kinship,* edited by Sandra Bamford and James Leach. Oxford: Berghahn.

Wagner, Roy. 1975. *The invention of culture.* Englewood Cliffs, N.J.: Prentice-Hall.

Wagner, Roy. 1977. Analogic kinship: A Daribi example. *American Ethnologist* 4: 623–42.

Wagner, Roy. 1986. *Symbols that stand for themselves.* Chicago: University of Chicago Press.

Wagner, Roy. 1987. Figure-ground reversal among the Barok, in *Assemblage of spirits: Idea and image in New Ireland,* edited by Louise Lincoln. New York: George Braziller, in association with the Minneapolis Institute of Arts.

Wagner, Roy. 1991. The fractal person, in *Big men and great men: Personifications of power in Melanesia*, edited by Maurice Godelier and Marilyn Strathern. Cambridge: Cambridge University Press.

Walden, Ian. 1995. Preserving biodiversity: The role of property rights, in *Intellectual property rights and biodiversity conservation: An interdisciplinary analysis of the values of medicinal plants*, edited by Timothy Swanson. Cambridge University Press.

Warnock, Mary. 1985. *A question of life: The Warnock Report on human fertilization and embryology*. Oxford: Basil Blackwell.

Weatherall, Kimberlee. 2001. Culture, autonomy and *Djulibinyamurr*: Individual and community in the construction of rights to traditional designs. *Modern Law Review* 64: 215–42.

Weiner, James. 1991. *The empty place: Poetry, space and being among the Foi of Papua New Guinea*. Bloomington: Indiana University Press.

Weiner, James. 1993. Anthropology contra Heidegger, II: The limit of relationship. *Critique of Anthropology* 13: 285–301.

Weiner, James. 1995. Technology and techne in Trobriand and Yolngu art. *Social Analysis* 38: 32–46.

Weiner, James. 1999. Culture in a sealed envelope: The concealment of Australian Aboriginal heritage tradition in the Hindmarsh Island Bridge affair. *Journal of the Royal Anthropological Institute*, (NS) 5: 193–210.

Weston, Kathleen. 1991. *Families we choose: Lesbians, gays, kinship*. New York: Columbia University Press.

Wexler, Nancy. 1992. Clairvoyance and caution: Repercussions from the human genome project', in *The code of codes: Scientific and social issues in the human genome project*, edited by Daniel Kevles and Leroy Hood. Cambridge, Mass: Harvard University Press.

Whimp, Kathy, and Mark Busse, eds. 2000. *Protection of intellectual, biological and cultural property in Papua New Guinea*. Canbera (Australia): Asia Pacific Press.

Wilson, Richard, ed. 1997a. *Human rights, culture and context. Anthropological perspectives*. London: Pluto Press.

Wilson, Richard. 1997b. Representing human rights violations: Social contexts and subjectivities, in *Human rights, culture and context. Anthropological perspectives*, edited by Richard Wilson. London: Pluto Press.

Winch, Peter. 1958. *The idea of a social science and its relation to philosophy*. London: Routledge and Kegan Paul.

Woodmansee, Martha. 1984. *The author, art and the market: Re-reading the history of aesthetics*. New York: Columbia University Press.

Woodmansee, Martha. 1994. On the author effect: Recovering collectivity, in *The construction of authorship: Textual appropriation in law and literature*, edited by Martha Woodmansee and Peter Jaszi. Durham, N.C.: Duke University Press.

Ziman, John. 2000. *Real science: What it is and what it means*. Cambridge: Cambridge University Press.

# Author Index

# Subject Index

relational knowledge, 7, 8, 11
relational view of the world, 3, 10, 37, 38, 43,
    76, 169
relationality, viii, 7, 13, 41, 46, 48, 84, 121
relations, as concrete and abstract, 64, 70, 71,
    72
    categorical and personal, alternative to
        conceptual and (inter)personal, x, 7, 8,
        84, 89. *See also* conceptual and
        (inter)personal relations
    conceptual, 63–64, 66, 67, 69, 75, 84
    intellectual, 75
    non-epistemic, 85–87, 89, 91
    personal, 64, 66, 67, 75, 84
    procreative, 66
    social, 64, 75
    to explore, 7
    two forms of, 7, 13, 32, 48, 83, 91
relationship, 10, 27, 126, 127, 128, 132, 170
'relative' (for kinsfolk), 7, 51, 64, 67
relatives, 31, 43, 49
representations, 85, 145
reproduction, 68, 70, 105, 137, 143, 147, 148, 151,
    153, 177
reproductive, capacity of, 150
    choice, 16
    interest, 147
    medicine, 16
    rights, 125
    technology, 24, 174. *See also* assisted
        conception
responsibility, 28, 30, 33, 36, 61, 74, 152
    as author, 61
    in relationships, 53
rhetoric, 136
right, of property, 118
    to designs, 189
    to reproduce, 107, 108, 150, 154
rights, 125, 149, 160. *See also* human rights
ritual, as technique, 121
Romantic individual, 135, 194
royalties, 138
rules, observance of, 142

sacred objects, 149, 160
same-sex parents, 18
same-sex relations 143, 145, 146, 149
scale, 47, 63
science, 9, 17, 33, 34, 39, 41, 43, 183
'science's relation', between the constructed
    and the given, 9, 11, 13, 62, 63, 84, 184. *See*

*also* connection and co-implication;
    culture and nature; invention and
    discovery
    as 'third duplex', 8, 11
science, and society, 10, 12, 17, 33, 35, 43, 49,
    169, 170
    policy, 33, 71
    tacit or embedded, 33
scientific, approach as, 38, 40, 44
    authorship. *See* authorship, scientific
    knowledge, 9, 11, 35, 44, 48, 61, 83, 171
    revolution, 8, 10, 34, 46, 62, 63, 65, 91
    thinking, 38, 42
'scientific kinship system', 12, 46, 67
scientists, as creative, 87. *See also* invention
self-construction, 152
self-embodiment, 156
selfishness, 17, 19, 25
self-organisation, 41, 63
self-ownership, 136, 156
self-verifying, 39
several persons, 157, 158, 161
sex-affiliation, 143
shaman, 144, 197
single parent family, 16, 23
single woman, and IVF, 17
singular person, 126, 145
sister's child, 122, 125, 130, 140, 154, 159. *See also*
    maternal kin
'skin', as body, 93, 98, 105, 197
skull in a netbag, 123
slavery, 116, 191
social anthropology, 8, 10, 11, 13, 14, 34, 35, 37,
    38, 40, 41, 42, 43, 47, 62, 83, 130, 131, 163
social anthropology, British, 43
social class. *See* class
social contract, 33. *See also* science, and
    society
social science, 38, 39, 40
social and biological relations. *See* biological
    and social
sociality, 7, 9
society, 11, 13, 15, 18, 42, 43, 157
society, and nature. *See* nature, and society
society, and science. *See* science, and society
Solomon Islands, Papua New Guinea, 192
song, 125, 145, 147, 151, 197
South Pacific Commission, 198
sperm donation, 18, 31, 168
    frozen, 191
Spinoza, Benedictus de, 30, 171

spirit, 127, 148. *See also* Tamberan
statistical methods, 38
statistical, and mechanical models, 47
stem cell research, 17
stillbirths, 141
structural functionalists, in social
    anthropology, 40, 41, 172
structuralists, in social anthropology, 40
subject position, 159
subjectivity, 30, 153
subject and object. *See* object and subject
substance, nurturant and procreative, 83, 126,
    127, 142, 143
surrogacy arrangements, 32, 52, 55, 57, 77, 168,
    174
systems, of classification, 39, 40, 42, 44, 171
systems, of knowledge, 13, 41

Tabar, New Ireland, Papua New Guinea, 188
Tamberan spirit, 148, 196
Tamberan songs, 149, 196–197
tangible, and intangible, phenomena, 147, 150

taxonomy, 172
technologies, new medical, vii, 10, 18, 25
technology, 84, 92–109, 174, 180, 185, 186
    and nature, 102
    of enchantment, 94–107, 185. *See also*
        enchantment of technology
temporality, in bodies, 141
text, 105, 106
theft, of authorship, 58
thing, 63, 89, 152, 154, 156, 161, 177, 192
    in English law, 118–120, 177
thing-image, 126
things, and persons, 111–133, 191
    as relations, 63
    classes of, 122
    of the world, 156, 177
    personified, 121
time, and space, 97
tissue, fetal, 164
tissue, human, 117, 118, 120, 191
Tolai, New Britain, Papua New Guinea, 160,
    199
tool, of analysis, 6, 7, 8, 9, 42, 83, 84, 90, 94,
    163, 180. *See also* duplex
Torrens system of land registration, Australia,
    198

totems, 144, 146. *See* emblems
Trade Related Aspects of Intellectual Property
    Rights (TRIPS) agreement, 100
trademark, 95
tradition, 89, 118, 129, 131, 146
tradition, and modernity, 115–116, 129,
    132
traditional knowledge, 149, 160, 199
traditional owners, 160
transactions, 148

'unclear family', 22
UNESCO, 146, 165, 170, 198. *See also* Universal
    Declaration
unilineal descent groups. *See* descent groups
unique points of view, 140
unit of comparison, 38
Universal Declaration on Cultural Diversity
    (UNESCO, 2001), 165
Universal Declaration on the Human
    Genome and Human Rights (UNESCO,
    1997), 165–6, 170
universalism, 114, 131, 182, 193

validation, 44, 47, 62
validation, two kinds of, 34, 48. *See also*
    verification
Vanuatu, 132, 193, 196
verification, 34, 38, 40, 46, 47, 61, 65, 83. *See
    also* validation
Vezu, Madagascar, 195
visiting rights, 16, 24, 31
vitality. *See* life

warfare, 128
Wari', Amazonia, 83
Warnock Report, on human fertilisation and
    embryology, 18
wealth, 121, 123, 127
Wesley, John 70
wholeness, of person, 116–125
wholes and parts. *See* parts, and wholes
will, 153, 155, 156
World Conference of Science, 169
World Council of Indigenous Peoples, 177
World Intellectual Property Organisation
    (WIPO), 100, 146, 198
World Summit on Sustainable Development,
    169

4043860R00134

Printed in Great Britain
by Amazon.co.uk, Ltd.,
Marston Gate.